D0927973

POVERTY AND CAPITALISM IN PRE-INDUSTRIAL EUROPE

PRE-INDUSTRIAL EUROPE 1350-1850

General Editor: Dr Geoffrey Parker,
Reader in Modern History, University of St Andrews

PRE-INDUSTRIAL EUROPE, 1350–1850 is a series of historical studies which provides an introduction to the central themes of European economic and social history in the pre-industrial age. Each volume has been commissioned from a leading British, European or American scholar, and each presents a synthesis of the latest research, both published and unpublished, on a selection of critically important subjects related to the theme of the series, which is the gradual erosion of the traditional agricultural society of medieval Europe by a number of influences, chief among them the growth of capitalism.

By 1850, a new society had emerged in Europe, one that was capable of accepting and adjusting to the machine age. But it would be wrong to believe that industrial change caused this new society; on the contrary, the prior erosion of the traditional society and its values was an essential precondition of rapid industrialization. It is therefore a matter of some importance to understand how fundamental social changes came about in Europe (and nowhere else) in the five centuries before 1850. By focusing attention on the key areas of change, this series aims to provide an explanation which will be of interest to scholars, students and the general reader.

POVERTY AND CAPITALISM IN PRE-INDUSTRIAL EUROPE
Catharina Lis and Hugo Soly
CRIME AND PUNISHMENT IN EARLY MODERN EUROPE
Michael Weisser

Other titles in preparation
DEATH AND DISEASE IN PRE-INDUSTRIAL EUROPE
Paul Slack
THOU SHALT NOT: THE CHRISTIAN CHURCHES AND SOCIAL CONTROL
Bruce Lenman and Geoffrey Parker
BROADSHEET AND CHAPBOOK: POPULAR LITERACY AND POPULAR LITERATURE
Peter Burke
ARISTOCRACY AND SOCIAL CHANGE IN PRE-INDUSTRIAL EUROPE
Charles J. Jago

POVERTY AND CAPITALISM IN PRE-INDUSTRIAL EUROPE

Catharina Lis

Senior Assistant, University of Brussels

Hugo Soly

Senior Assistant, University of Ghent

HUMANITIES PRESS

First published in the USA in 1979 by

HUMANITIES PRESS INC.

Atlantic Highlands, New Jersey 07716

Library of Congress Cataloging in Publication Data
Lis, Catharina
Poverty and capitalism in pre-industrial Europe.
(Pre-industrial Europe 1350-1850; 1)
Bibliography: p.
Includes indexes.
1. Europe – Economic conditions. 2. Europe – Social conditions. 3. Poor – Europe – History. 4. Capitalism – History. I. Soly, Hugo, joint author. II. Title. III. Series.
HC240.S654 1979 330.9'4 78–26731

ISBN 0–391–00959–1

Translated from the Dutch
by James Coonan

Printed in Great Britain by
Bristol Typesetting Co Ltd,
Barton Manor, St Philips, Bristol

June '80

Contents

Chapter 4

CHANGING ECONOMIC PATTERNS AND THE UTILITY OF POVERTY

(c.1630 – c.1750)

Chapter 5

ECONOMIC GROWTH, PAUPERIZATION AND THE REGULATION OF THE LABOUR MARKET

(c.1750 – c.1850)

List of Tables

List of Figures

Acknowledgements

No academic enterprise can be deemed a product of isolated scholarship; one always builds upon the work of innumerable predecessors. Nor can one disengage from the values, conscious or not, of one's society. This is particularly true in an essay which treats a much debated problem and is based primarily on published material. Hence, we are indebted to those many scholars whose work we have, literally, plundered for ideas and information. Masses of footnotes would be required to repay that debt, but, conforming to the layout of this series, we have gathered together the foremost sources in an unavoidably selective bibliography, arranged by chapter.

Above all, we are deeply indebted to Dr Geoffrey Parker, our friend of many years. He has not only shown great patience with two authors who repeatedly delayed delivery of their manuscript in order to incorporate new data, but he also found time to read through the whole text and to comment in detail. His encouragement and sensible advice, freely given, have been of the greatest help to us. James S. Coonan took on the difficult task of setting our often awkward and obscure Dutch phrases into English prose. Many improvements in the text are the result of his constructive criticisms, for which we express our gratitude. We alone, of course, are responsible for our errors.

Note on Spelling, Usage and Metrology

Where there is a recognized English version of a foreign place-name (Antwerp, Florence, Geneva, Vienna and so on) we have used it. Otherwise, we have preferred the style used in the place itself (Ieper, not Ypres; Mechelen, not Malines). We have followed the same system with personal names: where there is an established English usage (Francis I, Frederick the Great, Catherine II) we have adopted it. In all other cases the style and the title employed by the person concerned have been used.

To avoid confusion, we have not translated terms such as *pauperes Christi, popolo minuto, manouvriers, Habnits* and others for which there is no English counterpart. The terms concerned are explained in the text when introduced for the first time.

All weights and measures have been converted into metric units.

	British standard
1 metre	1.09 yards
1 hectare (10,000 square metres)	2.47 acres
1 kilometre	0.62 miles
1 square kilometre	0.39 square miles
1 litre	1.75 pints
1 hectolitre	21.9 gallons
1 kilogram	2.2 lb
1 metric quintal (100 kilograms)	220 lb
1 metric ton (1,000 kilograms)	0.98 ton

Foreword

Since the 1960s, the realization has grown that poverty in western society is not a thing of the past. There is abundant evidence to show that economic growth has not brought about universal prosperity; even in countries with a high national *per capita* income, large numbers live at or under the officially determined poverty line, and social inequality appears to be increasing rather than diminishing.[1] Yet, most relevant activity in the social sciences is not concerned with the fundamental causes of poverty but merely with the definition, measurement, and description of 'marginal' groups and sub-groups, who, once defined, measured, and described, are conveniently labelled 'minorities'. Moreover, the euphoric belief in the saving grace of economic growth has led many investigators to characterize poverty as the result of underdevelopment, temporary and localized backwardness, or individual disability – 'insular poverty' and 'case poverty', to use the terminology of J. K. Galbraith. The total failure of the 'war on poverty' in the richest country in the world, the USA, has not undermined these presuppositions. Many sociologists take as an article of faith the concept of a 'culture of poverty', but, in contrast to Oscar Lewis, who coined the term, they portray the living conditions and patterns of behaviour of the poor as the outcome of the personal inadequacy or inferiority of families locked into the poverty trap.[2] Some exceptions aside, more attention has been paid to the specific system of values of the poor than to the economic and political structures which lie at the roots of social inequality and cultural segregation.

The acute problem of poverty has not been ignored by historians. Just as the crisis of the 1930s stimulated investigation of long-term trends of prices, wages and incomes, growing concern for the social tensions of today has led to the proliferation of studies on the nature and extent of poverty in pre-industrial society. However, just as current problems determine in large measure the themes of historical investigation, they also strongly influence methods of inquiry. Since economic growth is generally viewed as the ultimate goal and a cure for every ill, it is scarcely surprising that most historians describe the *ancien régime* as underdeveloped, marked by 'the failure to provide acceptable levels of living to a large proportion of a country's population, with resulting misery and material privation'.[3] The main features of such a society, so it is said, are the structural inability to raise agricultural productivity substantially and the natural tendency of the population to increase on a limited supply of land. Thus, every phase of demographic expansion led necessarily to an insupportable tension between population and food supply, a 'bottle-neck', resulting in starvation and crises of mortality. Poverty in pre-industrial Europe is thus reduced to a 'natural' phenomenon, inherent in a 'society of scarcity' which was characterized by technological backwardness and a tendency towards uncontrolled demographic growth. But this is merely a description; it certainly cannot be deemed an explanation. It does not make clear why conditions leading to long-term stagnation gripped the whole of the Middle Ages, while they were gradually overcome in some early modern societies. The whole case is implicitly founded on a neo-malthusian model, the deterministic character of which is never questioned.

Like the many proponents of the 'culture of poverty' approach, historians too have the inclination to analyse poverty as an eternal phenomenon, and to represent its external manifestations as characteristics of the poor themselves. Thus, during the *ancien régime*, elite groups ascribed the presence of great numbers of the poor primarily to individual misfortune or disability, or to the existence of charitable institutions which, being over-generous, removed all incentives to labour: many historians have taken over, in whole or in part, this point of view. They base their conclusion on three observations: the proliferation of public and private sources of relief; the great extent of begging and vagabondage; and the predominance of the ill, crippled, widows and families with many children among the poor on relief. These authors apparently never ask themselves precisely what it is which they are evaluating. Is it the 'nature' of poverty? Or is it really the mechanics of a specific system of poor relief?

Although such approaches (or, rather, presuppositions) have found support, not all historians concur. Some investigators have sharply criticized the validity of neo-malthusian models for explaining long-term socio-economic changes in pre-industrial Europe. Others have shown that charitable institutions, due to their restricted financial means, could have supported only an extremely small portion of the needy and that consequently the 'poor lists' drawn up by the relevant administrations give an inaccurate picture of the social reality. But the most important questions of all still remain unanswered: why was poverty a 'structural feature' throughout the *ancien régime*? Why was the extent of destitution in regions which were economically backward similar to that in areas which were economically advanced, and in periods of both population growth and stagnation? Why was poverty not everywhere paired with capitalist development? Why, in some parts of Europe and at certain times, were large-scale reorganizations of poor relief carried out, while in other regions or periods everything remained as it was? Why did the majority of the supported poor consist at one moment of the young and of healthy adults, at another moment of infants, the aged, the infirm?

To answer these questions demands an holistic approach, that is a diachronic and comparative study of entire societies. Obviously, an analysis of long-term movements is required to come to generalized assertions on the causes of impoverishment and changes in social policy. Otherwise there is the danger that common features and crucial differences would not be evaluated properly. Although in recent years excellent monographs have been written on various aspects of the problem, as yet no attempts have been made to synthesize the results of these more detailed investigations. All works undertaking an overall picture are at least a half century old and focus upon charity.[4]

Comparative investigation is just as necessary as the diachronic approach (unless one proceeds from the axiom that poverty was a 'natural' phenomenon during the *ancien régime*). It is necessary to examine whether or not similar economic, demographic and political developments brought forth equivalent social outcomes and, conversely, whether or not divergent structures resulted in marked shifts in the division of wealth. Although these questions seem obvious, most studies of poverty in pre-industrial Europe have avoided them. That is true even for the few authors who have systematically discussed either medieval or early modern manifestations of destitution. Certainly they make geographic distinctions when describing transformations of socio-political regulations, but not when dealing with poverty itself. These authors make it appear that the social problem was everywhere determined by the same 'objective mechanism'. This point of view, which comes down to nothing more than historicist fatalism, rests on unfounded *a priori* assumptions.[5] For exactly those reasons, impoverishment processes can only be explained by studying the development of societies *in toto*, taking account of economic and demographic factors as well as changing class relations, the role of the state, and socio-cultural dimensions. In this way, common and specific characteristics, continuous and discontinuous trends, and independent and dependent variables can all be discerned. In short, the problem of poverty must be incorporated into the more general framework of the discussion on processes of historic transition.

General transitions consist of two distinct processes of historic evolution: 'First, in the central passage from one mode of production to another. Secondly, in the transformation undergone by a society in its entire structure, in the precarious equilibrium of its social forces, which makes it pass successively, *within* a given mode of production, through different social or socio-economic formations.'[6] Since the purpose of this series is to elucidate why a total social transformation took place in Europe – and nowhere else – in the four or five centuries before 1850, we have focused on the first sort of transition. Concretely, this means that, without denying the importance of other periods, the 'long sixteenth century', which witnessed the triumph of commercial capitalism, and the century after 1750, characterized by the gradual but irresistible growth of industrial capitalism, were the most thoroughly investigated. It also means that all parts of Europe were not treated evenly in this essay: areas east of the Elbe were only occasionally brought into the discussion because they were consigned to centuries of structural stagnation, a result of the rise of a true manorial economy from the later Middle Ages on. For similar reasons, some countries receive more attention at some periods than at others. A central place is assigned to Flanders and northern Italy, for example, in the treatment of urban manufacturing within the feudal mode of production, while England and France stand at the centre of interest in the chapters on early modern Europe. Finally, while certain aspects of poverty are focused upon, others are peripheral; thus, collective mentalities of the poor are mentioned only in so far as they help to clarify changes in the structure of surplus extraction relationships and subjects such as popular culture, rebellions and criminality, however important they may be for an understanding of pre-industrial society, receive less attention than one would perhaps expect.

To reduce a mass of new and old scholarship to a single manageable volume is a difficult task. We have chosen to organize our material more or less chronologically, rather than to follow one issue after another over time. This method risks obscuring the nature of long-term developments within particular sectors, but, on the other hand, it allows the complex of characteristics of a specific stage of development to be revealed. Each chapter has roughly the same structure. First, the various causes of socio-economic inequality among peasants and urban craftsmen are studied. Given the overwhelming importance of agriculture in the *ancien régime*, relatively more room is provided for discussion of agrarian structures than for analysis of industrial organization, which is, however, treated in increasing detail for the period which witnessed the definitive breakthrough of the capitalist mode of production.

At last the poor themselves arrive on stage. Who were they? Did their number increase in the course of time? Were there fundamental changes in the external manifestations of destitution? Over what resources did the pauperized masses dispose in order to relieve or even to escape their miserable lot? What did they think of themselves? Were they conscious of their common misfortune? Two introductory remarks ought to be made in this regard. First, the intention, as said above, is not to present an exhaustive analysis of the living conditions of the lower classes but rather to focus on phenomena which can be measured and compared objectively, in particular the division of total wealth, the number of 'fiscal' poor and those on relief, the quantity and quality of average *per capita* food consumption, migrations and so on. Second, it must be emphasized that it is impossible to give a rigorous definition of poverty acceptable for every century. As will be shown, the actuality of the concept varied from period to period and even place to place. This ambiguity does not affect the essential results of this investigation, because officialdom always employed extremely strict criteria to catalogue someone as poor, and generally they fell short of subsistance minima.

Every chapter ends with an extended section on poor relief. Most historians have ascribed changes in social policy during the feudal-capitalist transition chiefly to religious influences and humanitarian considerations. Successive reforms of public support, they assert, testify to the growing concern of elite groups for the extraordinary poverty of rural and urban masses. But such idealistic verdicts are totally unsatisfactory. The problem is misconceived. We should really be asking which factors produced the more empathetic stance of the upper classes towards the poor. What requires explanation is why the expansion of poverty did not always and everywhere lead to basic reorganization of poor relief; why the measures undertaken differed so strongly from country to country; why poor relief was generally limited to the towns; why traditional conceptions of private charity survived in some parts of Europe until the end of the *ancien régime*, while elsewhere they had long before made way for a more 'rational' perspective, emphasizing public support.

To handle so many complex problems in a single short volume is an ambitious undertaking; indeed, some might call it foolishly ambitious. Nonetheless, the task is begun in the hope that the question of poverty and impoverishment can be removed from its past history of ambiguity and confusion and henceforth be approached on a sounder basis.

May 1978

Chapter 1

FEUDALISM, POVERTY AND CHARITY *(c.1000–c.1350)*

By the eleventh century, Europe had developed a complex political, socio-economic and cultural structure, characterized by the fragmentation of sovereignty, a distinctive organization of agricultural production, and the spiritual monopoly of the Christian Church. Yet in spite of the hierarchy of mutual rights and obligations, the availability of land for all, and the authority of religious strictures, this society contained inbuilt contradictions. These contradictions formed the basis of developments within feudal society which resulted in increasing social differentiation.

1. The smallholder: the axis of feudalism

How and why feudalism of the western European variety developed falls outside the scope of this essay, but for an understanding of the causes of impoverishment in the Middle Ages, it is necessary to outline the social implications of this specific type of surplus extraction.

The peasantry of the High Middle Ages was not an undifferentiated mass. Despite regional differences, a significant part of the agrarian population of Europe was made up of unfree peasants; some were descended from full slaves (*servi*), others from the *coloni*, the bulk of the peasantry of the late Roman Empire, who, despite their dependence on large landowners, were still free in legal terms; other medieval villeins were the descendants of free smallholders who had come, at some time or other, under the authority of a landlord. In the Carolingian Empire and Anglo-Saxon England alike, the pressure of the *potentes* on the *pauperes*, free but marginal peasants, steadily increased. Many large landowners broadened their estates with allods, holdings originally subject to the jurisdiction of Church and State alone, acquiring them through purchase, in exchange for protection, or, frequently, by force. This gradual process of acquisition, which was by no means completed in the eleventh century, was an important aspect of the development of villeinage. In the course of time, the juridical distinctions among the diverse dependent groups were ironed out. In western Germany, England, most of France, numerous parts of Italy, and Spain, all dependent peasants who were subject to specific hereditary obligations were in the end deemed unfree and brought under one rubric: serf.

At the same time, the opposite tendency appeared in some areas. The clearance of new land and the founding of new villages, especially from the eleventh century onwards, played to the advantage of the peasants concerned, who received land on particularly favourable conditions. The connection between clearance of woods and waste on one hand and the rise in the number of peasants who enjoyed a certain measure of freedom on the other may be taken as a commonplace in European agrarian history.

Juridical distinctions, however, were much less important than economic inequality. In general a distinction can be drawn between farmers who disposed of sufficient land to feed a family and those whose holdings were too small. In eleven English hundreds (subdivisions of shires) where villein as well as free holdings are known, the land was parcelled out in 1279 as follows:

Table 1.
Distribution of peasant holdings in eleven English hundreds, 1279

Size of holding (in hectares)	*Number*			*Percentage*		
	Free	*Villein*	*Total*	*Free*	*Villein*	*Total*
Under 3	2,689	2,240	4,929	47	29	36.5
3 (¼ virgate)	759	715	1,474	13	9	11
6 (½ virgate)	1,018	2,430	3,448	18	31	25.5
12 (1 virgate)	835	2,308	3,143	14.5	30	23
Over 12	438	72	510	7.5	1	4
TOTAL	5,739	7,765	13,504	100	100	100

Source: E. A. Kosminsky, *Studies in the Agrarian History of England in the Thirteenth Century* (Oxford, 1956), p. 228.

It is clear from this table that almost half of the total tenant population disposed of holdings of only three hectares or less. It is equally clear that more free than unfree peasants fell below this minimum: 47 per cent compared with 29 per cent. Indeed, there was greater social differentiation among the free peasants – they were more numerous at the top as well as at the bottom of the table of wealth. However it is the poor who concern us here: those who did not possess the four hectares of arable land which constituted the minimum necessary to support a family of four in the thirteenth century.

What caused the extreme fragmentation of landholding which we find all over western Europe in the thirteenth century? The phenomenon definitely cannot be ascribed to the spectacular population growth which took place between 1150 and 1300. Such growth undoubtedly augmented the subdivision of holdings, yet it can in no sense be viewed as the fundamental cause: in the ninth century there were already enormous differences in the extent of holdings. In the region around Paris and in northern and central Italy miniscule and very large production units co-existed. The same held true for England: according to Domesday Book, at least one-third of the peasants were smallholders in 1086, their plots lying alongside the great estates of the tenants-in-chief.

There was in fact a far more basic reason for the proliferation of smallholdings: the nearly landless fulfilled an essential function in the feudal mode of production. Since they had too little land to support a family, they either hired out their labour or starved. The position of the cottar or *manouvrier* had two distinctive features: 'On the one hand, he is the object of feudal exploitation. He holds his land from a lord, he pays rent for it, he owes various dues. On the other hand, at the same time he hires himself out to work and receives wages.'[1] The marginal peasant differed from the other tenants in that the latter received a 'natural wage' in the form of land as compensation for performing a number of obligations, while the former were paid partly in land, partly in allowances in kind, and partly in money. As a result, the exploited cottars were not true wage labourers: they did not live from the sale of their labour alone, nor could they ever dispose of that in complete freedom. At the same time they differed from the farmhands since they received no regular payment, and since they had their own morsel of ground from which the family could be partially supported. In short, the cottars formed a social category apart, which can be seen as half way between the feudally dependent peasants and the unfree farmhands.

Nearly all groups secured advantages from the expansion of

the mass of the nearly landless. Certainly, landlords held the right to demand services (*corvées*, labour dues) from their tenants. The services, however, were in large measure established by custom: that is, reduced or increased according to particular power relationships. Landlords had an interest, therefore, in being able to call on a large number of cottars, who, because of the insufficiency of their own small harvest, were obliged to take on supplementary work. For the owners of small manors in particular (and they made up the majority), the presence of cottars was indispensable, because they could lease out only a fraction of their land and were consequently compelled to employ extra workers for the proper exploitation of their demesne. The movement towards the commutation of labour services into rents in kind or in money, a complex process which occurred from the twelfth century on, was caused in part by this need for seasonal labour. Some landlords judged that work on the manor could be organized far more efficiently by hiring workers as needed. It was never easy to distribute the labour services in a rational fashion among an often unwilling tenantry; moreover the wages paid to casual labourers in general were lower than the commutation fees provided by the peasants who had formerly owed labour services. Finally, it would appear that for landlords it was as a rule more advantageous to have numerous cottars rather than a few prospering tenants, because smallholdings could be subjected to relatively heavier demands than larger ones.

In his masterly study of the *Crise du Féodalisme*, the French historian Guy Bois has recently shown that an increase in the number of the nearly landless was an absolute necessity for the prosperity of the wealthier peasants, known in France as the *laboureurs.* The maximum holding which a single farmer could cultivate with the help of his wife and two grown children was twelve hectares. If he were obliged to render labour services to his lord, this maximum was reduced. The *laboureur* was consequently forced to employ casual labour, not only at harvest-time but also for those time-consuming unskilled tasks such as threshing grain which cropped up throughout the farming year. Both socio-economic groups were thus bound together by a sort of umbilical cord: the *laboureurs,* who formed the backbone of the rural economy, could not do without the *manouvriers*, and vice versa. This stratification of the peasantry into two basic levels resulted from the dominant role played by small producers, for the unit of production characteristic of feudalism was not the *seigneurie*, which merely formed the jurisdictional framework of production, but the smallholding. The hegemony of this fundamental unit of production was rooted in the state of agrarian technology: no single organization of labour in this period was as efficient as that centred on the full use of a single plough team. Hence, the large estate was in a precarious situation: its evolution was subordinated, through the interplay of prices and wages, to the fate of the smallholding. Feudalism of the western European variety must therefore be defined as the preponderance of the small individual producer, subject to seigneurial surplus extraction exercised through extra-economic coercion.[2]

Thus the size of the peasant holding in part determined the socio-economic differentiation of the peasantry; equally crucial, however, was the weight of surplus extraction. Seigneurial dues affected the whole of the peasantry, both freeman and serf, in one way or another. The medieval peasant could be unfree in two respects: he could be obliged to render labour services, and he could also be forbidden to do certain things (such as leave the manor, marry, sell land or goods, or bequeath an inheritance) without the approval of the lord. The two forms of servitude, tenurial and personal, did not necessarily coincide. One might find peasants with free personal status holding villein land; one might also find serfs holding freeholds. Furthermore, the whole community of 'free' and 'unfree' was subjected to various exactions which were raised throughout the jurisdiction of the lord, particularly from the eleventh century onwards. These included tolls, market rights, fines, hunting and fishing rights, and above all the seigneurial monopolies – the obligation to use the facilities provided by the lord, such as mills, ovens, wine presses, breweries and the like. All peasants, finally, had to pay the *tallia* (tallage, *taille*). Originally collected irregularly and arbitrarily, the weight of these seigneurial exactions grew increasingly heavy as landlords tried in every possible way to compensate for the gradual diminution of their income from land rent, aggravated by the thirteenth-century inflation, through maximal exploitation of their territorial authority. Around 1300, to take a single example, the two greatest magnates of Staffordshire drew nearly 40 per cent of their income from the exercise of seigneurial rights.

Naturally, the peasants reacted vigorously against the continuous assault on their means of existence. Numerous lawsuits testify to the frequent and often sharp clashes between lord and peasant; the free sometimes won their suits, but the unfree usually lost. By the end of the thirteenth century the burden became unbearable: extra-manorial obligation (tithes for the Church, occasional royal taxes) aside, the money dues of a villein tenant siphoned off about 50 per cent or more of his gross output. Even the serfs who disposed of sufficient land to feed a family, in many cases retained too little to break even after subtraction of all dues.

Free peasants *could* do better than serfs: they owed no labour services, were not bowed down by a plethora of personal duties, and were less subject to arbitrary taxation. Moreover, in general they paid lower rents than serfs. The result was that 'even if, in the aggregate or on the average, freeholders and sokemen were not better provided with acres than villeins, an individual villein would be poorer, perhaps much poorer, than an individual freeholder with a holding of the same size'.[3] The portion of surplus extracted from the gross output of freeholders probably amounted to not much more than 25 per cent, half that of the serfs. However, as stated above, there were absolutely and relatively more smallholders among the free peasantry than the unfree, and the material circumstances of these men were far from rosy. Hence, we do not find socio-economic differentiation along the divide between freeman and villein. Only the holder of sufficient land could take full advantage of his freedom. In the first place, given that the majority – the smallholders – found it impossible to live off their own plot of land, their 'freedom' to deal in land implied considerable vulnerability: free land not only allowed partible inheritance but was at the same time exposed to the destabilizing effects of the market. If free smallholders needed cash, due to harvest failure or other calamities, then they might be able to negotiate loans or sell rents on their property, but usually that sealed their fates. Their meagre incomes seldom proved sufficient to redeem debts, so they were eventually forced to lease or even to sell their holding to professional moneylenders, landlords, or well-to-do freeholders. Free peasants with twelve hectares or more could quite easily lay up reserves, since their surplus was great enough to cope with rents and taxes without much difficulty. In the second place, rent and taxes did not increase proportionally with size of holding; indeed, these charges grew comparatively lighter the greater the size of the freehold.

The evolving nature of seigneurial exactions also led to socio-economic differentiation. Changes in the *taille* from the twelfth century onwards is a case in point. Seigneurial exactions in large measure had a levelling impact so long as they were collected irregularly and arbitrarily; but the moment that the *taille* became periodic (in general, yearly), and the amount was fixed (*taille abonnée*), a change occurred. The lord demanded, in exchange for his approval of the arrangement, that the *taille* take on a real value, that is, proportional to the possessions of the inhabitants. Since proportionality was not observed beyond a certain acreage, wealthy peasants reaped the main benefits of the change.

The same held true for the so-called 'charters of liberty', agreements concluded between landlord and village community, by which seigneurial rights were defined. In the course of the twelfth and, above all, the thirteenth centuries, numerous villages, semi-urban centres and towns throughout western Europe received charters of this sort. Although their scope varied, these collective privileges show some common features. They fixed the conditions and the limits within which the lord might in future demand contributions and services associated with the power of the ban; they guaranteed a certain mobility of persons and property; and they granted specified forms of administrative autonomy. This movement of enfranchisement had significant results. First, the debt burden of the peasantry worsened. Redemption often cost so much that many had to take on long-term loans and fell into the hands of moneylenders. Second, the enfranchisement of some implied reinforcement of others' lack of freedom, so that in many places, the thirteenth century witnessed some restoration of serfdom in connection with the spread of franchises. Social differentiation of the peasantry as a result advanced both directly and indirectly.

Commutation of labour services into money rents had similar results. The growing needs of landlords for ready cash, the greater impact of the urban economy on rural areas, which stimulated production for the market, and the desire of the better-off peasants to profit as much as possible from the rising demand for cereals, wine, livestock and meat: all these encouraged commutation, which put peasants in a freer relationship to their landlords and augmented their opportunities for accumulation. On the other hand, they faced greater dependence on the market and thus increased vulnerability. To pay their rents in cash, an extra part of their surplus had to be sold. Since rents were not collected at the times most convenient for the producer, small peasants frequently saw themselves forced to sell below the 'normal' market price, while they in turn could seldom profit from the high prices of dearth years because of their small output. Moreover, it must be remembered that many peasants were simply too poor to buy themselves out of labour services. They lost on all fronts. Lacking time, they could not work their land more intensively and, due to their inability to accumulate savings, they secured no technical aids unless they took on loans. In short, only a minority of wealthy peasants benefited from commutation.

Unmistakably, all changes in surplus extraction strongly differentiated and even polarized an already unequal peasantry. In the end, only a small minority profited from the growth of the rural economy, which took place wholly at the expense of smallholders, free and unfree alike. To cite Georges Duby:

> The regularizing of the *taille* and the sale of franchises, the spread of fixed rents on land, even the facilities for borrowing the necessities of consumption, all these many ways by which the money economy spread, enmeshed the less well off peasants in a web of debts and bound them in effective slavery to the towns or to their better-off neighbours.[4]

The fourteenth-century crisis would show the limits of such evolution.

2. Urban manufacturing and socio-economic dependence

There was an upsurge in the urban life of Europe from the tenth century. Detailed figures are scarce, but numerous indirect data, such as the increase in the number of parishes and the construction of ever-larger town walls, indicate that population between 1000 and 1300 grew faster in the towns than in the country. To grasp the results of this development, one needs only to note that in the early fourteenth century Europe numbered four towns with more than 50,000, thirty-seven with more than

20,000, and seventy-nine with more than 10,000. The number of small centres also increased spectacularly: in Germany alone, around 1300 there were some 200 towns with several thousand inhabitants each. Moreover, innumerable villages had expanded into local markets. In England, the Crown conferred no less than 3,000 grants of market during the thirteenth century. Nevertheless, the vast bulk of European population lived in the countryside: at least 70 per cent in the most 'urbanized' areas (Flanders and northern Italy), 85 to 90 per cent nearly everywhere else. Despite their small quantitative weight, however, the towns would largely determine the course of subsequent economic development. There, not in the countryside, commercial capitalism was born.

Although the causes of the 'urban revolution' cannot be investigated here, the rise of new towns and the expansion of the old was clearly not the result of the revival of international trade, as Henri Pirenne postulated in his magisterial synthesis. His view implied a fundamental opposition between town and country, with the market as the sole motivating principle, the sole catalyst in an otherwise static society.[5] The basic weakness of this dualist thesis is that it completely ignores the decisive importance of the rural economy. Before towns arose, there had to be a substantial increase in agrarian production, more efficiently concentrated in the hands of a more highly differentiated aristocracy and a small but significant peasant elite. The essential pre-condition, in other words, was increased quantity and disposability of agrarian production. Significantly, many towns were founded by feudal lords; a marketplace offered them, directly or indirectly, a supplementary income. It should be remembered that towns could develop in Europe only because of the extreme fragmentation of sovereignty which characterized feudalism – the first mode of production in history 'to allow . . . an autonomous structural place to urban production and merchant capital'.[6] Finally, it must be noted that urban populations could grow only through continuous immigration of uprooted countrymen, seeking a livelihood, protection, or freedom. In short, the internal dynamic of the feudal mode of production favoured expansion of the market and consequent urbanization, but increasing production for the market disrupted the peasantry and accelerated the process of social differentiation.

The export industries which flourished in a number of towns formed the basis for the rise of commercial capitalism, characterized by the divorce of capital and labour, by the dependence of legally free wage labourers on employers, and by the realization of profit. These profits derived mainly from the commercial activities of merchant-entrepreneurs, but also partially from the surplus value produced by wage-labourers and expropriated by merchant-entrepreneurs. This development was of importance for the future because it meant the proletarianization of a steadily increasing number of people alienated from the land. It is necessary to sketch out this preparatory phase.

Cloth manufacture existed in Europe before the eleventh century, but it expanded spectacularly from then on, concentrating above all in the towns. By 1300 woollen industry had developed in numerous towns spread throughout western and southern Europe: Flanders, Brabant, the Meuse region, the Rhineland, Picardy, Ile-de-France, Champagne, Normandy, Languedoc, eastern England, northern Italy, and Catalonia, the two most industrialized areas being Flanders and northern Italy. Their preponderance was due to a combination of factors. The fertility of the soil made possible an enormous population explosion in both areas, leading to the growth of a large reservoir of labour, which, due to existing rural property rights, could not make a living from agriculture. Sheep-farming in the immediate surroundings provided wool, the most important raw material, to start up cloth-manufacturing of more than local significance. Both areas, finally, were particularly favoured geographically: Italy as a bridge between Europe, North Africa, and the Near East; Flanders as a crossroad of land and sea routes, linking the North Sea with the Atlantic, and England with Italy and Germany.

The significance of these export industries for the urban economy can be deduced from the number of persons involved in cloth production. At Ghent, the portion of workers in wool in a total population of 64,000 amounted to at least 60 per cent in the middle of the fourteenth century, some 25 per cent out of Brugge's 40,000 or so in 1338 to 1340, and 33 per cent of Florence's 90,000 around the same time, according to the chronicler Giovanni Villani. How was the labour of the thousands of weavers, fullers, shearers and other producers organized? The vast majority of them were dependent on a small group of merchants and entrepreneurs. In the first place markets were dispersed and elastic, so that direct contact between producer and consumer was extremely difficult. Due to competition on the international market, risks were high, especially for the uninitiated; also many expensive raw materials, such as English wool, dye-stuffs or alum, had to be imported. Since most artisans, with their low productivity and consequently low profits, could not bring together the requisite capital, they relied on merchants to supply small quantities – mostly on credit. Hence, merchants controlled both the first and last phases: the purchase of raw materials and the sale of finished products. In the second place, processing wool into cloth was an extremely complicated process. Thirty to thirty-two different operations had to be performed, each entrusted to specialized craftsmen: sorting, beating, washing, combing or carding, spinning, warping, spooling, weaving, fulling, tentering, raising, shearing, dyeing, finishing and so on. This extreme division of labour implied that no single craftsman wholly controlled the production process. Some operations, however, required relatively expensive tools and considerable technical expertise, so that the producer in time gained a dominant position in the textile industry. Such was the case with weavers, whose wide horizontal pedal loom was by far the costliest machine in the woollen industry. In every town with a prominent export industry, some weavers worked their way up to be entrepreneurs. These Flemish *drapiers*, English drapers, and northern Italian *lanaiuoli* became the intermediaries between merchants and local producers. From the former they purchased raw wool, which was processed by the latter at piece-rates, after which they offered the finished products on the local market or sold the cloth, undyed, to merchants who had it finished and then put it on the international market.

There was no question of concentrating the diverse subsidiary processes in a single enterprise. The small workshop of the craftsman, who practised his calling together with a few journeymen and apprentices using relatively simple tools, completely dominated the thirteenth-century textile industry. The *lanarii* employed the putting-out system. They disbursed material successively to each craftsman responsible for a specific phase of production. Thus not only were fixed costs lowered, since the home of the workers was simultaneously their working place, but production could also be easily adjusted to the fluctuations of the market. The supply of labour was so great as a result of continuous immigration of the possessionless, and wages were consequently so low, that there was no particular stimulus to organize the production process in a more rational way.

Contrary to a commonly held notion, until the fourteenth century merchants and entrepreneurs remained two largely distinct groups. It is possible that some international traders appeared as entrepreneurs in the woollen industry, but the few examples cited in this connection are not conclusive and form, in every respect, exceptions. Thus, Jehan Boinebroke of Douai is the most famous case cited in support of the hypothetical penetration of commercial capital into industrial production during the second half of the thirteenth century. But it has recently been demonstrated that Boinebroke was neither *drapier* nor merchant employing wage labourers; he was a vendor of raw material, selling it on credit, and a purchaser of half-finished cloth, buying it from independent producers, after which he had it finished at piece-rates for sale on the international market.[7]

Why indeed would merchants have taken an interest in cloth manufacturing in the High Middle Ages? In the eleventh and twelfth centuries, the number of traders was so small and the market so broad, the gulf between supply and potential demand so immense and the distribution network so primitive, and the dependence of most regions on a few highly developed areas so large, that every trader could, with any luck, make easy and huge profits. From the thirteenth century on, things changed. The 'commercial revolution' signified long-term diminution of the individual merchant's profit possibilities. Rise in the number of merchants, improvement of the organization of the supply system, growth of more competitive markets and industrial centres: the concurrence of all these phenomena caused a growing disparity between the goods which this society could produce and distribute on the one side and those which it could consume on the other. The time of nearly unbounded commercial profit was definitely past: opportunities now had to be created artificially.

Merchants, of course, chose the easiest way. In the first place, they excluded outsiders, especially craftsmen, from the most profitable commercial branches. Most Flemish, English, and

Tuscan towns determined that membership of a mercantile guild was incompatible with the exercise of an industrial activity. Their intention was clear. The well-to-do master craftsmen were potentially dangerous competitors for professional traders, whose ability to exploit the producers in the last instance depended on the extent to which they controlled the import of raw materials and the export of finished products, a trading monopoly, therefore, best guaranteed the dependence of producers. In the second place, merchants turned all available means towards lowering cloth prices. They tried, via municipal authorities, to forbid every form of agreement among producers which could result in higher prices. This was possible because, in every town with an important textile industry, the most prominent merchants nestled into town government or exercised influence through family relations. In many places, thirteenth-century craftsmen were prohibited from joining together in guilds, even those with purely religious or humanitarian aims, for conspiracies could still be launched covertly. If the authorities did approve the foundation of confraternities, they took care that such organizations could never be turned against the merchants by requiring, for example, that their weekly contributions be handed over to the magistracy. In various towns, the authorities emphasized the 'right to work': at times of labour shortage, the master craftsmen had to hire sufficient apprentices to raise production. The real intent of all these strictures, of course, was hidden behind the mask of consumer's interest.[8]

Producers reacted against such measures. Above all, they tried to gain a greater voice in municipal government: only in that way could the commercial monopoly of the merchants be broken and the organization of labour be regulated in a way more advantageous for producers, that is for the more important master craftsmen. Both targets caused growing tension between artisans and patriciate, wherein the merchants were strongly represented. The attempts of the master craftsmen to transform the organization of labour meant concomitant oppression of the *popolo minuto*, the mass of semi-skilled and unskilled workers, whose socio-economic dependence was a precondition of the enrichment of the former. The social tensions arising from this structural antithesis could, however, easily be turned against the patriciate. Hence, the *popolo minuto* initially strove alongside the more important master craftsmen for entrance to municipal government and against the dominant position of the merchants.

Growing economic saturation, mirrored in the concentration on the manufacture of luxury clothes at the expense of lighter and cheaper materials, put the producers in a position to reinforce their demands. From 1280 on the first wave of revolts broke out. Nearly all the Flemish towns, and many in France, the Rhineland, Tuscany, and Catalonia were shaken by serious conflicts between *popolo* and patriciate. Except in Florence, where craftsmen gained a limited measure of political participation, these revolts were everywhere bloodily suppressed. The socio-economic transformations were, however, too fundamental for the trend to be restrained. During the first half of the fourteenth century textile workers nearly everywhere won places in the magistracy. But 'textile workers', meant only the independent artisans: wage labourers might function as shock-troops, but after the 'democratic revolution' of their employers they remained deprived of all real power, just as before. How could it be otherwise? The wage labourers were in a precarious position due to continuous replacement of the labour reserve by penurious immigrants; they lived in permanent insecurity due to fluctuations in the international market; they were closely watched by all other social groups; they were scattered over hundreds of workshops; and they were divided by the distrust which existed between and within professional groups. In these circumstances workers could scarcely take a broad view which fundamentally questioned social relationships, let alone assault them. Only after the demographic collapse of the fourteenth century would the *minuti* throughout Europe revolt against the *meliores*.

3. The many faces of poverty

Although data concerning the distribution of wealth in the Middle Ages are extremely scarce, all available evidence points in the same (not unexpected) direction: wealth was concentrated in the hands of a minority. From an *estimo* (direct tax) of 1243, it seems that 20 per cent of the households in Piuvica, a rural community near Pistoia, owned half of all taxable wealth, while 30 per cent owned a bare 14 per cent. An even more striking example: at Rumilly-lès-Vaudes, a village in the south of Champagne, the two highest assessed peasants paid as much as the forty-five least-taxed, who nonetheless made up one-third of the total number of taxpayers. Numerous figures concerning land distribution in the thirteenth century show that this was no exception. The series of data published by E. A. Kosminsky shows that nearly half of the tenantry in six English counties covered by the Hundred Rolls lived at or even under subsistence minima. Manorial evidence confirms this proportion: on 104 manors from eight estates in differing parts of England, 3,141 of the 6,924 customary tenants, or some 45 per cent, disposed of three hectares or less – too little to support a family. On twenty-five Winchester manors the number of landholders with less than four hectares amounted to somewhat more than half of the population. In certain parts of Lincolnshire, cottars with less than two hectares made up as much as three-quarters of the total. The lot of most French peasants was certainly not much better. At the end of the thirteenth century, 30 to 40 per cent of the tenants in Picardy exploited snippets of seven to ten *ares*. Yet, there too, one needed at least three to five hectares of land in order to avoid misery. Summarizing the data, Robert Fossier drew a picture of rural society in Picardy around 1300 in which 12 per cent of the population consisted of landless paupers and beggars, dwelling in huts outside the village, living off wage labour; in which 33 per cent cultivated a morsel of ground and were likewise obliged to market their labour to make ends meet; in which 36 per cent were poor, not owning a plough-team of oxen or horses, but generally succeeding in buying off labour services; in which 16 per cent had a holding sufficiently large to escape all difficulties; and in which 3 per cent dominated everyone else. In the southern Low Countries, the bulk of the rural population lived in similar penury. In 1289 nearly 58 per cent of the tenantry in the region of Namur disposed of only three hectares or less – nearly 19 per cent did not even have a single hectare. Around Ghent, over half the peasants held a bare three hectares in the first decade of the fourteenth century. In the bailiwicks of Veurne, Sint-Winoksbergen, Kassel, and the rural area around Brugge, the holdings of between 50 and 60 per cent of the peasantry in 1328 were smaller than 2.2 hectares.[9]

In short, around 1300, 40 to 60 per cent of western European peasants disposed of insufficient land to maintain a family. Their holdings were seldom larger than two or three hectares and had to be cultivated by hand, with low yields. Raising productivity was out of the question, since the requisite capital was lacking. Hiring a plough-team would risk the surrender of even more of the meagre harvest or sale of labour, due to the lack of cash. Raising an annual and perpetual rent on the holding would bind them completely for the future, because of the impossibility of repurchase. Stockbreeding on a small scale could provide a solution, but smallholders were deprived of common lands as much as possible by seigneurs, well-to-do peasants, and even the village community. For most of the poor, there was nothing besides wage labour. Those recruited as a full-time farmhand or *famulus* on an estate were possibly the best off: not only were they fed, but they also received a regular wage. The bulk of cottars, *manoperarii, manouvriers*, or *Höldner*, the precursors of the later rural proletariat, however, had to live off casual work. All this still took place within the feudal nexus, but, gradually, the umbilicus was cut. From the thirteenth century, the number of *extranei* or *vagantes*, landless paupers trekking here and there in search of work, grew at a sharp pace.

Social inequality was no less pronounced in the towns. At the end of the thirteenth century, 44 per cent of Parisian taxpayers consisted of *menus*, who all told contributed barely 6 per cent of total taxation. A quarter of a century later, the number in six parishes of Reims varied between 40 and 60 per cent. At about the same time, Toulouse counted as many *nihil habentes* as tax payers in 1335. Differences in wealth among the latter, moreover, were considerable: while 7.5 per cent held about 61 per cent of all taxable property, nearly 51 per cent held scarcely 6.5 per cent. In Bar-sur-Seine, for example, six burghers in 1339 together paid nearly as much as the 146 least taxed, who represented 53 per cent of all those taxable. Thanks to the rich Tuscan archives it is possible to estimate social contrasts in one town with an important textile industry. By 1300 around eighty companies of merchants with altogether 500 to 800 members comprised Florence's *Arte di Calimala*, and some 300 great textile manufacturers grouped together in the *Arte della Lana*. Since around 30,000 Florentines lived off the wool industry, approximately one-third of the population was thus directly or indirectly dependent on a thousand or so businessmen, who, including their families, made up at most 5 or 6 per cent of the total population. In the first half of the fourteenth century, concentration advanced even further: between 1308 and 1338, the number of workshops dropped from three hundred to two hundred, although the value of the combined production rose from 600,000 to 1,200,000 florins. In the same period, the *lanivendoli*, small businessmen specializing in the purchase of raw wool which they had washed and beaten before sale to the *lanaiuoli*, were eliminated.

Without a doubt, the majority of Florentine artisans in the thirteenth and fourteenth centuries endured bitter poverty. Though censuses are lacking, some indirect evidence points out the massive extent of pauperism. According to Villani, the chronicler mentioned earlier, a rich burgher ordered in September 1330 that six pennies should be distributed after his death to every poor person in the town: 430 pounds were disbursed, so that 17,200 persons, or 19 per cent of the population, received alms. The figure does not seem inflated, for the charitable society of Or San Michele alone supported in June 1347 no less than 7,000 paupers. The main cause of urban poverty was undoubtedly under-payment, itself a result of the unfavourable evolution of socio-economic relationships. Ch.-M. de la Roncière investigated the daily wages paid to gardeners, masons' labourers, and masons in fourteenth-century Florence, expressed in wheat. He multiplied the least, the highest, and the average daily wage by 280 (i.e. by the annual maximum working days in the *ancien régime*) and then divided the product by 365. Finally the figures were expressed in kilograms of wheaten bread, the staple of the Florentine diet, and in the corresponding number of calories. By this method, it is possible to see whether various working groups earned enough to live. A child under fifteen needs about 2,000 calories per day, an inactive adult 2,500, and a manual labourer 3,500. The figures have been divided by four to see whether wages sufficed to feed a family of four – two adults and two children. Let us first look at the standard of living of gardeners, the working group more or less comparable to rural workers (Table 2). To interpret these figures, two factors must be considered. First, no individual worker could devote his wages exclusively to food – 20 to 30 per cent went on rent, fuel, clothing, and other less important items. Second, a balanced diet does not consist solely of carbohydrates: without a minimum consump-

Table 2.
Purchasing power, expressed in calories, of gardeners in Florence, 1326–39 and 1340–47

Wage	*Number of calories per capita per diem*			
	Bachelors		*Families*	
	1326–39	1340–47	1326–39	1340–47
Minimum	5,325	3,115	1,330	780
Maximum	9,550	6,300	2,380	1,375
Average	7,015	4,725	1,755	1,180

Source : Ch.-M. de La Roncière, *Pauvres et pauvreté*, vol. II, p. 674.

tion of proteins and fats, physical and psychological debilitation soon sets in. However calories provided by meat, fish, butter, cheese, or oil are much costlier than those from grain. It is no exaggeration to say that the purchase of non-cereal foodstuffs accounted for around 10 per cent of wages. In short, workers could not devote more than 60 to 70 per cent of their income to wheaten bread. Therefore, the daily wage of an unmarried worker had to equal 5,000 calories to lead a 'normal' life, that is to do heavy labour, to enjoy a reasonably varied diet, to pay rent regularly, to replace worn-out clothes occasionally. With 3,000 to 4,000 calories, he could feed himself, but was obliged to economize on all other items. A daily consumption of 2,500 calories sufficed to stave off starvation, but excluded all other expenses and implied permanent malnutrition. As for a married labourer with two children, he had to earn the equivalent of around 3,500 calories per day per person to provide for all his family's needs. If he brought home enough for 2,000 to 3,000 calories per person, then the family could be fed 'properly' only if all other expenses were kept to a strict minimum; with wages any lower, the family was always underfed, even if everything was spent on bread.

On this basis, we can evaluate the estimated living standards of Florentine gardeners. Bachelors earned not only enough to live in the 1320s and 30s, but some of them even had funds to spare. In contrast, in the years 1340 to 1346 all except the best paid had to prune their expenditures for clothing, rent and the like in order to buy food, but even then they probably did not face hunger. The situation was completely different for families. A family of four disposing of an average income during the whole period under consideration lived in extremely precarious circumstances. Even if the father's wages were completely devoted to bread, the spectre of hunger still threatened. In the 1340s the situation was absolutely hopeless: not one gardener could feed a family; even work done by his wife changed nothing as a woman received scarcely half as much as an unskilled man.

Table 3.
Purchasing power, expressed in calories, of masons' labourers in Florence, 1326–32 and 1340–46.

Wage	*Number of calories per capita per diem*			
	Bachelors		*Families*	
	1326–32	1340–46	1326–32	1340–46
Minimum	3,875	3,025	975	750
Maximum	10,750	7,000	2,700	1,750
Median	8,750	4,000	2,185	1,000

Source: Ch.-M. de La Roncière, *Pauvres et pauvreté*, vol. II, p. 679.

Masons' labourers did not do much better. (Table 3). Most bachelors seldom confronted destitution. Only the poorest paid had to trim their supplementary expenditures in 1326–32 in order to enjoy a varied diet. During the 1340s, the majority had to do so, but they probably did not face hunger. Yet, just like a gardener's wages, the mason's labourer could not support a family of four. By the mid-fourteenth century, the family of a mason's labourer was even worse off than a gardener's: no one could survive on 1,000 calories per day, even if the mother provided an extra 500 calories. The most highly skilled construction workers, master masons, likewise did not succeed in providing a family of four with a decent standard of living; in 1326–32, the equivalent of their daily wage amounted to less than 2,500 calories per family member, and in 1340–46, barely 2,000. Some general conclusions emerge from these data. Poverty did not limit itself to the working groups studied. The range of nominal wages in each professional category was so great that the lowest remunerations in all sectors of economic life lay beneath subsistence minima. Living standards declined along with job qualifications, and most immigrants led a miserable existence for many years. Bachelors were least threatened with hunger, but families generally existed in a state of chronic need. Marriage for most workers brought misery, and the unskilled in particular had to tighten their belts at marriage. Workingmen's children suffered permanent malnutrition. Even if the head of household had a relatively well-paid job, his income hardly provided bread for two children, and a working woman encountered the severest poverty if her husband died; she seldom earned enough to feed herself, let alone her children.

4. Charity: mortgaging the future

How did the elite react to the structural poverty which manifested itself in town and country alike? In the early Middle Ages the concept *pauper* was not understood to refer to a man in need, nor to a slave or serf. He was a free man whose freedom had to be guaranteed. The foremost characteristic of the pauper was his dependence, which could take on various forms: it might result from physical debility (youth, old age, illness), mental deficiency, or a certain status (orphan, widow), but it could also be a conscious choice – there were the *pauperes Christi*, men and women who followed Christian teachings literally, living near churches and cloisters in voluntary poverty. Only one form of dependence was implicitly ascribed to economic circumstances: free smallholders whose incomes, as a result of plundering or other misfortune, were insufficient to match the demands of the *potentes* were labelled *pauperes.*

The Church was not unduly perturbed by the existence of this group: they formed a normal constituent of a society which was of necessity hierarchic. Adversity was a personal ordeal set by God, who offered the pauper as well as his benefactor the chance of salvation. Hincmar, Archbishop of Reims, and his followers opposed only those excesses which endangered the means to support large numbers of paupers; they condemned *avaritia* and *cupiditas*, the roots of all evil in society. These sins led ecclesiastics to squander the property entrusted to them and led the laity to steal from the Church and from their neighbours. Above all, *potentes* who misused their position of power in order to lay their hands on ecclesiastical property or to ruin free smallholders drew complaints, because their lust for wealth threatened order and peace. Perceptions of poverty penetrated no further. In a society which considered *paupertas* a normal way of life and alms a normal means of subsistence within a 'gift-economy', the structural opposition of *potens-pauper* could scarcely be recognized.

Charity remained a monopoly of the Church, especially monks, well into the eleventh century. Every large Benedictine abbey had its almshouse, where bread was disbursed on feastdays; its infirmary, where the sick or lame were admitted; and its pilgrims' shelter, where travellers found temporary lodgings. Although the significance of this form of poor relief ought not to be underestimated, it was in fact the sole refuge of the needy. The laity seldom gave alms; they limited their charity to donations to abbeys and other ecclesiastical institutions. But from the twelfth century, a change gradually showed itself. Traditional charitable foundations enlarged their scope of action and, more important, the laity began to concern itself with poor relief. Innumerable hospitals, pilgrims' shelters, leper-houses, and almshouses sprouted up in and around the towns.

This proliferation of charities may be ascribed to two closely related factors. First, economic development, as said above, resulted in growing social disparities. Smallholders could no longer subsist; they were forced to take out usurious loans, eventually losing their lands to their creditors and creating a surplus population which drifted to the towns. Released from the land, the pauper no longer enjoyed the protection of the village community, which may have disdained but never abandoned him. In town the uprooted pauper was only an anonymous stranger, who as a wandering beggar could spread disease and, even worse, as an unemployed pauper could cause trouble. Consequently, many towns set up reception centres, where the sick, lame, poor, and passing travellers received temporary material and spiritual aid. The newly rich, the *burgenses*, were interested in the security of the town where they lived and worked, hence it was often they who first brought together the necessary financial means to found charitable institutions. Since burghers thus *de facto* retained control of the funds, they gradually expanded their powers over areas which had traditionally been controlled by the Church. Second, evangelism flourished during this period. The growing seriousness of the phenomenon of poverty stimulated the search for spiritual solutions. Return to the gospels, the key word of twelfth-century religious movements, signified return to the material and spiritual poverty of the Church. The exaltation of voluntary poverty was not a goal in itself but a means directed against earthly temptations; consequently it had a sanctifying character. A conscious connection was made between contemplation and action: individual ascetics could actually contribute to the relief of others' material impoverishment. This religious development deeply influenced collective mentalities. Were not the poor, the suffering members of the body of Christ, the privileged intermediaries between believers and the Saviour, whom, on account of their need, they most closely approached of any mortals? This inclination grew even stronger in the thirteenth century through the activities of the mendicant orders, mindful of the word of St Francis of Assisi: *Nudus nudum Christum sequerere*, naked follow the naked Christ.

The sanctification of poverty justified the *status quo*: the poor were nailed to a cross at the bottom of society. Since they brought about the necessary mediation between this world and the other, their place on earth seemed indispensable. The fundamental distinction between rich and poor was consequently unquestioned; for the souls of the rich sufficed an inner poverty, expressible in good deeds. Thus the poor were reduced to the passive agents of a spiritual action which completely escaped them. The alms they received brought spiritual value to the donors alone, for whom *caritas* functioned as an 'investment in the hereafter'. In short, the 'social contract' of the High Middle Ages came to this: since to be saved the rich needed the poor, the poor had the duty to remain poor, while the rights attached to their status implied the duty of submission to the rich. Did not Christ, the apostles, and St Francis cheerfully endure their poverty? Hence widows, the sick and lame, and beggars who accepted their lot were seen as the chosen of God, and the poverty of underpaid wage labourers was noted with approval (if at all).

It is evident that these conceptions rested on a choice, whether conscious or not: some exceptions aside, ecclesiastics emphasized certain texts out of Scripture (Luke 16:19–31, Matthew 5:3 and 25:31–36) while passing over others (especially James 5:4). Portraying poverty as a virtuous condition to be accepted with resignation, they subverted the apostolic mission of the Church in favour of the rich. How could it be otherwise? Ecclesiastics directed themselves towards the group which had the means and the power to relieve the most crying needs. It could scarcely be expected of merchants and entrepreneurs, whose activities focused on their own enrichment, to release the poor from their misery, since the poor formed the backbone of the work force necessary for today's profits, and tomorrow's. There was an obvious compromise: rich and poor needed one another; spiritual and

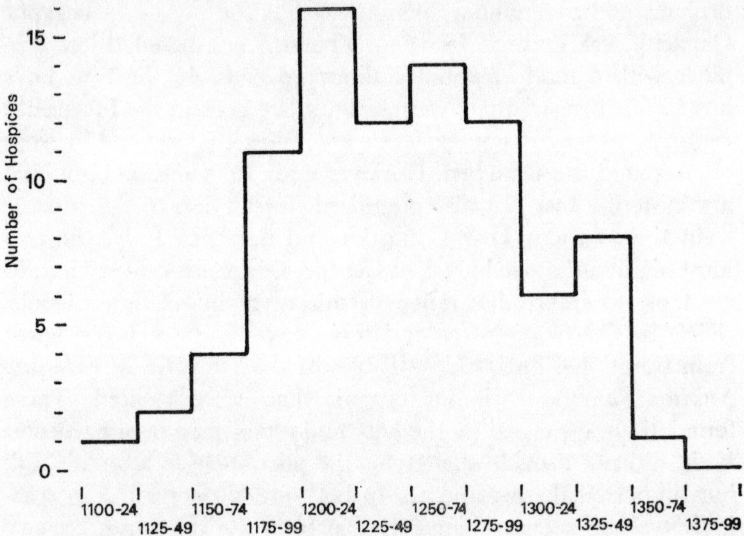

Fig. 1 Number of hospices founded in the region of Paris, 1100–1399.

Source: based on M. Candille, 'Pour un précis d'histoire des institutions charitables, quelques données du XIIe–XIVe siècles,' *Bulletin de la Société française d'Histoire des Hôpitaux*, 30 (1974).

Note. The data refer to the area covered by the *départements* Seine, Seine-et-Marne and Seine-et-Oise.

material poverty were complementary. And, after all alms assured more than the soul of the donor. They also guaranteed the continued existence of the labour market and the maintenance of a social equilibrium.

This dual function of relief gained importance as fast as the number of poor grew. The thirteenth century witnessed a spectacular augmentation of charitable institutions and a systematic extension of existing foundations. Hospitals were enlarged, their personnel adjusted and administration reorganized. To understand medieval poor relief, one must realize that these institutions fulfilled wholly different functions from today. Health care was of secondary significance. Expenses for medicines represented only a fraction of their budget – many hospitals did not even retain a physician. Emphasis lay on *hospitalitas*, especially for the needy. This included the sick and lame, travellers and pilgrims, orphans and pregnant women, as well as the poor and beggars. Capacity was limited. In 1339, Florence numbered thirty hospitals with a total of about a thousand beds. In the Sint-Jan's hospital in Brugge, there were seventy-five beds in the fourteenth century – meagre figures, even assuming that several persons often shared the same bed. However, most hospitals had not only a ministering task but also organized distribution to the poor.

In the southern Low Countries and northern Italy, the two most highly urbanized areas of Europe, thirteenth-century burghers took an impressive range of initiatives in relation to poor relief. In dozens of towns and their surrounding villages, apart from traditional institutions, Tables of the Holy Ghost (*Mensae Spiritus Sancti*) or similar organizations were created. These foundations, governed by the laity and established on a parochial basis, did not provide shelter for the poor such as hospitals did, but supported them at home. In both areas, poor relief increasingly took on a controlling function from the thirteenth century onwards, since, in the heavily populated centres economic fluctuations had greater and more dangerous social repercussions.

The close connection between economic changes on one side and social control on the other can be clearly seen in the 'charitable' actions of municipal authorities in Ieper. The foundations of hospitals (1226, 1270, 1276 and 1277) in this textile town corresponded to short-term but severe economic crises. The background was always the same: lack of raw materials (English wool) for local industry and subsequent high unemployment. The new institutions were intended to meet the needs of the urban labour market. The number of admissions varied: in periods of full employment they discharged the poor who in the preceding years had been admitted. Thus thirteen-century Ieper's charitable provisions arose not only from impulses of social justice among the patriciate, but also from material circumstances; since marginal labour potential could easily be lost in case of long unemployment, refuges for temporary relief were set up.[10]

From all available evidence, it seems incontrovertible that the burghers intended to do no more than save the poor from total starvation. During the first half of the fourteenth century the two most important charitable institutions in Florence, the society Or San Michele and the hospital San-Paolo de Convalescenti, disbursed bread, clothing and small amounts of money at regular intervals to a mass of beggars; also, they supported about a thousand selected 'stable' poor. The chosen received from the governing boards a ticket (*polizza*), granting assistance. The aid given to the stable element was much more extensive than that given sporadically to the anonymous group. Yet the bulk of the poor received *in polizzis* for two months a sum only equal to a day and a half's wages for an unskilled worker – enough to buy only six to seven kilograms of wheaten bread, or about 15,000 calories. Spread over a year, that gave less than 250 calories per day. Since most of those receiving such relief were married and had children, this quantity had to be portioned out to several people, so each member of a family of parents and two children received the daily equivalent of sixty supplementary calories, or a thirtieth of the subsistence minimum. In the Low Countries, *per capita* support was even lower. Around 1330, a thousand poor, supported by the Table of the Holy Ghost in the Sint-Niklaas parish of Ghent, the most thickly populated quarter of the largest town in the Low Countries, received a yearly average of 2.7 kg of wheaten bread, or 7.4 g per day. One must remember, however, that almsmen in most Netherlands towns also received yearly a pair of shoes, several ells of linen, and a small amount of meat. Hence the poor relief there, just as in Florence, was chiefly intended as a supplement for insufficient family income.

Charity at its best merely saved the recipient from immediate starvation; nowhere was a serious attempt made substantially to better the lot of the needy. Altruism, religiously inspired and expressed, was present, but the disinterestedness of most donors manifested itself only within well-determined limits, roomy enough to sanctify poverty, but restricted enough to relieve only minimal needs. The social problem was reduced to a moral question, and was collectively perceived chiefly from a tolerant but repressive perspective. A fundamental crisis was essential to make clear to the *potentes* that the unity of material and spiritual poverty was nothing more than a mental construct.

Chapter 2

CRISIS, SOCIAL PROBLEMS AND POOR LAWS (*c.1350–c.1450*)

FROM around 1350 until the mid-fifteenth century, the whole of Europe passed through a general crisis. Catastrophic dearth and epidemics were accompanied by long and devastating wars, while a dramatic rise in mortality and a sharp drop in the birth rate caused the greatest demographic collapse since the Dark Ages. Within a century, European population diminished by some 30 to 35 per cent. Innumerable villages were abandoned and massive migrations took place. Nor was the urban economy spared: although international commerce retained its fundamental characteristics, the drastic fall in population meant a contraction of the overall volume of business, and there were changes in the orientation of trade and location of industries. Taxes rose systematically, and a general shortage of precious metals repeatedly led to debasement of coinage, aggravating even further the effects of the crisis. Simultaneously, the internal conflicts of feudal society were pushed to the limit: rural and urban areas alike were the stage for violent revolts.

1. Social inequality and the limits to growth

The causes of the fourteenth-century crisis fall outside the scope of this book, but it is important to realize that these causes are not to be found either in external factors (changes in climate for example) or in a simple supply-and-demand demographic model. The first point needs little explanation. The possibilities and limitations inherent in specific modes of production largely determine the impact of external factors. To cite Pierre Vilar: 'What is of significance is the response of an agrarian society to a meteorological challenge and in the information which that response gives concerning the society involved. . . . The problem begins on the social plane, it does not end on the climatological plane.'[1]

The second point deserves more attention. Many historians, M. M. Postan among them, have postulated that a general disruption of society was inevitable, given that population continuously increased while productivity in the long run fell, due to the exhaustion of marginal land, primitive agrarian technology and organization, extensive fragmentation of holdings, and low levels of investment. In these circumstances, it is argued, the law of diminishing returns came into play, leading to a 'bottle-neck'. However, this is a description of the crisis, not an explanation: its proponents do not make clear why conditions conducive to long-term stagnation continued despite a substantial increase in population. Their entire rationale rests in the last instance on implicit acceptance of a neo-malthusian model, the 'natural', deterministic character of which stands unquestioned; yet a whole series of questions remain open. Why, for example, was economic growth in most of Europe limited to extension of arable ('widening of capital'), while productive investment ('deepening of capital') steadily gained in importance in Flanders? Intensification of agriculture, marked by improved rotation of crops and specialization in livestock, fodder and cash crops, was undoubtedly aided in this area by the early enfranchisement of the peasantry, who did not see their extra efforts negated by a proportional increase in surplus extraction. They were also encouraged by the proximity of extensive natural pasturage alongside coasts and rivers, and by the presence of numerous urban centres, steady customers and a source of fertilizer, tools and, eventually, imported grain. Hence the example of Flanders shows how technological improvements were possible in medieval agriculture. Certainly, raising the productivity of land and labour was initially attained only in the so-called *Intensitätsinseln* around the great towns, but in any case, it seemed possible to break through the law of diminishing returns. Despite extensive fragmentation of the land, the fourteenth-century crisis was much milder in Flanders than in other European countries. In short, the long-term tendency towards relative overpopulation was then, as now, not a 'natural' fact.

It is not our intention to minimize the role of demographic factors in the evolution of a society, much less deny it. But population growth never takes place in isolation: it must always be related to a specific mode of production. Simply to note that a significant part of the European population lived on the edge of starvation by 1300 does not imply that the preceding demographic expansion necessarily had to result in massive impoverishment, malnutrition, and mortality. The roots of the fourteenth-century crisis must be sought in the dynamics of the feudal mode of production. As Robert Brenner recently stated:

> Because of lack of funds – due to landlords' extraction of rent and the extreme maldistribution of both land and capital, especially livestock – the peasantry were by and large unable to use the land they held in a free and rational manner. They could not, so to speak, put back what they took out of it. Thus the surplus-extraction relations of serfdom tended to lead to the exhaustion of peasant production *per se*. . . . The crisis of productivity led to demographic crisis, pushing the population over the edge of subsistence.[2]

The tendency towards crisis was, in other words, built into the interrelated structure of peasant organization of production on the one hand and the institutionalized relationships of surplus extraction on the other. Considering that 50 per cent or more of the gross output of servile peasants was creamed off, and that landlords on the average applied only 5 per cent of their incomes for productive purposes, one is compelled to accept this explanation. The nobility, who disposed of the necessary means to employ technological improvements, squandered the vast bulk of the extorted surplus, while the peasantry, for whom deepening of capital was a question of life and death, could seldom accumulate sufficient reserves to take steps in that direction.

Furthermore, from the twelfth century both landlords and the well-off peasantry attempted to deny commons and *pascua* (wasteland) to smallholders, and, on the pretext of protecting commons and wastes, many seigneurs usurped the right to control the use of these lands. The more important peasants reacted, most often, by forming associations to back their claims forcefully. In some cases they lost, and the seigneurs extended their right to use common lands wholly or partially to their own advantage; in other cases they reached an accord defining mutual rights and obligations. Such a compromise, however, was often detrimental to the cottars, who could not assert ancient rights of usage, since their well-to-do neighbours had every incentive to engross as much meadowland as possible in order to increase their livestock to the maximum. Moreover landlords, stimulated by the high speculative profits of marketing wood, moved to limit or even to prohibit admission to forestlands in the early thirteenth century. Smallholders lost not only fuel, construction material and a little extra food, such as berries and small game, but also a place to pasture their few livestock. These deep-seated changes worsened demographic tensions.

Since economic growth had a predominantly extensive character for structural reasons, it had to lead sooner or later to a general blockage. A gradual diminution of the productivity of land and labour in these circumstances was simply unavoidable. The first symptom manifested itself by the end of the thirteenth century in the stagnation of population growth, or even, here and there, regression. As Guy Bois has shown, the critical threshold was crossed at the moment when the volume of seigneurial extraction began to show signs of weakening, that is, when the declining rate of surplus extraction could no longer be compensated for by economic and demographic growth. Landlords had to demand more socially, while economically the peasants could not spare a greater part of their produce. Every attempt to impose extra exactions on the peasantry, either through taxes or through plunder, aggravated this fundamental contradiction, affecting productive capacity and demographic potential.

If social inequality imposed limits to growth and, consequently, entailed large-scale impoverishment in the countryside during the period preceding the Black Death, what of the period after? With the drastic fall in population, was the burden of surplus extraction on the peasantry diminished, allowing, in addition to improved material conditions, productive investment towards the agrarian growth needed to avoid demographic catastrophes in the future?

Due to the strongly divergent socio-economic evolution of the various parts of Europe and the often inadequate sources, these questions cannot be answered with an unconditional yes or no. However, there was no simple causal connection linking demographic collapse and its related phenomena with subsequent socio-economic evolution, as can be seen from a comparison of eastern and western Europe. Although in both areas population dropped, serfdom disappeared gradually in the west, while it was newly imposed in the east. How is this contrasting development to be explained? Eastern European peasants could be more easily dominated by their landlords, because they had developed village community solidarity and local political autonomy in much smaller measure than western European peasants. The whole evolution of this area into a 'colonial' society, dominated by its landlords, seriously obstructed the emergence of peasant power and peasant self-government. When lardlords, confronted with economic crisis and relative scarcity of labour, attempted to secure their incomes by imposing coercive controls on the peasantry, the peasants could not in the long run resist their lords. Even less so because the princes formed no effective counterweight. The once powerful monarchies of Poland, Bohemia and Hungary had virtually disintegrated by the early fifteenth century. There was a brief restoration of royal power in the middle of the century, but fifty years later the nobility had definitely gained the edge over the princes and was able, in addition, to nullify municipal autonomies. Not surprisingly, the peasants, despite hopeless outbursts of violence, ultimately succumbed to seigneurial reaction and the imposition of serfdom. For the first time in history, a true manorial economy arose in the East. The focus of production shifted gradually to the great demesne, parcelled out to feudal entrepreneurs, at the expense of the once important *rolniki* or well-to-do peasants, now completely eliminated. The ratio of demesne to peasant cultivation on noble estates rose to unprecedented levels; in Poland, for example, the average fluctuated between 2:3 and 4:5 in the period 1500–80. The outcome was what André Gunder Frank called the 'development of under-development'.[3] The large amounts of uncultivated land and, above all, the availability of forced labour, whose services could be intensified, discouraged the implementation of agricultural improvements, while the growing squeeze on the peasants by landlords excluded the growth of an internal market for industrial goods. Progress in eastern Europe was henceforth limited to extension of arable. Dependence on the export of grain to the west was, in the last analysis, the result of economic backwardness inherent in a feudal system based on the large scale estate as fundamental unit of production. While the West headed towards a period of unparalleled expansion, the East consigned itself to centuries of structural stagnation.

Nor was the outcome of the fourteenth-century crisis predetermined in western Europe, as the example of England shows. Although the labour market was already tight by the middle of the fourteenth century, real wages rose substantially only from around 1380, when the legal status of the peasantry improved as well. The first reaction of many English landlords to demographic collapse was in essence an attempt to control the peasants and rural labourers, who found themselves in a favourable negotiating position. New laws held wages low, migration was blocked as much as possible, and old obligations were increased. This policy was fairly successful for a few decades: real wages increased only minimally, and the higher nobility in the 1370s drew only 10 per cent less income from their lands than in the 1340s, although the population meantime had fallen by some 30 per cent. The reversal of the trend around 1380 was due in large measure to the resolute and sometimes bloody resistance of village communities against the seigneurial reaction. Without this struggle, the material improvement of the peasantry would have been delayed even longer.

Although the evolution of society after the Black Death was far more complex and varied than a simple neo-Malthusian model would lead us to suppose, the living conditions of the western European peasantry did improve in certain limited respects. Notably, the last remnants of servile status gradually lost their real significance. The extent and intensity of that process depended on the fluctuations of the balance of power between lord and peasant; thus the lessening and eventual disappearance of serfdom differed from country to country and even from manor to manor, but by the end of the fifteenth century the great majority of western European peasants had lost the stigma of personal servility.

Two economic factors also benefited the peasant: the drop in real terms of fixed payments and the declining interests of landlords in direct exploitation of estates affected by falling grain prices and rising wages. Numerous demesnes were wholly or partially parcelled out, giving the peasantry the opportunity to rent land. Obviously, renting land could bring losses as well as gains; everything depended on the terms of the lease, which could, according to circumstances, be permanent or renewable. Excepting Italy and part of France where half the harvest went to the landowner (*mezzadria, métayage*), the system of money rents in place of rent in kind seems in general to have favoured the peasantry in the fourteenth and fifteenth centuries: due to the drop in grain prices and the numerous devaluations of currency, rents almost everywhere declined.

In a different way, some marginal agricultural labourers also benefited; though the rise in real wages varied in its timing and intensity, it was a general and highly pronounced phenomenon. In England around 1400, for example, the wages of a relatively well-paid worker, such as a ploughman, together with the earnings of his wife and child, equalled the income to be drawn from the cultivation of eight hectares of land. Even where wage rises were far from spectacular, the economically weak could buy more foodstuffs than before thanks to a sharp decline in grain prices.

Yet the impact of these benefits was restricted, for the peasantry as a whole was still not able to provide a level of investment which would ensure the growth of agrarian production. Social differentiation within the peasantry had increased rather than decreased after the Black Death, despite favourable conditions, and every peasant could not make use to the same degree of the economic possibilities offered during the phase of disruption. The well-to-do naturally disposed of the necessary means to buy up abandoned land, to rent demesne, to introduce technical innovations, to switch over as necessary to raising cash crops or livestock – in short, to accumulate land and capital. This minority, whose possessions steadily increased, became by the end of the fifteenth century the most dynamic 'upper class' in the countryside. They alone were able to contribute to increased productivity.

Peasants with a small or even a middle-size holding were not. In the first place, they were able to profit from the growing land market only to a very limited extent. Lacking reserves, they were no match for the competition of their better-off neighbours and rich townsmen. Moreover, grain prices fell farther and quicker than the prices of other agricultural products; the same holds true for all agrarian prices *vis-à-vis* industrial goods. Certainly, all peasants were confronted with relatively high expenses for wages and tools on one side and with relatively low profit margins on the other. However, any possible answer to the decline of income, such as switching over from less profitable grain to more profitable cattle raising, was beyond the reach of those without capital. Furthermore, the expansion of cattle-breeding which began at the end of the fourteenth century brought more disadvantages than advantages to most rural inhabitants, for both landlords and the rural upper class tried more than ever to lay their hands on the commons. Moreover, cattle, as opposed to grain, required a small labour force, so that this specialization endangered rural employment. Secondly, peasants with small and middle-sized holdings grew more subject to the vicissitudes of the market. The best means for smallholders to avoid the effects of dropping grain prices was undoubtedly to change over to cash crops, which made possible relatively high yields on a small area of land. Increasingly, in the fourteenth and fifteenth centuries, western European farmers turned to the cultivation of wine, hops, oil-bearing seeds, flax and dye-stuffs, profiting from the relatively high prices of industrial products. The reverse of the coin was that they became completely dependent on the market for the sale of their produce and purchase of foodstuffs – a twofold dependence implying greater insecurity. Caught between the scissors of increasing social inequality and the growing tyranny of the market, not only could the western European peasantry as a whole not invest on a large scale in agrarian growth, but in many areas they even faced an actual deterioration in material conditions during the decline of serfdom.

2. The golden age of the craftsman?

It is generally agreed that the century after the Black Death witnessed a redistribution of wealth and economic activity from one region to another. In some respects this process signalled a loss for the towns in general; a clear example of that trend is the spread of rural industry, which emerged in many areas, at the cost of urban production. Alternatively, some centres lost ground because others grew in importance. An important shift took place in the hierarchy of manufactured goods; traditional industries declined as new ones came on the scene. There are considerable differences of opinion, however, over the level of business activity during this period. While the proponents of a depression in the Renaissance do not deny many signs of local prosperity, they emphasize that 'the rapid progress of a few younger countries may be insufficient to make up for the slow decline of the old economic giants', but others contend that there was only 'a reshaping of the international division of labour', and that the growth of new businesses in most cases compensated for the decline of the old.[4] However important this debate may be from the economic point of view, socially it is of little relevance. For artisans who lost opportunities for profit – or even employment – it was scant comfort to know that other regions or industries profited, and major shifts in the structure of industrial production during this period ensured that all but the elite of skilled workers faced the threat of severe setbacks. As urban industry shifted to production of luxury goods, the craftsman in his supposed 'Golden Age' encountered both competition from the emergence of rural industry and a growing tendency towards economic concentration within the towns.

From the first half of the fourteenth century, the older centres of Flanders, Brabant, and northern Italy concentrated increasingly – and often exclusively – on the manufacture of expensive cloth of the finest wool, neglecting less expensive fabrics. Their example was quickly followed by smaller and younger centres of production. Growing foreign competition undoubtedly played an important role in the move towards higher quality. With the persistently high level of mortality due to endemic plague, and with the weakening of transcontinental trade which led to a further contraction of the total market, competition between the various manufacturing centres in the second half of the fourteenth century became particularly stiff. Thus English competition brought about a reorientation of the Flemish and Brabant cloth industry, which tried to compensate for low production costs in England (above all cheap wool) by making the demand for their luxury woollens less elastic. Luxury industries emerged, producing for international consumption and dependent on highly skilled workmen and fashionable refinements. This choice was made possible by the advanced technical infrastructure and the great supply of human capital available in the southern Netherlandish towns.

Other factors besides foreign competition were also involved in the renovation of the industrial life of the major textile centres, which had, in fact, begun before English competition made itself felt. The costs of production and of distribution had risen, as labour and credit grew more expensive and transport more insecure, favouring goods with high unit value and a low proportion of labour costs. Second, a shift in the structure of demand must be taken into account: population decline affected the lower income groups much more than the higher, while the 'inheritance effect' led to an even more distorted division of wealth. Many *homines novi* of the previous century had withdrawn from the export trade, due to its greater risks and fewer chances for profit, so that more capital became available for consumption. The strengthening of central authority, culminating in the unified Burgundian State, called into being a luxurious court with an extended and well-paid officer corps, while the enrichment of the 'middle classes' must not be forgotten. Although this group presumably declined in number, it augmented its portion of the total wealth.[5] Thanks to these favourable circumstances, the great towns of Flanders and Brabant managed to survive the crisis.

This shift towards luxury goods strengthened the social position of skilled workers on two fronts. By emphasizing the creativity of the craftsman and by manufacturing cloths destined exclusively for the elites, they grew less dependent on economic fluctuations and, consequently, on merchants. This structural factor was without doubt a decided advantage for the prosperous guild masters in their struggle to secure a place in town government. At the same time, they were more than ever given the opportunity to strengthen their grip on the workers. Advanced specialization meant tight control of the manufacturing process, particularly of the labour involved. In all great textile centres, industrial regulations and guild organization became an integral part of economic life in the course of the fourteenth century. Conditions of production were fixed; the quality of fabrics was inspected by an official specially appointed for the task; wages in all occupations were strictly controlled; admission to a guild was regulated in a draconian fashion – henceforth, no one could become a master without producing a masterpiece, the execution of which became steadily more difficult and more expensive. An admission fee was required, and this was steadily raised. All these protectionist measures favoured the more important masters and justified their privileged status. Thus the protection of individual trademarks of quality sharpened social distinction.

The triumph of urban corporatism gradually spurred the merchants to divert their activities to the countryside. From the end of the thirteenth century, production of cheap cloth in quantity began in many rural areas of western Europe. Attempts by Flemish towns during the first quarter of the fourteenth century to obstruct this expansion had few results, since the counts and landlords of Flanders protected rural industry for the financial advantages which it brought them. In the Italian countryside also, woollen weaving expanded quickly. Francesco Datini, head of a large commercial firm at Prato, employed more workers in the surrounding countryside than in the town by the early fourteenth century. In England too, after the Black Death, the cloth industry took refuge in rural areas, where the introduction of the fulling mill increased physical productivity, pushing costs down. Linen weaving in particular was successful in many areas, at the expense of urban production. In southern Germany and north-eastern Switzerland, an industrial complex arose: in innumerable villages south of Lake Constance pure linens were produced, while the rural population of the area bounded by Ulm, Augsburg, Kempten, and Ravensburg concentrated on fustians made from a flaxen warp and woollen weft. From 1400, rural linen weaving also developed in the area around Chemnitz, in Westphalia (above all between Münster and Osnabrück), in a large part of Flanders, and in Hainaut, Brittany, and Burgundy.

The gradual but steady growth of rural industry must be ascribed to the concurrence of two factors. First, merchants tried to compensate for their declining margins of profit by turning to cheap labour. Since subsistence costs were lower in the countryside than in the towns, and since the guilds exercised no influence, relatively low wages could be paid to rural workers. Moreover, the absence of corporate controls allowed production to match the demands of the market, especially introduction of new fabrics destined for less well-off consumers, while the smaller fiscal demands made on the countryside militated in favour of rural industry. Secondly, many small farmers sought to supplement their income following the decline in grain prices. As their economic situation worsened, they became interested in 'marginal' activities.

The fourteenth century in no sense witnessed a diminishing influence on the part of the merchant-entrepreneur; on the contrary, merchants in this period dealt directly with woollen and linen weaving, not (or only secondarily) in the towns, where an aristocracy of guild masters controlled the manufacturing process, but rather in the countryside, where a cheaper and more willing workforce was at hand. Since the peasants who turned to weaving were generally too poor to buy the requisite raw materials, most of them soon depended on the merchants, without whose command of the market they could not dispose of their produce. The most telling example of the growing impact of commercial capital on rural industry is undoubtedly the *Grosse Gesellschaft* of Ravensburg: this merchants' association, founded around 1380, by the fifteenth century monopolized the linen and fustian production of whole cantons.

The expansion of rural industry had a feedback effect on the towns: urban industries outside the major, long-established centres were adversely affected by the competition of the cheaper products of the countryside, as were those sectors in the major centres which proved unable to switch over to luxury goods. European demand for cheap cloth was limited, and it was sufficiently met by rural industry, so that most smaller centres were crushed during the decline of the traditional cloth industry upon which they had almost exclusively depended.

The elite among skilled workers, however, managed to survive the crisis relatively unscathed; concentration on luxury goods, in fact, offered several thousand craftsmen the opportunity to climb up the social ladder. Technical proficiency and personal creativity were more than ever highly rewarded, but two important reservations must be made. Although statistics are lacking, there can be little doubt that the number of artisans who made a living or even grew rich from the booming luxury industries in no sense balanced the mass of producers (masters, journeymen and apprentices) who, as a result of the collapse of the old cloth industry, were excluded from the production process. The skills required in industries such as painting, sculpture, wood-carving, furniture-making, tapestry-weaving, leatherwork, embroidery, arms manufacture and the like, were totally unattainable for the overwhelming majority of the labouring population. Moreover one must remember that the exclusiveness of many guilds made upward social mobility extremely difficult. Above all, the greater political power of the more important masters led to concentration of economic activities. In Frankfurt-am-Main, for example, 8 per cent of the master weavers in 1432 were responsible for nearly a quarter of the urban textile production, while 37 per cent of the master weavers had to be satisfied with scarcely 12 per cent of the total. In the construction industry, socio-economic differentiation could be even more pronounced: in Brugge between 1388 and 1410, two masons and four carpenters were responsible for more than 80 per cent of all public works executed.[6]

The polarization of urban society had begun. The very men who had led the revolt against the patriciate turned into the greatest exploiters of apprentices and journeymen. The distribution of officers in town government clearly shows that the majority of artisans were not represented. In Florence, the money-changers, bankers, and drapers (*cambio, calimala, lana*) regulated the whole of public life by the middle of the fourteenth century, and in Toulouse scarcely 27 per cent of the aldermen (*capitouls*) belonged to the secondary guilds by 1380. In the Flemish and German towns, the 'humble folk' scarcely had a voice in the government: at Ghent, the weavers had reduced the fullers to second-class citizens around 1360, and at Cologne the Wool Guild (*Wollen Amt*) by the end of the fourteenth century dominated the weavers, whose help they had summoned in the coup against the patricians. The tensions resulting from this political tutelage were augmented by the growing exclusivity of many guilds following the 'democratic revolution'. The rank of master was often limited to a fixed number and, moreover, reserved for the children of actual masters, who enjoyed advantages such as lowered entrance fees, exemption from the required masterpiece, and so on.

The proletariat quickly realized that it had been deceived, and the economic difficulties of the 1360s and 1370s, aggravated by growing unemployment and dearth, brought latent social tensions to a head. Between 1378 and 1382 a flurry of revolts broke out. In many parts of France, Flanders, England, Italy and the Empire artisans rose up against the authorities and their employers. The movement failed abysmally, but it definitely sealed the union of an aristocracy of guild masters with the public authorities, whose intervention often had been a prerequisite for the restoration of order. The struggle also furthered journeyman solidarity. Despite the distrust of their employers, they gradually began to unite on a professional basis, initially under the cover of pious confraternities and associations for mutual assistance. However, they soon created *compagnonnages* (secret and illegal organizations) which forced all journeymen in a craft to join the group and exercised strong discipline over them – two indispensable conditions for successful resistance to the employers' cartels. Nonetheless, opposition to the growing power and concentration of capital was unable to halt the processes of impoverishment at work.

'The golden age of the craftsman' is a totally inadequate description of the fourteenth and fifteenth centuries. Certainly, in many areas of western Europe, real wages were two or three times higher than before the Black Death, but one must remember that wage labour in the countryside was generally only a supplementary source of income, and it is doubtful whether the rise of real wages made good the loss of income due to declining grain prices. As for urban workers, the Belgian historian Raymond van Uytven has shown that the undoubted prosperity of a minority protected by corporate restrictions was by no means typical of all workers. Besides, even the privileged professional categories did not live entirely without a care. Although the prices of foodstuffs declined in the long run, they fluctuated widely, bringing workers regularly to the edge of subsistence – or even below. In the period 1362 to 1483, the journeymen and apprentices in the construction industry at Brugge had to tighten their belts one year in three, and even that calculation assumes that they worked around 250 days each year. This was, however, seldom the case, for from detailed accounts it appears that more than half of Brugge's builders spent no more than four weeks on the same construction site. The Flemish Primitives, just like Italian Renaissance artists who filled their canvases with building workers happily toiling in the sun, painted only a fragment of the social landscape (see Figure 2).

3. The persistent threat of destitution

Some social groups, skilled workers, merchants, well-to-do peasants, and so on, certainly bettered their positions during the demographic decline and subsequent stagnation; changes in property relationships in the countryside clearly show this. Thanks to unusually rich sources, this evolution can be followed in detail in England (Figure 3). Nearly everywhere, the number of large

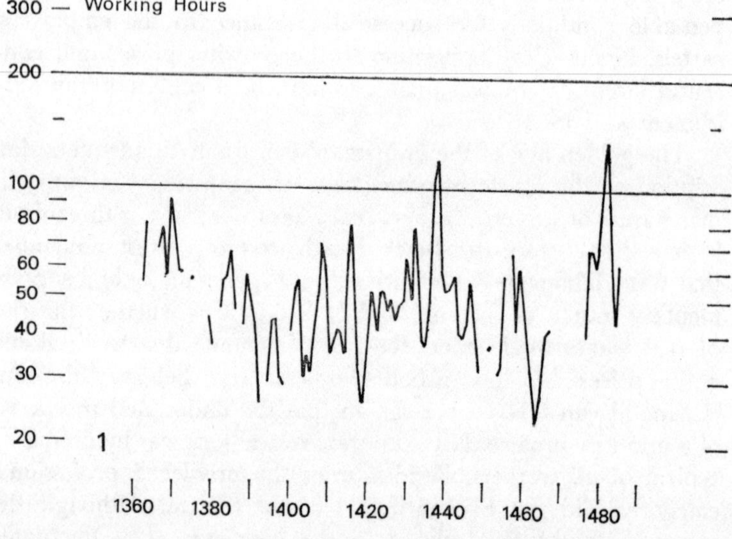

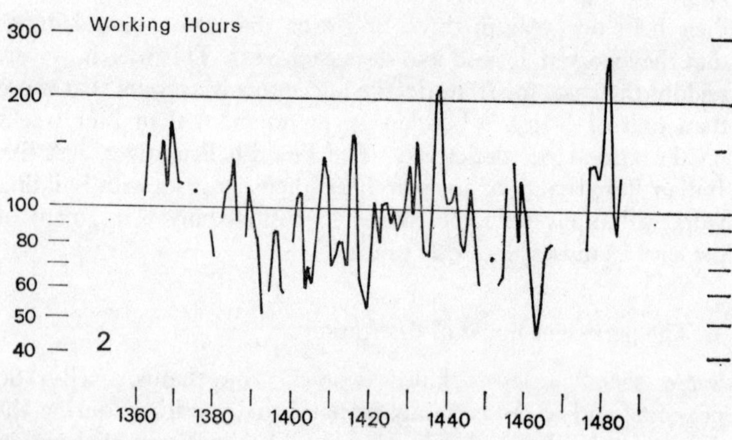

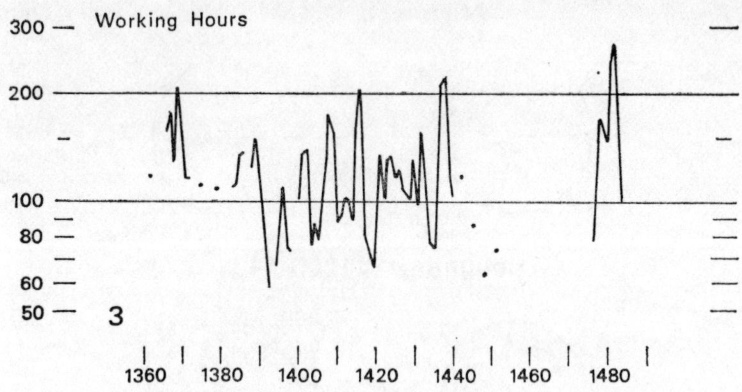

Fig. 2 Purchasing power of building workers in Brugge, 1362–1485.

Source: J.-P. Sosson, *Les Travaux publics de la ville de Bruges, XIVe–XVe siècles* (Brussels, 1977), pp. 308–9.

Note. Supposing that a labourer could work roughly 3,000 hours *per annum* (250–300 days of 10–12 hours), and that his family consumed some 12 quintals of wheat *per annum*, then the exchange of 100 working hours for one quintal of wheat was a critical threshold. Master carpenters (1) exceeded this barrier only in the year 1437–39 and 1481–83. Free journeymen (2) and labourers (3), in contrast, lived in misery during forty-six of the 101 years for which information is available.

holdings (twelve hectares or more) grew during the fourteenth century, as seen in Stoneleigh, Weedon Beck, Wistow and Houghton. Some fragmentary evidence shows that Flanders and France evolved similarly, though on a more modest scale. In the area around Kortrijk, 6.5 per cent of the peasants in 1382 owned more than thirteen hectares each, while the number of similar holdings in the nearby bailiwicks of Veurne, Sint-Winoksbergen, Kassel, and the Franc of Brugge in 1328 averaged only 2 per cent of the total. At Gorges in the Ile-de-France, the number of tenants with more than five 'parcels' of land increased from 12 per cent in 1351 to 17 per cent in 1405, and, at Ouges near Dijon, the majority of the tenants in 1455 disposed of ten to twenty *journaux*, versus four or five in 1409. In the parish of St Nicholas in Normandy, finally, the proportion of holdings of more than six hectares rose between the end of the fourteenth

Wistow, 1252-1414

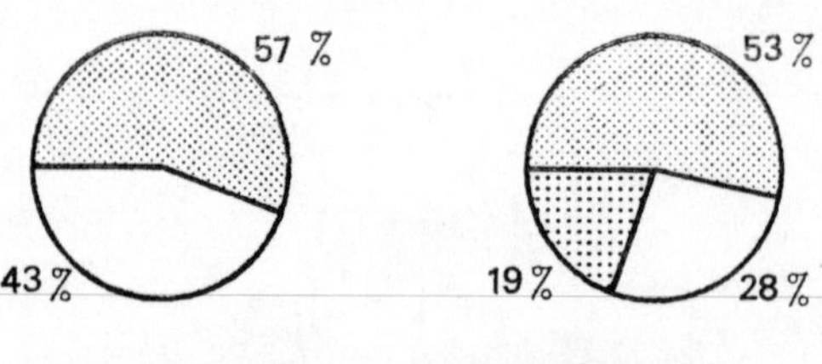

Houghton, *c.* 1260–1403

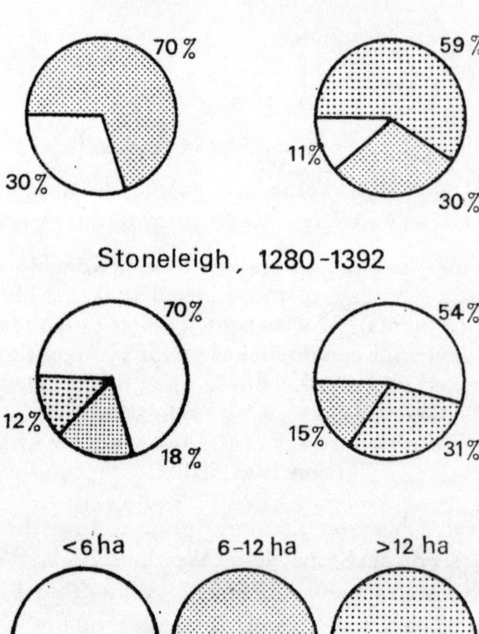

Fig. 3 Percentage distribution of holdings in three English villages before and after the Black Death.

Sources: R. H. Hilton, *The Stoneleigh Leger Book* (Oxford, 1960), p. xli, and J. A. Raftis, *Tenure and Mobility, studies in the social history of the medieval English village* (Toronto, 1964), pp. 19–20.

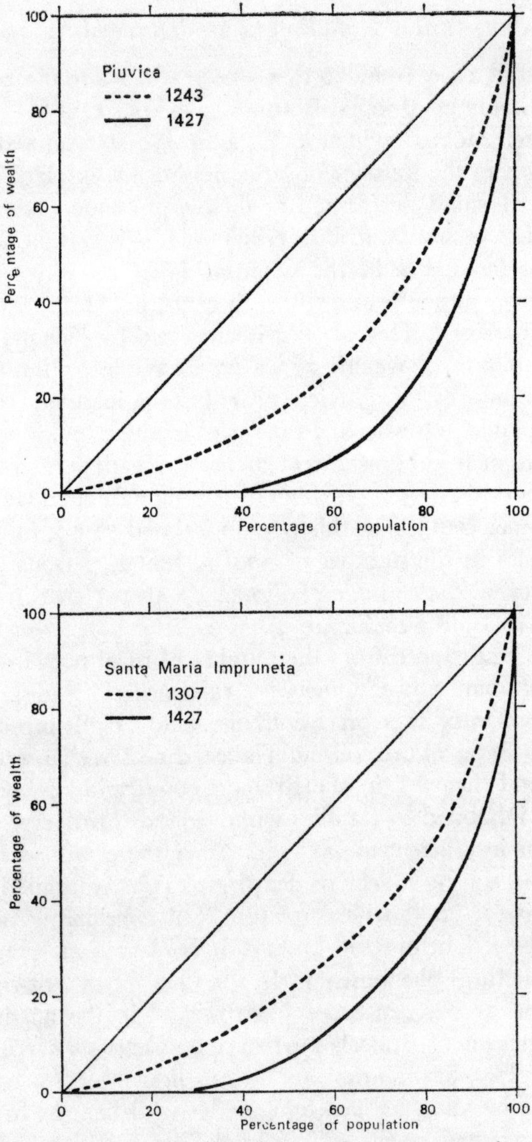

Fig. 4 Lorenz curves, showing the growing concentration of wealth in two rural communes in Tuscany, 1243–1427.

Note. The diagonal line is the line of equal distribution of wealth. The area enclosed between the diagonal and the curves is a measure of the inequality of distribution.

Sources: Based on D. Herlihy, *Medieval and Renaissance Pistoia* (New Haven and London 1967), pp. 181–3 and 'Santa Maria Impruneta: a rural commune in the late Middle Ages', in N. Rubinstein, ed, *Florentine Studies* (London, 1968), pp. 259–60.

century and 1477 from 52 to 58 per cent, while the proportion of small holdings dropped from 48 to 42 per cent.[7]

Through lack of evidence, it cannot be determined whether the growth in the number of large holdings took place chiefly at the cost of small peasants, or whether in some cases they too managed to secure land. But, either way, it is certain that socio-economic inequality in the countryside in no way diminished during the fourteenth and fifteenth centuries; it appears, rather, to have increased. That at least is suggested by such evidence for the distribution of wealth as we have. While no family in the rural community of Piuvica near Pistoia in 1243 completely lacked taxable possessions, 30 per cent of the population in 1427 existed in such circumstances; at the same time, a minority of 20 per cent raised their portion of the total estimated wealth from 50 to 74 per cent. That this was no isolated case is indicated by the increase in the number of *nihil habentes*, persons exempted from taxes, in the *contado* of Florence: 46 per cent in 1364, 53 per cent in 1388 (see Figure 4).

As can be deduced from the number of rural poor in fifteenth-century Brabant and Flanders, the existence of 20 to 30 per cent of the peasantry was precarious, in spite of all improvements. In 1437–38, ducal tax collectors labelled no less than 30 per cent of the total 'hearths' in the Brabant countryside as 'poor', that is to say, inhabited by families without landed property and with an income insufficient to pay taxes. Since the census was partially carried out during a year of dearth, it might be argued that the figures give a far too bleak picture, but considering only those areas surveyed before the famine, it is clear that such poverty was a structural phenomenon. In the Quarter of Antwerp, there were some 21 per cent poor hearths, and in the northern part of the Quarter of Brussels 26 per cent. Censuses carried out in Walloon Flanders show that these figures were completely 'normal': in 1432, 22 per cent of the total hearths in fourteen villages were poor in the bailiwicks of Lille, Orchies, and Douai: in 1449, the number had grown to 27 per cent. In the county of Flanders, finally, poor hearths in all the parishes surveyed made up an average of 25 per cent of the total in 1469. Given that this last census was not taken in a crisis period, the proportions deserve particular attention: even in 'normal' years, at least 20 per cent of the peasantry in one of the most prosperous areas of mid-fifteenth-century western Europe were poor according to fiscal definitions. We do not know the criteria by which officialdom categorized someone as poor and an assessment probably varied from one region to the next, perhaps even parish to parish, but that all areas reported a similar order of magnitude indicates that the problem of poverty had reached acute levels in those rural areas characterized by highly specialized agriculture.

In the towns, socio-economic contrasts were even sharper than in the countryside, as the examples of Pistoia, Volterra, and Florence indicate (Figure 5). At Brugge, from a tax raised in 1394–96, one concludes that around 83 per cent of the inhabitants belonged to the lowest taxed category; 54 per cent among

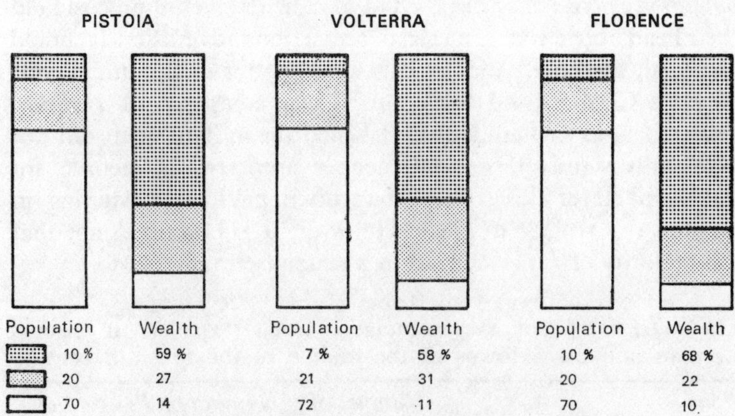

Fig. 5 Percentage distribution of population and estimated wealth in three Tuscan towns, 1427–9.

Sources: Based on C. M. Cipolla, *Before the Industrial Revolution: European society and economy, 1000–1700* (London, 1976), p. 10 and D. Herlihy, 'Family and property in Renaissance Florence', in H. A. Miskimin, D. Herlihy and A. L. Udovitch, eds, *The Medieval City* (New Haven and London, 1977), p. 8.

them paid at most a ninth of the daily wage of a skilled worker. The members of the 'upper-class', in contrast, contributed one to four times such a daily wage. The upper class, scarcely one per cent of the population, was made up of 59 per cent merchants and bankers, and 41 per cent master craftsmen; 87 per cent of textile workers fell into the lowest tax division. All studies concerning the divisions of urban wealth in the Low Countries have yielded a more or less equivalent result. Everywhere, half or more of the wealth was concentrated in the hands of a small minority. In eight towns – Mons, Diksmuide, Leuven, Ninove, Eeklo, Ostend, Soignies and Namur – one-fifth of the taxpayers contributed between 48 and 85 per cent of the total sums around 1400. Since the percentages include tax*payers* only, social polarization was in reality even more pronounced.

Various 'property statistics' show that the contrast between rich and poor in fifteenth-century German and Swiss towns was just as overwhelming. Nearly everywhere, half or more of the taxpayers consisted of citizens owning less than one hundred florins in property (see Table 4). Such families were at best *potentially* poor: they disposed of too few reserves, if any, to hold their head above water in case of any serious adversities. It should be noted, moreover, that at least one quarter of the inhabitants of most German and Swiss towns was composed of *Habnits*, 'have-nots', as contemporaries labelled them. This term did not necessarily signify those with neither property nor income, for the members of this social group often paid taxes, varying in amount from place to place. However, it is beyond doubt that the majority of *Habnits* lived in a state of chronic need.

Table 4.
The *potential* poor* as percentage of total taxpayers in selected German and Swiss towns in the middle of the fifteenth century

Town	*Year*	*Number of inhabitants*	*Number of taxpayers*	*Per cent of potential poor*
Augsburg	1475	*c.* 20,000	4,485	87
Basel	1446	*c.* 10,000	2,841	68
Constance	1560	*c.* 6,000	1,487	61
Esslingen	1468	*c.* 6,000	1,101	48
Görlitz	1443	*c.* 5,000	997	60
Hall	1460	?	1,040	59
Kaufbeuren	1479	*c.* 3,500	613	65
Lübeck	1460	*c.* 20,000	5,600	52
Memmingen	1450	*c.* 4,500	1,096	63
Ravensburg	1473	*c.* 5,000	1,416	70
St Gall	1447	*c.* 4,000	1,011	64
Ueberlingen	1444	*c.* 4,500	1,177	61

* the term '*potential* poor' refers to those taxable citizens owning less than one hundred florins in property.

Sources: see p. 233.

Some striking evidence concerning the living conditions of the very poor can be drawn from the demographic history of the northern Italian towns. Endemic plague struck every social group and age cohort, but some were 'more equal' than others; mortality was highest among the poor and the young, and worst of all among the children of the poor. The impact of socio-economic inequalities on demographic development can be illustrated by a single striking example. In 1427, in the countryside around Pistoia, material welfare and the number of children were closely connected: the richer the household, the greater the number of children under the age of fifteen. In the towns, socio-demographic contrasts were even more pronounced. In Florence, for example, the woman/child ratio (i.e. the proportion of married women aged between fifteen and forty-four to children aged four or below) amounted in 1427 to only 101 for families without taxable wealth, but to nearly 150 for those with property above 3,200 florins. Taking all women between fifteen and forty-four into account, the proportions were 84 among the poor, 116 among the rich.

Some quantitative data concerning the numbers of urban poor in Brabant and Flanders illustrate the effects of the fifteenth-century structural shift in industrial production for certain centres and social groups. We have already noted that the decline of the traditional cloth industry, begun by the end of the fourteenth century, came to a climax in the reign of Philip of Burgundy (1419–67); that the southern Netherlandish towns were consequently obliged to reorient their industrial production; and that this shift took its course in the smaller centres much less smoothly than in the larger. This is confirmed by the different evolution in the number of poor. In 1437 the small and large towns of Brabant counted 9 per cent and 10.5 per cent poor hearths, respectively; some forty years later, these figures amounted to 27 per cent and 14 per cent. In 1469 the situation in the small centres of Flanders was not much better; 26 per cent of the families were then on relief or were officially categorized as poor.

Much investigation remains to be done before a general and detailed picture of the impact of the economic contraction emerges. Two conclusions, however, are unavoidable. First, socio-economic inequality remained a constant factor after the Black Death in both town and country, and considerable evidence points towards an increasingly distorted distribution of wealth. Second, poverty remained a structural phenomenon. Everywhere, a notable part of the population in the fifteenth century, as before, lived in circumstances which even contemporaries admitted to be extremely precarious. Despite demographic decline, the threat of want and need was a daily reality.

4. Labour shortage, poor laws and social tensions

As seen in the concentration of urban industrial activities in fewer and fewer hands, in the great number of the potentially poor, and in the growth of large holdings, the material divide between rich and poor was widening during the fourteenth and fifteenth centuries. And as the profile of social stratification shifted, conflicts between the two poles emerged. The rich tried to make the poor pay for the dislocations of the fourteenth century while, for their part, the poor were no longer quite so willing unquestioningly to accept the rich as their masters. A 'glacial programme of exploitation' brought about the first episodes in the radicalization of the poor.

From the middle of the fourteenth century, a structural shortage of labour and, consequently, demands for higher wages confronted employers in nearly every European country. To cope with the problem the authorities in many areas published ordinances which restricted the migrations of servants and day-labourers, froze their wages, and in large measure limited their claims to relief. In England, Edward III's Council in 1349 proclaimed an 'Ordinance of Labourers' which established the duty of all able-bodied men to work. Begging nonetheless increased. Hence, in 1351, Parliament added new provisions. The major objective of these famous and repeatedly re-enacted Statutes of Labourers was to ensure an adequate supply of labour at wage levels current before the Black Death, determining that all able-bodied men and women under sixty and without means of support were obliged to accept employment at wage rates equal to the average between 1325 and 1331. Landlords had a pre-emptive right to the labour of their tenants; all servants and day labourers were strictly forbidden to abandon their masters during the period of their contract, and no one might hire anyone who had done so. No landowner or contractor could pay higher wages than those customary. Last, but not least, it was strongly forbidden to give alms to sturdy beggars who 'do refuse to labour, giving themselves to idleness and vice, and so that they may be, through want, compelled to labour for their necessary living'. Disobedience was to be severely punished. As shown by thousands of prosecutions, these provisions were enforced and, conversely, frequently disobeyed. Still, the envisioned goal was largely attained: wages did rise above the legally determined level, but much less than they would have in a regime of free competition.[8]

On the Continent similar steps were taken. In 1349 Pedro IV of Aragon commissioned an investigation to find ways to restrict wage rises. A year later, the *Cortes* of Aragon, the representative body of landlords, ecclesiastics, and urban patriciate, set the legal maximum and threatened those asking or paying more with banishment, enforceable by summary jurisdiction without right of appeal. In Castile an ordinance was proclaimed in 1351 against begging, which obliged all able-bodied men older than twelve to work and fixed their wages. For a transgressor to be punished it was necessary merely for a complainant and two witnesses to swear his guilt on oath. In 1381 Juan I went a step further: anyone could capture a wandering beggar and set him to work for one month without wages. The Portuguese Crown proceeded in an even more draconian fashion: between 1349 and 1401, at the behest of secular and ecclesiastical estate owners, a whole series of laws were proclaimed, forcing labourers to work for the same wage, in the same way, and in the same place as they had done earlier; and a passport system was established to hinder migration and control begging. The *Lei das Sesmarias* of 1375 even bound workers to their traditional calling. In France, too, the authorities intervened. Beginning in 1351, King John the Good offered all sturdy beggars in Paris the choice of finding work immediately or leaving town in three days. The king stipulated that in future only the sick, lame and aged might be given alms. A new ordinance, published in November 1354, indicated that the rural labour market was particularly critical at that moment. Large landowners complained not only about 'the great dearth of day labourers', who refused to accept the old wages, but also about the recalcitrance of rural workers, who trekked *en masse* to the towns with an eye towards better pay.

Hence, the king ordered all unemployed, able-bodied men without means of support to be driven out of the towns without delay. German princes followed suit. Ludwig von Wittelsbach, ruler of Upper Bavaria and the Tyrol, published in 1352 mandates for each of his territories to counter a serious shortage of labour in the countryside. The Bavarian ordinance stated 'that we have seen the weakness and the harm which have been brought about in our land of Upper Bavaria by farmhands and workers, that every man seeks the highest wage he can secure and will undertake no cultivation'. The prince judged it essential to fix wages. In a similar mandate for the Tyrol, Ludwig determined that servants and day labourers could not migrate, on pain of loss of property; they had to stay with their old employers, at the old wage.[9]

Thus with a stroke of the pen states attempted to crush the hopes of the poor for better living conditions and to remove the sole benefit bequeathed by the millions of cottars, servants, and day labourers mowed down by epidemics. Princes, who had never before been concerned with such matters, coordinated a system of social control designed to protect the interests of a rich minority. The ban on migration, the obligation to accept the old wage levels, the expulsion of sturdy beggars from the towns, and their exclusion from alms all aimed to regulate the rural labour market and thus to support seigneurial reaction. Town magistracies, on their side, fixed maximum wages yet made no effort to halt the influx of unskilled labourers, because they considered demographic recovery to be the best way to depress wages. The sole problem posed by migration for the towns was the potential threat to their security. Hence many local authorities took steps to control begging more efficiently after the Black Death.

But in the long run these measures could not be maintained. With such high demand for labour, many employers eventually saw the need to break the law and pay higher wages. Due to recurrent epidemics and the concomitant dislocation of the rural economy, migrations could not be stopped. Nonetheless, sustained opposition by the peasantry and day labourers against seigneurial reaction and the forms of social control coupled to that reaction was just as effective for their enfranchisement and the improvement of their working conditions as the structural shortage of labour. Attempts to make the poor pay the costs of the fourteenth-century crisis brought on stiff resistance indeed. Disturbances grew more frequent, often turning into rebellions. Although revolts could nearly always be suppressed, they made clear to the wielders of economic and political power that serfdom and exploitation could not be maintained without endangering – perhaps even radically disrupting – the precarious social balance.

The ordinances concerning migration, begging and wage levels, published at the height of the crisis, thus had a limited, temporary effect; but for the later evolution of western European society they were of great significance. For the first time a sharp and explicit distinction was made between paupers, who had a right to assistance because of their physical weakness, and sturdy beggars, to whom alms might in no circumstances be given. This discrimination implied a break with earlier attitudes; collective glorification of poverty as such belonged *de facto* to the past. The duty to work was the harbinger of a new ethic: the exaltation of self-employment directed towards the production of material goods. Moreover, for the first time secular authorities were concerned about begging. Thus the basis was laid for the appearance of a coordinated system of social control directed by public authorities in place of private persons. Since the clergy, traditional refuge of the poor, raised no protest, the way lay free and open for a gradual secularization of charity.

During the fourteenth century, the poor began to consider their position. In Florence numerous legal processes and dossiers show that the economically weak drew the connection between manual labour and poverty from the 1340s onwards: the terms *pauper* and *laborator* became freely interchangeable. Unlike the rich, they emphasized human needs. Further, they considered *impotenza* as the fundamental characteristic of poverty – the inability to pay taxes, to avoid debt, or to support a family. This impotence, according to one spokesman, crippled whole groups, which consisted not simply of those in need. Poverty was, in other words, not the lot of a minority, but the way of life of a majority. Obviously such ideas clashed with those of the elite, who emphasized individual misfortunes caused by external factors and considered total indigence as the sole criterion for poor relief. As socio-economic polarization advanced, the poor became more conscious that their interests in no sense coincided with those of the rich. They began to realize that they formed an extremely large group with its own characteristics and its own dynamics.[10]

In the countryside a similar radicalization process took place. From the middle of the fourteenth century ideas of social equality and personal freedom spread in rural areas, while the misuses of the Church drew more complaints more openly than before. In England and on the Continent, peasants and rural labourers began to ask themselves,

> When Adam delved and Eve span
> Who was then the gentleman?

Peasant revolts in northern France, Languedoc, southern England, the Rhineland, Spain, Bohemia, and Scandinavia leave no doubt how the rural folk, often strengthened by a rudimentary evangelism, answered that question.

In short, we can discern slowly but surely changing attitudes towards *paupertas* among both rich and poor during the fourteenth and fifteenth centuries; the former increasingly identified poverty with begging and disorder, the latter with inequality and impotence. Although nearly all revolts drowned in blood, the collective recognition of the fundamental opposition between rich and poor could not be undone.[11]

Chapter 3

ECONOMIC GROWTH, IMPOVERISHMENT AND SOCIAL POLICY *(c.1450–c.1630)*

THE disappearance of famine and the eclipse of the Black Death in the second half of the fifteenth century and the early sixteenth century set off a population explosion. Demographic recovery in turn brought agrarian expansion. Everywhere, abandoned land was again put to use; there were large-scale clearances in many areas; and the organization of agricultural production was improved: the qualitative innovations brought in here and there during the preceding century were now widely diffused. The short-term rise in the productivity of land and labour resulting from such changes enabled the peasant holding to bear new fiscal demands for several decades. The recovery of transcontinental trade and the genesis of intercontinental trade gave a further impetus to the western European economy, laying the basis for the emergence of a world economy and favouring the growth of capitalist forms of organization. Increased demand for manufactured goods, a result of greater marketing outlets and increased population, strengthened the already present tendency towards concentration and rationalization. Growing demand, consequently, went hand in hand with qualitative transformations in the organization of industrial production.

The transition from medieval to modern was also characterized by increased urbanization. Town dwellers still represented a small part of the total population in most European countries, excepting the Netherlands and northern Italy; nonetheless, the portion undeniably grew higher during this period. Thanks to the maritime revolution, numerous old and new centres prospered, while the rise of the centralized state with its extensive bureaucracy stimulated the growth of capitals. Around 1600 Europe had twelve towns with more than 100,000 inhabitants; there had been only five around 1500. Through the variety of their functions, their extraordinary accumulation of wealth and their massive consumption, these colossal concentrations of people played a strategic role throughout several centuries of western European economic life.

Sixteenth-century expansion offered new and greater opportunities for enrichment to some social groups. Many entrepreneurs and financiers built up enormous fortunes. The democratization of international trade, based on the generalization of participation and commission business, favoured the multiplication of small and middle-sized firms. As for the agricultural sector, a large body of evidence shows that this period witnessed consolidation and perhaps even the extension of a 'peasant aristocracy'.

Hence it is generally recognized that the long sixteenth century was a time of secular economic expansion. But what about the mass of humanity? What impact did all these developments have on the living conditions of the cottars, smallholders and rural labourers, the artisans, journeymen, unskilled workers and servants?

1. The social cost of agrarian change

Although the nature of agrarian changes differed from country to country, even province to province, overall they had the same social effect: an absolute impoverishment of the rural masses, who, besides marginal 'solutions' such as settlement in forested areas or recruitment as mercenaries, had a choice of three alternatives: wage labour, cottage industry, or migration. The peasants paid a high price for their release from serfdom, for by the sixteenth century the shift from personal to economic dependence was far advanced, rendering them liable to landlord oppression. Economic dependence could be onerous indeed, according to differences in tenurial systems.

By this period French peasants had relieved themselves of all stigmata of personal servitude, and some 40 to 50 per cent were landholders. But their ownership was never complete: the seigneur always retained his rights, symbolized by the *cens*; at every transfer of property, whether through inheritance, sale or exchange, the seigneur exacted his due. In addition, all peasants, as before, were subject to the royal *taille* and the ecclesiastical tithe. Nonetheless, with an hereditary right to their land, peasant proprietors enjoyed greater security than simple tenants, who formed the majority in many areas. The relatively great extent of peasant proprietors in France can be ascribed mainly to the protective role of the monarchy, which saw therein possibilities of broadening its power. Peasant production, through non-parliamentary taxation, functioned as a direct source of the income needed by the Crown to strengthen its autonomy. Peasant ownership and the absolute state thus evolved in mutual dependence. Conflicts between peasants and landlords over property rights were nearly always adjudicated by the French monarchy to the cost of landlords: the integrity of the *cens* and hereditary tenure was generally confirmed. Landlords were seldom able to expropriate vacant holdings held by this form of tenure, consequently they were compelled to buy up innumerable small-holdings in order to acquire a consolidated estate, which, in practice, appears to have been extremely difficult.

In western Germany a similar process took place. Here the princes were the real winners of the great peasant wars, winning not only against the peasants but against the Emperor and the nobility as well. The western German princes carried out a conscious policy, *Bauernschutzpolitik*, protection for peasant proprietors, with the goal of providing an independent tax base for themselves. They did what they could to protect the security and the extent of peasant holdings: hereditability of tenure was established or restored; dues were fixed. At the same time, princes tried to reconstitute the scattered parcels of peasant lands into unified *Hüfen* and to restrain farmers from subdividing their holdings. With their finances based on peasant proprietors, the rise of 'mini-absolutisms' in western Germany made it extremely difficult for the nobility to enlarge their demesne at the expense of small landholders. Thus the peasantry of western and southern Germany was given the opportunity to acquire some 90 per cent of the land.

The property rights of the English peasantry, in contrast, were extremely limited. The English monarchy evolved from the fifteenth century onwards in close association with landlords, as seen in the contemporaneous growth of parliamentary institutions, while they decayed in France. Therefore English landlords frequently succeeded in seizing peasant holdings vacated during the fourteenth century crisis and joining them to their estates. Large parts of the land were simply transferred from the customary sector to the leasehold sector, 'thus thwarting in advance a possible evolution towards freehold, and substantially reducing the potential area of land for essentially peasant proprietorship'. This development significantly advanced economic growth in England: 'With the peasants' failure to establish essentially freehold control over the land, the landlords were able to engross, consolidate and enclose, to create large farms and to lease them to capitalist tenants who could afford to make capitalist investments.'[1] R. H. Tawney masterfully analysed the dispossession of the English peasants, above all focusing attention on the most numerous group in the manorial population: the customary tenants, mostly but not always copyholders, that is, farmers with property rights dependent on and in conformity to the custom of the manor. While leaseholders and tenants-at-will could easily be evicted, two aspects of customary tenure were of importance for the position of the copyholder: 'First, whether he had by it an estate of inheritance, or merely an estate for years, for life, or for lives; second, whether his payments were fixed or unalterable, or whether they could be increased at the will of the lord.' Copyholds for life or lives were more common than copyholds of inheritance, while fixed entrance fines were the exception, variable fines the general rule. Landlords forced copyholders to surrender their copies and to accept leasehold in exchange; they also systematically drove up fines. The embittered verdict of the affected peasants was that: 'They take our houses over our heads; they buye our groundes out of handes, they reyse our rents, they levy great, yea unreasonable fines.'[2] In short, the ability of English landlords to profit from the general rise in land values depended in large measure on their power to alter the terms of tenancy by which their land was rented out. Given that this evolution was determined by economic fluctuations, by changes in the composition of the incomes of large landowners and by the balance of power between peasant and landlord, regional and chronological differences were quite large. In some areas and during some periods, landlords considered it more profitable to exchange tenures-at-will for rents on long terms because the peasants involved had more security and as a result were inclined to raise their output; afterwards, the greater surplus could still be skimmed off by rent adjustments. In general it appeared that the large rented farmstead, worked by capitalist peasants on commercial principles, offered the best opportunities for high rents. Therefore most landlords gradually exchanged small farmsteads for larger holdings, so that copyholders with insufficient reserves were driven off the land.

The greater or lesser vulnerability of western European peasants resulted, of course, not only from the nature of the property rights which pertained to their land; just as significant were the size and rentability of the holding, opportunities to exploit it, admission to common ground, and, last but not least, the existence of alternative sources of income, such as wage labour and home industry. In most parts of France, smallholdings formed by far the majority. All monographs concur: 80 to 90 per cent of peasant holdings were smaller than five hectares, the minimum necessary to support a family. The presence of rental property seldom offered salvation to small farmers. In the Cambrésis in northern France, for example, smallholdings made up some 86 per cent of the total around 1600, yet they occupied scarcely 28 per cent of the ground cultivated; ecclesiastical institutions, nobles and townsmen controlled the remaining 72 per cent, of which only a small part consisted of holdings of less than five ha. This unequal distribution of the land had far-reaching results. The bulk of peasant proprietors disposed of insufficient land to feed a family, while they could not rent a large farmstead due to lack of capital. Due to the enormous discrepancy between the number of smallholders on one side and the available number of small, rented farmsteads on the other, the price of the latter was systematically pushed sky-high. The existence of land for rent provided most peasants with only a single advantage: opportunity for wage labour.

In some regions the small peasant proprietors could hold their heads above water more easily than in others, thanks to specialization. In Alsace, Burgundy, the Ile-de-France, Languedoc, along the Atlantic coast, and the Loire valley, viticulture expanded during the sixteenth century. The same holds for the cultivation of cash crops. This development, begun in the later Middle Ages, was strongly stimulated from the end of the fifteenth century onwards by the expansion of trade and the growth of towns. The advantages and disadvantages of such specialization have already been discussed: on one side, higher yields and thus larger harvests; on the other, increased risks, which could only be avoided by the simultaneous cultivation of different crops. Accordingly, an increasing number of merchants invested capital in agriculture, rendering cultivators more than ever at the mercies of speculation.

The situation of most tenants was even less rosy. Share-cropping, which propagated itself rapidly from the second half of the fifteenth century onwards in much of France (*métayage*) and northern Italy (*mezzadria*), was undoubtedly the form of land tenure most detrimental to the peasantry: the owner of the farmstead provided half or even two-thirds of the capital (seed, tools, and eventually the livestock), but drew in return half of the *average* grain harvest. Often the tenant had to surrender a part of the wine harvest as well, and was forbidden to consume any of the produce. *Métairie* diffused throughout the Gâtine, a part of Poitou, between 1450 and 1550, illustrating the dramatic expansion of this system of land tenure. The extraordinary demands of landlords, enshrined in draconian contracts, quickly reduced most *métayers* to simple workers. Moreover, many peasants were chased off their land by frequent transformations of villages into consolidated estates. The combination of both impoverishment processes led to structural overpopulation. Most serious of all, the system brought on agrarian stagnation. Neither tenant nor owner put any fundamental technological innovations to work: the former, squeezed by his rent, lacked the requisite capital, while the latter saw no need for deep investment so long as exploitation of the peasantry was sufficiently profitable.

The 'ordinary' tenant in France, who rented a farmstead for a fixed sum in money or kind, was not much better off. Even tenants with a holding averaging some forty ha. situated on fertile land in the region of Paris seem to have found it extremely difficult to hold their heads above water. After subtraction of seed, labour costs, rent, royal taxes, ecclesiastical tithe and seigneurial dues, they retained an insufficient surplus to support a family even in good years. If they did not dispose of supplementary income (stock-raising, wine, rental of ploughteam, etc.), then their holding was not viable in the long run. Only those who rented a farmstead of 120 ha. or more were in a position to realize a substantial profit. Such *coqs de village*, who regularly brought a notable surplus to market, also collected seigneurial dues, provided credit and bought up holdings burdened with debt; they represented, however, scarcely one per cent of the peasantry.

Not surprisingly, the socio-economic position of the bulk of French peasants in the sixteenth century steadily worsened. The system of perpetual tenure undoubtedly protected smallholders against seigneurial reaction, against periodic evictions. Their holdings were, however, generally so small, their dues so heavy, the opportunities to rent a farmstead so limited and rent so high, that most were barely able to support their families, let alone retain anything for the market. Any serious setback almost automatically began the infernal spiral of loan – debt – loss of property. One example: around 1540 the peasants south of Paris held some 40 per cent of the land; one century later they held only 28 per cent. The majority of tenants did not escape impoverishment, and as for the *métayers*, in the first half of the sixteenth century, 27 per cent in the Gâtine of Poitou were forced to abandon their contracts, but no less than 52 per cent during 1560–1600.

In other parts of western Europe as well, dispossession of the peasantry reached new heights by the second half of the fifteenth century or so. By 1500 peasant proprietors in some of the villages around Florence and Siena had nearly disappeared. Surrounding Parma and Piacenza smallholdings were to be found only in the foothills, the least fertile area. In Modena the duke, nobility and Church together controlled no less than 80 per cent of all arable in 1546 and, in the *contado* of Padua, the peasants around the same time possessed a mere twelfth; in New Castile, the peasant proprietors in the 1570s held at most 25 to 30 per cent of the total cultivated surface area.

In England the expropriation process paired itself to fundamental changes in agrarian structure caused by the enclosure movement, 'large-scale enclosure of common fields and commons, usually undertaken by wealthy tenants or proprietors without the poor commoners' consent, and often involving depopulation'.[3] This transformation in the organization of landholding, begun around 1450, had far-reaching results. For smallholders it was of crucial importance whether or not they could graze their few livestock on the communal waste. Their own holdings were too small for cattle-breeding; nearly 37 per cent of English tenants disposed of less than 2 hectares. Just as vital were claims on woodland, the undergrowth and quarries of the common, which provided building materials and fuel. In many parishes smallholders had the right to catch fish and fowl on the commons, or to pick berries and herbs. Tampering with these rights endangered the means of subsistence of the peasantry; all enclosures, whether they bore upon common fields, waste, or pasture, robbed them of an irreplaceable source of income.

Although historians dispute the causes, extent, and results of the enclosure movement, it undeniably turned many small farmers into beggars. Although the complaints of contemporaries equally referred to rackrenting and engrossing (joining farmsteads together into a single unit), the most inflammable situations arose with the seizure of commons and their conversion into sheep pasture, for this blow to the peasants' elementary means of subsistence accelerated their impoverishment. In all areas where a systematic shift from arable to pasture took place the demand for labour dropped drastically. Underemployment and unemployment rose. The enclosure movement undoubtedly favoured economic growth in England by promoting changes in agrarian structure which brought along greater efficiency and specialization, but these technological improvements were to the cost of small farmers and rural labourers, who not only lost their rights to the commons in many areas, but simultaneously were confronted by fewer opportunities for work.

In other parts of western Europe the expansion of livestock raising had equally unfavourable social outcomes. In Denmark the nobility during the sixteenth century increasingly concentrated on livestock, with an eye on export. In 1536 some 30,000 cattle were sold; by the early seventeenth century the number had risen to 80,000. The expansion of cattle-breeding was paired with a systematic expropriation process. Supported by the Crown, the Danish nobility increased their portion in the land from 25 per cent to more than 40 per cent. Schleswig-Holstein evolved similarly. Given the capital resources of the Holstein nobility, who were active not only as cattle-breeders but also as merchants and financiers, peasant holdings disappeared in favour of *latifundia* on an even greater scale than in Denmark. The growth of commercialized sheep-breeding in Saxony, one of the most important wool-producing areas of central Europe in the sixteenth century, not only affected the commons but also exhausted the land, lowering the living standards of the peasants in the long term. In Languedoc and Provence, in various parts of Italy, and in Spain, transhumance (the seasonal migration of often colossal herds of sheep) brought enormous damage to the fields on either side of the line of march. In Castile, the Mesta (the sheep-owners' guild) had no less than 3,000 members in the early sixteenth century, with some three million merino sheep. This powerful organization of sheep-breeders was in fact dominated by a small group of great secular and ecclesiastical landlords, each owning 25,000 to 40,000 beasts. The attack on the common land, the fixing of prices for pasture, prohibition of technological improvements in agriculture, and exaction of high export duties on victuals all fit into the policy by which the interests of arable were totally sacrificed to sheep-breeding. In the long term, these measures led to rural depopulation, deforestation, agrarian stagnation and consequently, structural poverty.

Finally, many peasants were adversely affected by the increasing grip of townsmen on the countryside. The land hunger of the bourgeoisie was, it is true, an old phenomenon, yet in the sixteenth century it manifested itself in a more forceful way than ever before, in conjunction with the spectacular commercial expansion and rapid growth of the towns. Merchants, financiers and entrepreneurs put some of their capital into real estate. Besides prestige, four motives dominated. One was to give some security to their acquired riches. Capital in the form of commodities and promissory notes provided indisputably high yields but was threatened every moment by bankruptcy, shipwreck, confiscation and other disasters. When put into farms or houses, it was out of immediate danger. Second, the elite strove for assured and regular incomes. The Fuggers, for example, owned in Swabia alone about a hundred villages with a joint area of 230 to 250 square km and a value of two million florins. Exploitation of these lands brought in a yearly average of 6 per cent, not an extraordinary profit, but all the more attractive when the small risks in such investments are considered. Third, real estate fulfilled credit functions: the owner could not only mortgage it to stave off payments due but could also sell redeemable annuities (*rentes constituées*) and thus negotiate a long-term loan at relatively low interest. Fourth, speculative interests ought not to be underestimated. Many merchants bought farmsteads in the hope of realizing windfall profits during dearth, and numerous financiers from Antwerp and southern Germany in the 1530s and 40s provided sizeable amounts of capital in the reclamation of polders in Zeeland for speculative reasons.

The example of Valladolid shows the disastrous consequences which the growing interests of rich townsmen in agriculture could have for the peasantry. In the first half of the sixteenth century, many peasants sold *censos al quitar* (fixed and redeemable annuities) on their farmsteads to improve their holding. The supply of capital was nearly as great as the demand for credit. Enticed by the prospect of fixed and regular incomes, numerous inhabitants of Valladolid bought *censos*. Most farmers, however, were eventually unable to pay the yearly sums, even less to redeem the *censo;* many were driven even deeper into debt to avoid eviction. Speculators took advantage of the situation to advance money in exchange for part of the coming harvest and realized astounding profits: the market value of the wine harvest generally lay two or three times higher than the capital loaned. Consumers as well as peasants were sacrificed to speculation. The former faced inflated prices; the latter were seldom able to profit from their increased efforts. Once the peasants realized that their surplus was siphoned away and that the speculators were interested only in windfall profits, productive investment gradually disappeared. The generalization of the *censos* system thus strengthened the tendency towards agrarian stagnation.

Although most peasants in western Europe in the sixteenth century were still established on small family plots and only occasionally sold their labour, these expropriation processes caused the number of landless who could feed themselves only through wage labour to rise in some regions to alarming proportions. In Tudor England, rural labourers formed one-fourth to one-third of the rural population; in the villages of the canton of Zürich in the early sixteenth century day labourers represented about half the inhabitants; in New Castile, too, half of the rural population around 1575 consisted of *jornaleros*. However, the bulk of the seasonal workers in most of sixteenth-century western Europe were recruited from the ranks of smallholders, whose incomes out of their own holdings were insufficient to support a family. Nearly 50 per cent of the peasants in Upper Swabia around 1531 disposed of less than fifteen hectares and an average of 30 to 50 per cent of their harvest was skimmed off. Since a family in this region needed at least eleven to fourteen ha., the vast majority of households were compelled to seek out wage employment. In all rural areas the rising number of peasants dependent on finding work incessantly affected real wages during the sixteenth century.

Rural woollen and linen industries, which had spread steadily in the century after the Black Death, expanded spectacularly from the mid fifteenth century onwards. The need of small farmers for a source of supplementary income played just as effective a role as the demand for rural labourers on the part of the merchants. Everywhere rural industry developed in close connection with the agrarian situation and the social organization of the peasantry involved. Woollen and linen weaving undoubtedly placed a number of small farmers in a position where they could hold their heads above water, but the opportunity to augment income undermined the demographic equilibrium of traditional communities; lower age at marriage pushed the birth rate upwards, so that the supply of labour soon began to exceed its demand. Merchant entrepreneurs naturally profited from demographic expansion in order to tighten their grip on rural producers. Thus the growth of rural industry in the long run brought on the proletarianization of large sectors of the peasantry.

Those with neither sufficient land nor recourse to wage labour or cottage industry could do nothing except migrate. Richard Gascon reckoned that 64 per cent of the 15,101 immigrants to Lyon between 1529 and 1563 came from the countryside. Yet, the 'urban' population was even more mobile than the rural: althought ten times less populous, the towns around Lyon provided half the number of immigrants provided by the countryside. Hence the attraction of the town in no sense took priority over repulsion out of the agrarian sector. The town was not only a refuge for the poor; it also generated the poor.[4]

2. The triumph of commercial capitalism

Despite the growth of mass production, the tendency towards concentration, rationalization of the manufacturing process and the emergence of new forms of organization, a revolutionary transformation of the economy did not materialize during the sixteenth century. Although in some sectors there was a notable increase in scale, the small or middling workshop run by a single artisan along with some journeymen and apprentices, using relatively simple tools, remained the typical unit of production. In some crafts productivity was raised, a result of improved organization (division of labour), not technological improvements (mechanization). The resilience of the traditional industrial structure was determined by the development of commercial capitalism.

In a pioneering essay the Japanese historian Kohachiro Takahashi pointed out that two paths led to the capitalist transformation of economic life. In one, producer and capitalist were the same: entrepreneurs, who owned the means of production, dealt directly with 'free' wage labourers, who owned only their labour. The capitalist entrepreneur produced directly for the market and subordinated marketing to industrial capital, a radical break with existing relations of production. In the second model, the merchant could become the capitalist. In that case, marketing by small-scale producers, who were not necessarily separated from their means of production, was controlled by merchant entrepreneurs, who dealt in manufactures within the bounds of their commercial horizon; that is, they subordinated industrial activity to their paramount commercial interests. Thus the second path implied the continued dependence of industrial production on the market. These two possibilities cannot be considered equally feasible solutions for the same problem: they responded to different interests, each to specific social groups.[5] This is clearly seen in the textile sector, the premier industry of the *ancien régime*.

Both merchants and master craftsmen naturally tried to draw as much profit as possible from the rising demand for cloth. Merchants could attain this goal by means of the putting-out system: they provided domestic workers with raw materials and, eventually, tools, bought woven materials at a piece rate, had the cloth finished by sub-contractors, and then sold it. This organization of production satisfied merchants because their profits and cashflow were chiefly determined by the fluctuations of the international market and by the place which they filled in trade circles, by the frequency and intensity of their relations with other centres. In contrast, the creation of large undertakings based on centralized production demanded heavy investments which could be written off only after long periods, and also demanded numerous subsidiary expenses of a lasting nature, such as maintenance of buildings. Substantial fixed capital, moreover, diminished the manoeuvrability of the merchants and, due to the high elasticity of demand, entailed considerable risks. Hence the putting-out system dominated the textile industry. There were a number of advantages: the sequence of manufacture could be split into separate processes; for most techniques of production, simple, cheap tools sufficed, tools which could be placed in the workers' houses by the merchant entrepreneurs easily and with little risk; the necessary skills were quickly taught; production was generally standardized, so that close oversight was superfluous; and, finally, the basic processes could be carried out by the family: children carded the wool, the wife spun thread, the husband wove. Not surprisingly, textile merchants more often chose the putting-out system than centralized production. Admittedly, some of them built up large businesses, with numerous looms under one roof, but such initiatives were exceptional in the sixteenth century.

The wealthy master craftsmen, in contrast, strove towards concentration of the means of production and labour forces. Since their profits derived from industrial activities, they had to produce as much, as quickly and as cheaply as possible. Towards this end they could depress wages, rationalize the production process by bringing their workers together into one room and sharing out the tasks involved, or introduce labour-saving devices. The first means often met with success, because the urban labour market was constantly fed with those uprooted from the agrarian sector, to be recruited by the master craftsmen in case his journeymen refused to work for the set wage. Such a policy, however, had its limits. Extreme pressure on wages led easily enough to strikes and disturbances which severely threatened public order. All other means of trimming costs and raising productivity could be employed only sporadically because many guild regulations had as their goal to prevent the uninhibited growth of large concerns. Although they often succeeded in circumventing restrictions, the well-to-do master craftsmen in the sixteenth century nowhere managed to bring about centralized production units on a large scale, a failure ascribable to the conjunction of several factors. First, local producers were dependent on large-scale traders for provision of raw materials and for the sale of their finished products on the international market. The traders, due to their wealth and business experience, were able to sell the goods concerned sufficiently slowly not to drive down prices; to strengthen their grip on manufacturers, moreover, merchants hindered craftsmen from trading outside their own areas. Second, the merchants were themselves all too conscious that, if the corporative restrictions relative to size of businesses were abolished, the more important master craftsmen could be dangerous competitors. Therefore they often supported small producers in their actions against attempted concentration. In many centres, the industrial politics which the great masters had earlier pursued were turned against them. The very measures master craftsmen had taken in the fourteenth and fifteenth centuries to protect their interests hindered them in the sixteenth century from competing efficiently with the merchant entrepreneurs. This handicap was even more serious given that the greater opportunities for profit resulting from increased scale put merchants in a position to accumulate more capital than had earlier been possible. Impelled by rising demand for manufactures, they attempted with every available means to gain control of the production of the most significant trade goods. Instead of impairing this trend, corporative restrictions aided merchants to reach their goal, since they held enterprising craftsmen 'in their place'. Finally, the socio-political implications of these conflicting interests must be taken into account. Lesser craft masters were still too numerous in most sixteenth-century towns for the authorities to be able to side with a few manufacturers without endangering public order. The putting-out system did not hold similar threats, because it gave the 'middle class' the illusion that nothing essential had changed. The very dispersal of domestic workers made impossible a clear appraisal of the network of dependence.

Centralized production dominated only a few branches of industry, such as shipbuilding, milling industries, metal-working, and mining. The case of mining is obvious: alum, coal, copper, silver and the like could be extracted in only a limited number of places. In the others, concentration was essential because production took the form of an assembly process, because the productive plant was a piece of fixed capital equipment to which raw materials had to be brought for processing, or because the plant was driven by energy, mostly wind or water, not transmissable over distances. From the perspective of employment, mining was perhaps the foremost form of centralized production. Thanks to substantial technological improvements, silver and copper extraction in the Harz around Goslar, in the county of Mansfeld, in Saxony, Bohemia, the Tyrol, near Salzburg, and in northern Hungary expanded rapidly from the second half of the fifteenth century. Technological improvement, however, increased the impact of commercial capital on the organization of production. The old cooperative society (*Gewerkschaft*), the members of which worked the mine themselves, could not provide the capital required for expensive machinery such as winches, hoists, pumps, tilt hammers, rolling mills and blast-furnaces. As a result, they lost out to the great concerns of capitalist merchant entrepreneurs, each holding a number of shares in the mine, *Kuxen*.

Commercialization of mining led not only to impoverishment of the earlier small producers but also created the first proletariat in the modern sense. In the mid-sixteenth century, 12,000 'professional' miners worked in the copper mines of Schwaz in the Tyrol, not counting day labourers. The flowering of most mining towns was nevertheless relatively short. The population of Jachymov, the foremost centre in Bohemia, dwindled from around 18,000 inhabitants in 1553 to scarcely 3,000 in 1613. One ought not to forget that demand in the sixteenth century for iron, tin, paper, and other non-textile manufactures was still too small and too elastic to stimulate large-scale production. Large undertakings with hundreds of workers undoubtedly existed, but the typical unit, even in the general category of centralized production, remained small.

Sixteenth-century capitalism was thus essentially commercial capitalism, extremely mobile due to minimal investment in durable means of production. Merchant entrepreneurs could withdraw their capital from one business or region and transfer it to another, quickly and with little financial loss. The development of western European industry, consequently, was characterized by a continuous 'redrawing of the map', in the words of Fernand Braudel.[6] Since commercial capitalism brought about so few technological improvements, no single town or region during its golden age took a qualitative lead sufficiently great to remain competitive when structural difficulties were confronted; instead, new better situated centres took over. At the national or international level, such transformations signified only replacement and compensation. At the local or regional level, in contrast, the results were disastrous, even more so since commercial capitalism had in the meantime impoverished broad social groups.

Every western European town with an important export industry evolved in a comparable way during the sixteenth century: in time, most craftsmen depended on the greater merchants, obliged to surrender their produce to them: thus craftsmen resumed the status of wage labourers. In 1584–85 only fifty of the 4,000 inhabitants of Antwerp who lived off silk weaving belonged to the propertied class; all others were 'poor folk [*schamele personen*] who do not have a thing if they have to cease work'. But, among the 380 dealers in fabrics and raw materials for the textile industry, no less than 302 (80 per cent) were propertied; the vast majority, some 239 (63 per cent), even belonged to the highest tax brackets. The Lyonese silk industry, established in 1536, was likewise controlled by a small group of capitalist merchants. By the middle of the century, about 12,000 inhabitants (20 per cent of the population) lived off silk. The merchants who imported raw silk and exported the finished product had the producers completely in their power. Scarcely ten years after the introduction of the silk industry, two merchants owned 220 looms. In 1576 two other large-scale dealers together provided a living for 800 to 1,000 workers.

One might object that neither example is representative, since both concern luxury goods and two of the most prominent commercial centres in sixteenth-century Europe. Given the high cost of raw silk, the susceptibility of this craft to economic fluctuations and the presence of a rich elite of foreign merchants undoubtedly explain the pace and intensity of the social decline of the Antwerp and Lyonese silk workers. However, in the small centres which produced cheaper textiles, craftsmen likewise suffered impoverishment and proletarianization. This can be seen in Hondschoote. From the mid-fifteenth century the manufacture of serge made of inferior worsted yarn spun from long-staple wool (known as the 'new draperies') became a boom industry in south-western Flanders. Hondschoote soon grew into the foremost centre: yearly production rose from 28,000 pieces in 1528 to an average of

100,000 in the 1560s. Drawn by the hope of a decent wage, thousands of uprooted farmers streamed into Hondschoote. From scarcely 2,500 inhabitants in 1469 the population rose to around 15,000 by 1560. Since the labour market was little regulated, if at all, the continuous immigration of the propertyless increased exploitation of workers by merchants. In the second half of the fifteenth century and the first decade of the sixteenth, most producers appear to have worked for themselves; in the course of the sixteenth century, however, the majority of them were proletarianized. Competition was so great that all without sufficient capital were lost. Gradually, the small master craftsmen were forced to provide themselves with the necessary raw materials on credit. Many even lost the ownership of their looms and had to hire them: they became wage labourers. Capitalist merchants eventually dominated the whole serge industry in Hondschoote. Some merchants exported to Antwerp a fifth to a quarter of the town's produce at a time.

Contemporaries were conscious that industrial growth was no synonym for prosperity. The Brugge rhetorician Cornelis Everaert in the 1520s and 1530s showed a deep understanding of the socio-economic relationships dominant in the textile industry. In his plays, repeatedly banned by the authorities, he unambiguously portrayed the underpayment of the textile workers and the scandalous practices of their employers, who paid in debased coinage or in produce. The German writer Hans Sachs, in his dialogue on avarice, castigated the merchant entrepreneurs who paid their workers so little that their wives and children lived in poverty. In a detailed report, dating from 1577, the town secretary of Leyden, Jan van Houtte, ascribed the poverty of the urban craftsmen to the organization of the cloth industry. He declared that the innumerable persons who lived off spinning, weaving, fulling, and other wool processes were totally dominated by a few rich and powerful *drapeniers*, who underpaid their workers and cheated them in every imaginable way. Resistance was impossible, since employers were supported by the magistrates: the two groups were interrelated. Van Houtte concluded with the verdict that 'the poor workers – better call them the slaves – after having worked a whole week, are compelled to beg on Sundays to supplement their wages'. Similarly, Robert Reyce wrote in 1618 about Suffolk that 'in those parts of this shire, where the clothiers do dwell or have dwelt, there are found the greatest number of the poor'.[7]

The construction industry in western Europe in the *ancien régime* was apparently one of the most labour-intensive concerns. The growth of urban population and the erection of new fortification stimulated construction in the sixteenth century, and rising production was responsible for the growing power of the large entrepreneurs. Since master contractors were generally paid at the completion of a project, they needed large amounts of capital to pay for wages and raw materials. As prices and wages rose and work grew more extensive, contractors were less able to cover their expenses; their rich 'colleagues' gradually gained the upper hand, a development illustrated by the evolution of the relations of production in the Antwerp construction industry.

The population of Antwerp increased from nearly 50,000 inhabitants around 1500 to about 100,000 in 1568, giving an enormous impulse to the building industry; between 1496 and 1568, no fewer than 5,700 houses were built. Similarly, commercial expansion proved a stimulus to public works; canals were dug, bridges built, markets founded, staple houses and auction halls raised. Simultaneously, the antiquated medieval town walls were demolished and replaced by bastions, to which a citadel was joined. How many contractors profited from this intense activity? Self-employed masons and carpenters constructed a third of all houses finished in the second quarter of the sixteenth century, but a mere 15 per cent of these builders engrossed more than half the business. Public works projects furthered the tendency towards economic concentration. In the middle of the century one contractor, Gilbert van Schoonbeke, took on the completion of the new walls, some 79,000 cubic metres of masonry, and contracted out 96 per cent in turn to six or seven subcontractors. This *de facto* monopoly was made possible by Van Schoonbeke's personal construction industry: fifteen brick factories employing 400 to 500 workers, an enormous peat-cutting effort with at least 100 workers, limekilns, and considerable forestry. Thanks to this enterprise, Van Schoonbeke halved his costs and thus eliminated all competition. Since he concluded contracts only with rich builders, the small craftsman, who could not take refuge in the private sector during economic depression, was put out of business. The construction of the Antwerp citadel, fifteen years later, went the same way. Nearly 80 per cent of all masonry and carpentry work was carried out by nine cartels, which grouped together some twenty-four contractors; the foremost associations were controlled by merchants and financiers. No wonder that in 1584–85 only 59 of the 353 master builders and carpenters belonged to the propertied class: all the others made up part of the poor community, the *arme ghemeynte*.

Only master craftsmen who produced for the local market or who manufactured luxury goods (which, because of the highly skilled labour required, were aimed at a limited market) could maintain their socio-economic position. Craft exclusivity ensured that the differences in fortune among such manufacturers remained quite small. On the other side of the coin, most journeymen could no longer climb upwards: permanent dependence was their lot. In short, the triumph of commercial capitalism implied the impoverishment of innumerable small master craftsmen, journeymen, apprentices, and casual labourers in the four most labour-intensive industries: textile, construction, mining and metallurgy.

3. Polarization of society

'Polarization' perhaps better than any other word characterizes the social evolution of early modern Europe. This period was, as W. G. Hoskins has remarked, 'a golden age for the Shearers, not to be paralleled until the late eighteenth and early nineteenth centuries when a combination of the new industrial capitalism with an age-old smooth and perfected system of political plunder left the Shorn with just enough on their backs to keep alive, and not always that'.[8]

Tax assessments show that the extreme socio-economic inequality of English rural society was already evident by the third decade of the sixteenth century. No less than 1,375 of the 2,277 inhabitants recorded in the Hundred of Babergh in southern Suffolk, one of the most industrialized parts of the country, possessed neither land nor house. Of the 902 whose 'lands' were taxed, 620 had only a cottage. Expressed differently, 87 per cent lived at or beneath the poverty line, and 1.5 per cent held more than 50 per cent of the land. The distribution of wealth gives the same picture: the lower half of the population owned at most

4 per cent of the total wealth, but the top 5 per cent had at least 50 per cent of all fixed and moveable property. In agrarian areas, the situation was not much more favourable. In the large parish of Constantine(3,247 hectares) on the Helford River in Cornwall, the great majority of inhabitants, apparently three in four, rented their dwellings. In the coastal Hundred of Happing in Norfolk, with its untouched farming and fishing economy, Hoskins's 'bottom people' owned scarcely 7 per cent of personal wealth, while 9.5 per cent of the population held nearly half. In the course of the later sixteenth century, the impoverishment process reached ever greater proportions in the English countryside. Before 1560 scarcely 11 per cent of rural labourers disposed of only a cottage and garden; after 1640 their numbers amounted to 40 per cent, and the proportion without livestock of their own

Table 5.
Size of peasant labourers' holdings in England, by percentages, before 1560 and after 1620:

Size of holding	*Before 1560*	*After 1620*
Cottage with garden or croft only	11	40
Less than 0.4 ha	31	23
Size of holding	*Before 1560*	*After 1620*
0.4 – 0.7 ha	28	14
0.8 – 1.1 ha	7	8
1.2 – 1.5 ha	11	7
1.6 – 2.0 ha	11	8

Source: recalculated from A. Everitt, 'Farm labourers', in J. Thirsk, ed., *The Agrarian History of England and Wales*, vol. IV, *1500–1640* (Cambridge, 1967), p. 402.

Note: The term 'peasant labourers' refers to those workers whose livelihood was based partly on their holdings and who were wealthy enough to leave inventories.

rose from 5 to 13 per cent. Expansion of the labouring population had a particularly unfavourable impact on wage levels. Since supply rose much more quickly than demand, employers could put maximum pressure on wages. Between 1500 and 1600 grain prices rose sixfold, while wages rose only threefold. Not surprisingly, workers and cottars were 'but house beggars' for Francis Bacon.

The living conditions of French peasants were scarcely better. Many were, it is true, owners of a small plot of ground, but this seldom sufficed to support a family. At Lespignan in Languedoc, 67 per cent of the peasants around 1607 harvested too little grain to feed four without supplementary income, compared to only 38 per cent at the end of the fifteenth century. The excessive

Table 6.
Percentage distribution of farms and arable land in Lespignan (Languedoc), 1492–1607.

	1492		*1607*	
	Farms	*Arable Land*	*Farms*	*Arable Land*
Less than 5 ha	38	8	67	15
5 – 10 ha	57	55	26	37
26 ha or larger	5	37	7	48

Source: calculated from E. Le Roy Ladurie, *Les Paysans de Languedoc* (Paris, 1966), pp. 240–3.

rise in the number of cottars dependent on wages augmented underemployment and unemployment, and blocked wage increases. Between 1500 and 1600, the purchasing power of rural workers diminished by some 45 per cent. Moreover, the greater number of men employed had a drastic impact on the wages of women: around 1600, they received only 37 per cent of a man's wage in place of 50 per cent in the early sixteenth century.

In New Castile, where approximately 50 per cent of the rural population consisted of landless labourers, wage labour and poverty were considered synonymous – 'the greater part of the inhabitants are poor, all being day labourers', ran the laconic summation of the social situation in many villages. The *relaciones topográficas* of the 1570s showed that workers in New Castile lived like animals: they were chronically underfed and lived in rickety huts of earth or wood, without furniture; men, women, and children slept crowded together on stamped earth. The moment seasonal employment began, thousands of hungry *jornaleros*, often with their whole families, trekked from village to village offering their labour. Since they had at most three or four successive months of full-time work, they had to try during most of the year to get by on odd jobs. The life of this pitiful mass was hence a daily struggle for mere existence – a struggle whose outcome was extremely uncertain.

Censuses show that the Low Countries had their share of rural poverty. In Holland south of the Ij, the poor in 1514 formed around 23 per cent of the 3,745 rural hearths for which information is available. To the north the situation was even more sombre: 31 per cent of rural households were designated poor. In Brabant, the tax receivers in 1526 counted around 27 per cent rural poor; this number lay somewhat lower than in 1480, when around 30 per cent poor hearths were registered. The small drop, as we shall later see (p. 78), ought to be ascribed to the emigration of many impoverished peasants into the great towns. In Walloon Flanders, the portion of rural poor rose between 1498 and 1544 from *c.* 30 per cent to *c.* 40 per cent.

For Germany west of the Elbe, we know the distribution of wealth in ten villages in Württemberg. In 1544 10 to 25 per cent of the population consisted of servants, 13 to 25 per cent of landless daylabourers, and 15 to 22 per cent of cottagers. Although the proportion of actual or potential poor thus differed strongly from village to village, even in the most favourable situation 65 per cent were economically dependent, living on the edge of subsistence.

Through lack of evidence, it is not yet possible to form an accurate picture of the changing daily life of the rural lower classes in the sixteenth century, yet there is no doubt that a growing number suffered from chronic malnutrition. Increased numbers of landless labourers and cottars dependent on wage labour as a source of supplementary income became a general phenomenon; since supply easily exceeded demand, a growing part of rural society was struck by unemployment and lower wages. The drastic decline of family income meant that expenses for necessities had to be severely limited. The poorest country-dwellers, who represented a fourth to a third of the peasantry, were progressively less able to buy a sufficient quantity of food even in 'normal' years. Many sixteenth-century chronicles relate that turnips, rape, roots, flowerbulbs, leaves, and grass were the only foodstuffs available in time of dearth. As the gulf between prices and incomes widened, the potential poor had to tighten their belts too. In Languedoc between 1480 and 1590 the diet of labourers, who were paid partly in kind and partly in money, was adversely affected not quantitatively, but qualitatively. In Sicily consumption of meat in the countryside dwindled from 16 to 22 kg per person per annum in the fifteenth century to between 2 and

10 kg in the period 1594–96. In Germany a similar process took place. In Swabia by 1550, Heinrich Müller wrote that

> in the past they ate differently at the peasant's house. Then there was meat and food in profusion every day; tables at village fairs and feasts sank under their load. Today, everything has truly changed. For some years, in fact, what a calamitous time, what high prices! And the food of the most comfortably-off peasants is almost worse than that of day-labourers and valets previously.[9]

For good reasons, the first picaresque novels had hunger as their main theme. The drop in personal consumption led to physical weakness and lowered resistance to contagious disease. It was symptomatic that famine was increasingly more often accompanied by epidemics from 1560 onwards, and that the number of victims rose.

Uprooted inhabitants of the countryside, having sought refuge in the towns, were confronted with a society in which socio-economic contrasts were much more pronounced. In 1549, a Councillor of Jachymov declared bluntly, 'One pays, the other labours'. Nowhere was the distinction between capital and labour expressed so sharply as in the metropoles. The gulf between rich and poor grew wider than ever before, widening both absolutely and relatively, due to the intensity of concomitant enrichment and impoverishment processes. From changes in the division of wealth in Turin and St Gall, an increase in social inequality can be seen from the second half of the fifteenth century. While one per cent of property owners in Turin raised their portion of the total wealth of the town between 1464 and 1523 from 13 to 21 per cent, 75 per cent saw their portion diminish from 25 to 21 per cent. In St Gall, with its linen export industry, the number of taxpayers with property of less than one hundred florins rose between 1471 and 1520 from 65 to 73 per cent, while the number of households with property of more than a thousand florins doubled.

Every available example indicates that, in all towns where trade and industry expanded, wealth was divided extremely unequally. That was not only the case in important textile centres such as Leyden, Coventry and Nördlingen (Figure 6), but also in commercial metropoles such as Antwerp and Lyon. In the richest town of the Netherlands, and perhaps of all Europe, the propertied classes represented only 24 per cent of the total population in 1584–85;

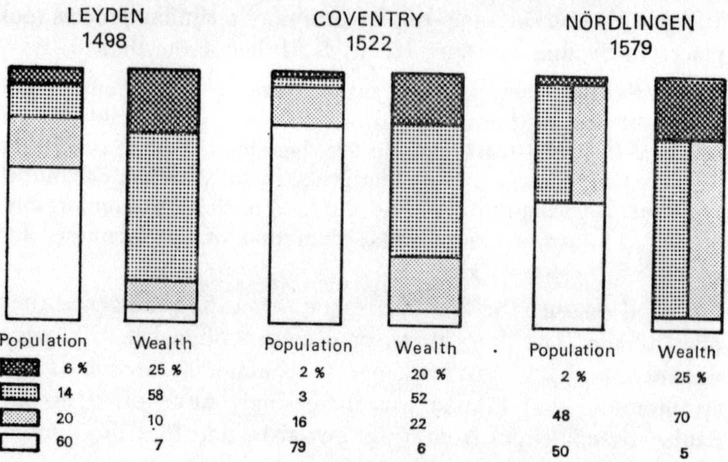

Fig. 6 Percentage distribution of population and estimated wealth in Leyden (1498), Coventry (1522) and Nördlingen (1579).

Sources: Calculated from N. W. Posthumus, *Geschiedenis van de Leidsche lakenindustrie* (The Hague, 1908), I, pp. 386–98; W. G. Hoskins, *The Age of Plunder* (London and New York, 1976), p. 40; C. R. Friedrichs, 'Capitalism, mobility and class formation in the early modern German city', *Past and Present*, 69 (1975), p. 28.

76 per cent belonged to the *arme ghemeynte*, the poor community, people who paid no taxes due to their low income. Lyonese society presented a similar picture: in 1545, around 75 per cent of the burghers were exempted from taxation because of their economic circumstances. As for the taxpayers, while 10 per cent owned nearly 53 per cent of total wealth, 60 per cent disposed of scarcely 21 per cent of urban assets; ten merchants, or 0.27 per cent of the taxpayers, together paid 7 per cent of the total.

These examples, which could be multiplied easily, show that economic growth went hand in hand with social inequality. The same held true for smaller towns and centres without export industries. Two in five persons in sixteen English country towns, averaging 500 to 600 inhabitants, in 1524–25 were wage labourers, generally owning no more than a tenth of the aggregate wealth. Nearly everywhere, the top 5 per cent of the burghers controlled 40 to 50 per cent of the total wealth. In eighteen small and medium towns in Lower Saxony, 30 per cent of the population in the mid-sixteenth century consisted of propertyless workers, who may be deemed 'unfree'. It is no exaggeration to conclude that half of western Europe's town-dwellers in the sixteenth century were a proletarianized mass which owned little or nothing besides their own labour. How could it be otherwise? In every important centre the triumph of merchant capitalism ensured the social degradation of the small producer and the total economic dependence of journeymen, and constant immigration of impoverished country-dwellers, quite prepared to work for low wages, gave employers the opportunity to push down further already low wage levels. Hence, wages trailed behind rising prices, and they steadily grew more and more insufficient. By 1600 the real wages of construction workers expressed in grain were universally 40 to 50 per cent lower than in the period 1451 to 1475. The real income of workers possibly sank even further: growing labour surplus steadily brought not only underemployment, but unemployment as well, drastically trimming the average number of work days available for every man, woman and child.

A recent estimate of the poverty line of Lyonese workers presumed that workers were employed 260 to 270 days per annum and had to support, on their wages, a family of four with some 2.5 kg of bread per day. The poverty line was exceeded when more than 70 per cent of wages had to be devoted to the purchase of bread. In that case no other staples, such as meat, wine, or oil, could be bought, and expenses for rent and fuel could not be covered. For three categories of building workers, the number of years their purchasing power lay below subsistence levels was investigated for the period 1475 to 1599 (Table 7).

Table 7.

Number of years in which Lyonese building workers fell below the poverty line, 1475–1599.

Period	*Free Journeymen*	*Mason's labourers*	*Casual Labourers*
1475–99	0	1	5
1500–24	0	0	12
1525–49	0	3	12
1550–74	0	4	20
1575–99	1	17	25
Total	1	25	74

Source: Gascon, *Grand Commerce*, vol. I, 402.

Even with full employment, casual labourers during twenty-four years in the first half of the sixteenth century were unable to support a family of four. From 1550 they endured biting poverty: in only five years did they rise above the poverty line. Masons' labourers after 1575 knew three difficult years in five. Only the wages of the most skilled workers remained sufficient to give four persons their daily bread, but if they went fifty days without work in a year, then they too would live in poverty, two years in five during the last quarter of the sixteenth century.

Every town in western Europe confronted increased poverty from around 1450 on. In Memmingen, a major centre of linen production in upper Swabia, the number of 'have-nots' leapt from 31 per cent to 55 per cent in 1521. In the metropoles of Brabant, the number of poor hearths rose between 1480 and 1526 from 14 to 19 per cent, and in the smaller centres from 27 to 29 per cent (Figure 7). The rise was apparently caused not only by the impoverishment of urban artisans, but also by the influx of the rural poor: in 1529, the prelates of Brabant declared: 'We find ourselves and the whole land in such great poverty that it is not possible to describe it. We cannot prevent the country dwellers from leaving, as they have already done in many places.'[10] In Leyden, about one-third of the population consisted of 'poor and miserable folk' in 1498; fifty years later, the number was set at 5,000 to 6,000, some 40 to 50 per cent of the total. London in 1594 had twelve times as many beggars as in 1517, although the population of the capital had risen scarcely fourfold. In Cremona the portion of registered poor in the total population around 1600 was three times greater than in the middle of the sixteenth century. In Lucerne the number of sedentary poor rose between 1579 and 1592 by 28.5 per cent. In French and Spanish towns too, poverty increasingly presented a social problem. In Lyon, during the dearth of 1531, more than 5,000 hungry, some 10 per cent of the inhabitants, had to be supported by the authorities. When the magistrates of Rouen in 1534 held an inquest into unemployment they reached the bewildering conclusion that the town housed around 7,000 needy and 532 beggars, adults and children; nearly 15 per cent of the population, in other words, lived below the poverty line. A census carried out in Troyes in 1551 brought to light that beggars and vagabonds alone comprised about 16 per cent of the inhabitants.

In Segovia, the foremost textile centre of the Iberian Peninsula, around 16 per cent of the population in 1561 consisted of resident poor, regularly aided by the authorities.

Not surprisingly, migration in these circumstances was nothing exceptional. Both rural and urban paupers left their homes in desperation, hoping to find work elsewhere, or at least some material aid. More and more, towns were merely temporary stops in a long series of moves on a doubt-ridden and often fruitless search for the most elementary means of existence. This swelling mass of wandering poor, driven by need to occasional crimes, filled contemporaries with horror and fear. In 1518, the magistrates of Coventry openly condemned 'these big beggars that will not work to get their living but lie in the fields and break hedges'. Twelve years later, a royal proclamation complained of the vagabonds, who 'have of long time increased and daily do increase in great and excessive numbers . . . whereby have insurged and sprung . . . continual thefts [and] murders'.[11] The same complaint was heard throughout Europe. In Germany, France, Italy, the Iberian Peninsula, the Low Countries, Switzerland: everywhere, migrations of the famished assumed alarming proportions, and the continual movement of hordes of 'masterless men' was seen by the propertied elites as a threat to public order. Growing realization that disease was not caused by corruption of the air or conjunctions of the stars but spread from one person to another focused suspicion on vagabonds and wandering beggars during an epidemic. Anxiety over the poor as potential carriers of disease spurred wealthy townsmen to avoid daily contact with them. In nearly all centres, a growing tendency towards spatial segregation manifested itself in the course of the sixteenth century. Everywhere massive immigration led to intense speculation in fixed property, sending rents soaring. Since workers had to devote an increasingly greater part of their budget to food, housing conditions worsened. Speculators, building contractors, and homeowners profited from the growing demand for cheap lodging, dividing up extensive areas into minute parcels, filling the gardens and courtyards of old buildings with hovels, and letting houses for the maximum rent possible. Afraid of disease, criminality and prostitution, the rich withdrew from the old city centres and established themselves in new residential areas. Where that was impossible for military or other reasons

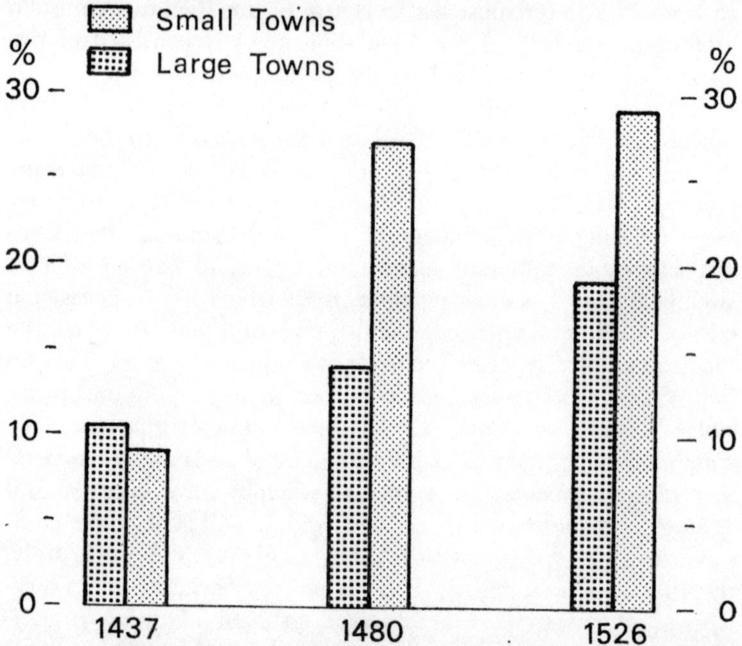

Fig. 7 Poor hearths as percentage of total hearths in the large and small towns of Brabant, 1437–1526.

Source: Based on J. Cuvelier, *Les dénombrements des foyers en Brabant, XIVe–XVIe siècles*, vol. I (Brussels, 1912).

the poor were driven to the periphery of the town or to special streets or quarters, which turned into ghettos. In the early 1580s, nearly a fifth of the population was concentrated in two of Antwerp's thirteen wards; most were poor: all the inhabitants of this part of town together paid scarcely 2.5 per cent of the taxes on property. Two other wards, the centre of the metropolis, held only 14 per cent of the burghers, but they owned more than 34 per cent of total municipal wealth. The ideal town designed by Leonardo da Vinci is a striking illustration of a mentality which increasingly translated social inequality into spatial terms. To quote the artist: 'In the upper streets, carts and similar vehicles may not pass; these streets are reserved for the notables. In the lower streets shall go the wagons intended for the use and supply of the populace.'[12]

Changes in public festivities likewise testified to the growing chasm between rich and poor. Coronations, carnivals, and royal marriages were the occasion for great feasts with processions through the town, but the decoration of floats and the themes treated by rhetoricians and musicians increasingly drew on a mythology and an aesthetic without significance for the bulk of the population. Festivities in Rome during the second half of the sixteenth century grew more and more exclusive: while the spectacles organized by spiritual and secular officeholders initially were open to all, they could be attended at the end of this period by a small elite alone. When the banker Tiberio Ceuli married off his daughter in 1603, a tournament took place in front of his palace in the presence of numerous cardinals, ambassadors and other VIPs. The people heard only the trumpets – the entrances to the area were closed off. Another sign of the times; at the feast given by Cardinal Aldobrandini in honour of the Viceroy of Naples in 1600 attendance was by invitation, a *bollettino*, only.

Increasing malnutrition among the lower classes undoubtedly influenced their physical development. The rich, in the words of Peter Laslett, 'must have been taller, heavier, better developed and earlier to mature than the rest'. If sixteenth-century paintings and engravings bear some relation to reality, the physical distinctions between rich and poor were indeed quite great. Thus, the belief of the elite in their 'inbred' superiority grew. Around 1600 every fair milkmaid in plays and stories seemed to be a princess in disguise. Even the medieval folk hero Robin Hood was rebaptized a disowned earl. For Cervantes too, himself the son of a poor physician, beauty was the hereditary prerogative of the propertied class: manual labour seemed more and more an activity of lesser worth, a sign of servility. Sir Thomas Smith declared that the 'commonwealth consisteth only of freemen'; day labourers and others without freeholds 'have no voice nor authority in our commonwealth, and no account is made of them but only to be ruled'. They who 'be hired for wages . . . be called servants'. In France similar conceptions won the day. Claude de Rubys of Lyon called surgeons, cobblers, leather-workers, even printers and goldsmiths 'squalid and indecent'. Bernard de Palissy felt obliged to excuse his 'meagre and despicable condition'. In Spain, where 'people of the middling sort' nearly disappeared, the debasement of manual labour was raised by the elite to a dogma.

'There are but two families in the world,' declared Sancho Panza's grandmother: 'the haves and the have-nots'. More and more contemporaries, rich and poor, subscribed to this interpretation. In Norfolk in 1540 the poor considered that 'it were a good turn if there were as many gentlemen in Norfolk as there be white bulls'. Half a century later, Thomas Deloney pronounced: 'The poor hate the rich, because they will not set them on work; and the rich hate the poor, because they seem burdensome.' Around the same time, Sir Walter Raleigh suspected that the poor, in case of a Spanish invasion, would say, 'let the rich fight for themselves'. How *did* the propertied classes neutralize growing social tension, to keep the poor under control? Together with Sir Fulke Greville, the historian might well argue that 'if the feet knew their strength as well as we know their oppression, they would not bear as they do.'[13]

4. The emergence of social policy

The growing numbers of transient poor wakened the curiosity as much as the fear of contemporaries; numerous books and pamphlets portrayed their 'monstrous' world. The *Narrenschiff* (*Ship of Fools*) of Sebastian Brant, the *Liber Vagatorum*, the *Propos Rustiques* of Noël du Fail, the *Fraternity of Vacabondes* of John Awdely, and many other works gruesomely pictured the evil practices, shameless customs, the hierarchy, and esoteric lingo of 'marginal' folk. The poor, beggars and vagabonds were tossed together, degraded to a single stereotype; the deceitful tramp, unworthy of charity, citizen of a kingdom apart, a negative characterization of 'civilized' society. Innumerable editions and translations testify to the extraordinary success enjoyed by this literature.

Research indicates that the stories of secret associations of rogues with their own hierarchies and vocabulary sprang mostly from the vivid imagery of contemporaries. Although such a substratum of organized roguery existed, its significance should not be overestimated. The vast majority of incessant wanderers consisted of paupers who migrated due to need, guilty only sporadically and out of desperation of 'misdeeds'. The 'subculture' of beggars and vagabonds was in great measure the imaginative creation of an elite which chose the easiest way to remove the uprooted poor from society yet simultaneously to analyse the poor in terms sensible to that society. Even around the Mediterranean, where banditry spread more widely than elsewhere, bands of criminals paled into insignificance besides the mass of the subsisting migrants. Parenthetically, it is notable how often banditry was indistinguishable from social revolt.

Anxiety over the transient hungry took hold from the second half of the fifteenth century on. Throughout western Europe, central and local authorities took measures against 'antisocial' elements. In 1459 the magistrates of Augsburg determined that all alien beggars had to leave within three days and that the local poor could no longer beg on workdays in the churches or at the homes of burghers. The same year, Philip the Good proclaimed an ordinance in Brabant, ravaged by bands of cashiered soldiers, that sturdy beggars must leave the duchy within three days, on pain of sentencing to the galleys; the edict followed shortly in Flanders, and perhaps in Holland and Zeeland as well. The magistrates of Strasbourg, who in the first half of the fifteenth century limited themselves to admonitions, took a whole series of measures against immigration of propertyless transients after 1460. The poor from the countryside might stay a mere three days in the town; excepting lame, sick, and old, all were forbidden to beg; infractions were threatened with corporal punishment. In 1473 the Parlement of Paris ordered forceful measures against vagabondage in the capital. Transient paupers were to be detained at once, and the incomes of suspected inhabitants fully investigated. During the following years steadily more repressive measures were taken, culminating in the ordinance of 1496, in which Charles VIII commissioned the courts to put vagabonds to the galleys. In England as well, attempts were made to stop the trek of the poor to the towns. The 'Acte against Vacabounds and Beggars', proclaimed by Henry VII in 1495, stipulated that beggars and other idlers were to be put in the stocks for three days, whipped, and sent back to their homes.

These measures did not go beyond repression; nowhere was an attempt made to deal adequately with the uprooted poor or to reorganize poor relief. The authorities sought only to sow terror: exemplary punishment to restrain the propertyless from flocking to the towns, which as storehouses of wealth and creators of poverty were particularly vulnerable. Given that most ordinances were reissued with great regularity, it seems that this policy showed few results. The shortcomings of the political apparat were too great for large-scale prosecution: there were too few officials; the tasks of the officers of justice included too many other things; cooperation between different juridical instances was out of the question; and many officials showed too little zeal, fearing reprisals from the lower classes, or because the poverty of the 'delinquents' rendered them unable to repay the expenses of their detention. At the same time the extent of the social problem grew so great that even a soundly organized and coordinated apparat of repression could not solve the problem. It did not suffice to drive transients out of town and forbid the sedentary poor to beg; the needy had to be dealt with one way or another. Traditional institutions could not cope with the tidal wave of demands for poor relief; hence, a more positive approach to poverty demanded a radical reorganization of its administration. Neither public authorities nor wealthy burghers were readily inclined to begin such steps. Rationalization of poor relief necessitated administrative reforms, which easily led to jurisdictional disputes. The propertied class, for its part, was conscious that more efficient social control would entail financial sacrifices. Consequently as long as it was possible the wielders of economic and political power supported traditional restraints.

The period 1520 to 1535 was the turning-point. Until then the necessities of life were relatively abundant and famines relatively rare, but the dearth year 1521–22 showed the writing on the wall. Demographic growth without 'problems' proved incompatible with the structure of agrarian production. Between 1527 and 1534 a series of harvest failures throughout Europe led to catastrophic famines and epidemics. Wars, financial crises and manipulation of currency depressed international commerce and, consequently, industrial production. Dwindling demand for manufactured goods caused underemployment, reducing yet again real income. The crisis of the 1520s and the earlier 1530s led to a temporary bridging of the gap between skilled and unskilled workers; the latter were undoubtedly hit the hardest, but the former were more embittered because they had significantly improved their economic position during the preceding phase of expansion. The traditionally revolutionary inclinations of the lower classes were strengthened by the frustrated middle classes.[14] Results were not long in coming.

From 1520, rebellious movements, often of dangerous proportions, pressed local and central authorities to act on social problems. Whole regions were set aflame: the *Communeros* in Spain in 1520–21, followed by the *Germanias* in 1525–26; the *Bauernkrieg*, the German Peasants' Revolt of 1524–26; the revolts of textile workers in south-east England in 1525–26 and 1528; the *Grande Rebeyne* at Lyon in 1529; the revolt of the *Straccioni* at Lucca in 1531–32; and the Pilgrimage of Grace in 1536–37, five revolts which gripped a great part of England. Also, in numerous Netherlandish regions (Land van Waas, Luxemburg, Limburg, Liège) and towns (The Hague, 's-Hertogenbosch, La Roche, Utrecht, Brussels, Amsterdam, Leyden), serious disturbances took place in the period 1520 to 1535. A count of the rebellious movements in the towns of the Empire demonstrates that social unrest welled up during the 1520s with an intensity until then unknown. Between 1451 and 1530, both west and east of the Elbe, Bohemia and Austria included, the Empire witnessed 96 urban revolts: 33 in the period 1451 to 1510, some 0.5 per annum; 18 in the second decade of the sixteenth century, 1.8 per annum; and not less than 45, nearly half of the total, in the third decade, 4.5 per annum. The centre of gravity between 1521 and 1530 lay in the large and middle-sized towns, specifically in the industrial centres. Protests against the exceptional concentration of wealth in the hands of a minority and the increasing domination exercised by capitalist merchant-entrepreneurs usually formed the main theme. Indisputably, middling sorts often played a prominent role in the rural and municipal revolts, but in the course of time many rebellious movements underwent a radicalization process and the lower classes secured the upper hand. Not surprisingly, the swelling armies of the poor were considered more and more as the pre-eminent threat to the precarious social order by the representatives of the 'establishment'. Quite rightly, the Duke of Norfolk, when asking a rebellious crowd in eastern England in 1526 to speak with their leader, received the answer: 'Since you ask who is our captain, for sooth his name is Poverty, for he and his cousin Necessity, hath brought us to this doing.'

The humanists applied themselves to the newly threatening

problem of poverty during the crucial period of the 1520s. In utopia, wrote Thomas More in 1516, begging would be forbidden and work obligatory for all sturdy poor, and this point of view quickly won the field in the next decade. Many humanists, anxious over the massive social need and fearful of revolts, proposed means to alleviate need and to counter vagabondage. In 1524 Erasmus aimed one of his *Colloquia* at the 'plague': begging was antisocial, abominable, and dangerous to public order. At the end of the dialogue he proposed that municipal authorities should take strong measures. A year later, the Spanish humanist Juan Luis Vives published at Brugge the most famous and detailed sixteenth-century treatise on poor relief, *De Subventione Pauperum*. He set out a whole programme: prohibition of begging, forced labour, centralization of relief funds, establishment of schools for the children of paupers, and so on. In 1527 Cornelis Agrippa noted sarcastically that, in imitation of classical antiquity, one should not pity the poor, but despise beggars and vagabonds instead. Thomas More broached the theme anew in 1527, this time expressing himself far less academically than in *Utopia*, painting a horrifying picture of the dangers incarnated in all those who acted

> with contempt of God and all good men, and obstinate rebellous mind against all laws, rule, and governance . . . For they shall gather together . . . and under pretext of reformation . . . shall assay to make new division of every man's land and substance, never ceasing if ye suffer them, till they make all beggars as they be themself, and at last bring all the realm to ruin, and this not without butchery and foul bloody hands.

After the traumatic experience of the Pilgrimage of Grace, pauperism in England stood at the centre of interest more than ever before. Thomas Elyot, Richard Morison (who drew a connection between impoverishment and rebelliousness), Thomas Starkey and other humanists were unanimous in their verdict: idleness is the devil's handwork; forced labour was the essential requirement for maintenance of the common good.[15]

Religious reformers were equally concerned with poverty during these years. However much Luther, Zwingli and Calvin differed, they agreed that poverty was neither virtuous nor sanctifying. Since each answered for his own fate, idleness was harshly judged; its opposite, work, was 'saintly'. The duty to work, grounded theologically, was not only preached but also put into practice. In 1523 Luther helped in the reorganization of poor relief in the Saxon town of Leisnig; three years later, Zwingli directed a plan for the reform of public welfare in Zürich; in 1541 Calvin established the precise working of poor relief in Geneva in a church ordinance. Although the three reformers differed on numerous points, the principles proclaimed and approved by them in this case followed the same general lines: prohibition of begging, forced labour, and centralization of poor relief providing minimum benefits. On that last point, Luther considered that relief had to be limited strictly to the level of subsistence.

Only one movement sounded another note at this time: anabaptism. Anabaptists opposed begging, but only because a true Christian community ought to be based on voluntary mutual aid, therefore contempt for the poor as well as intervention by the authorities in the sphere of welfare was wrong. The possibilities for spreading such ideas were limited. All princes viewed anabaptism as a 'cursed sect', composed of unlettered and poor men seeking to plunder the Church, nobility, bourgeoisie and merchants, in short, property owners, 'to make of all one mass'. Recent research has found that this description in no sense matched reality: anabaptists were recruited from all strata of society, hence the preponderance of the unpropertied; most of them recognized the right of private property. That the upper classes in the 1520s and 1530s so often and so explicitly saw a connection between pauperism and anabaptism, branded 'communism', shows how serious social problems had become and how far the potential explosiveness of the situation filled the authorities with fear.

Holding all these factors in mind, it is understandable that so many western European princes and municipal authorities fundamentally reformed their social policy from the 1520s onwards. In the preceding centuries there had been repeated prohibitions against begging and vagabondage, but, nonetheless, there was no systematic, coordinated social policy. Between 1522 and 1545 some sixty towns took the first steps in this direction: twenty to thirty in Germany, fourteen in the Low Countries, eight in France, six in Switzerland, and two in northern Italy. In the Netherlands (1531), France (1534), England (1531 and above all 1536), Scotland (1535), and Spain (1541), the central authorities proclaimed ordinances with various regulations concerning begging and/or poor relief for the whole realm. What were the most significant characteristics of the new dispensation?

In nearly all towns two principles dominated: strict prohibition of begging and, though not strictly formulated, the duty of the sturdy poor to work, regardless of age or sex. With one exception, Venice, the existing funds were centralized into a 'common box', *gemene beurs, Aumône générale, gemeinen Kasten.* Authorities in the French towns went even further: they compelled the well-to-do burghers to pay a regular 'poor tax'. The design of princely ordinances was more or less the same, though the concrete realization differed from country to country. In the Netherlands Charles V forbade all forms of begging; detailed regulations were, however, relegated to local governments. The emperor exhorted them to create immediately a *gemene beurs*, but this exhortion remained simply advisory. In England, in contrast, Henry VIII forbade not only begging but ordered each parish to bring together their charitable funds in 'common boxes', and in 1572 local authorities were pressed to levy a tax to provide a permanent source of income for the maintenance of the impotent poor. The Scottish law of 1535 specified that the able poor had to see to their own support; they could in no circumstances beg or claim aid. The 'aged and impotent poor' could seek alms, but only in their birth place. During the reigns of Francis I and Henry II in France, especially between 1516 and 1554, a whole series of ordinances were proclaimed with strong penalties for beggars and vagabonds. The most important decisions over poor relief, however, were taken locally. In Spain, finally, there was no strict prohibition of begging nor centralization of poor relief, much less a poor tax. Though the *Cortes* repeatedly complained in the 1520s and 1530s about the terrifying spread of vagabondage, the government restricted itself to the regulation of begging.

In short, excepting Scotland and Spain, the reorganization of poor relief had a common basis: strict prohibition of begging was an attempt to hinder the migrations of paupers and simultaneously to compel the local poor to accept work, of necessity underpaid work. In England this programme was emphasized by the famous *Statute of Artificers* of 1563. This elaborate code ticked

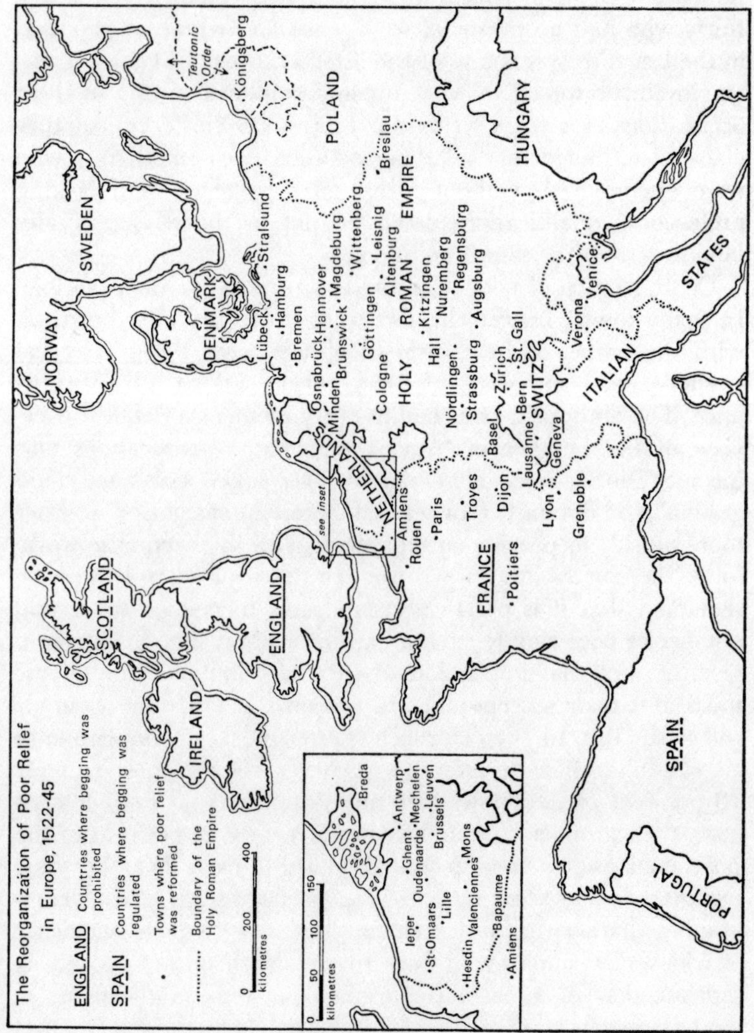

Fig. 8 Map showing the reorganization of poor relief in Europe, 1522–45.

Source: based on H. Soly, 'Economische ontwikkeling en sociale politiek in Europa tijdens de overgang van middeleeuwen naar wieuwe tijden', *Tijdschrift voor Geschiedenis*, 88 (1975), p. 591.

off a list of thirty occupations for which labour contracts had to be made out for at least a year. Everyone unmarried or under thirty who had no means of subsistence and who had practised in the last three years any of the listed occupations could, if unemployed, be forced to work for any employer in any of these occupations at a wage set by the Justices of the Peace. Another clause determined that all those between twelve and sixty who were unemployed, without means of subsistence, and lacking professional qualifications could be put in the service of any landowner, on the same conditions.

Centralization of poor relief made control of the poor possible. In many towns, henceforth, lists were to be carefully drawn up with the name, address, profession, age, civil status, physical circumstances, and wage of every person seeking public assistance. The authorities thus had at every moment a detailed overview of the number of 'true' needy, their qualifications and income. During economic expansion, *per capita* assistance could gradually be diminished or refused to certain categories, in order more quickly to provide entrepreneurs with their requisite workforce, thereby avoiding wage rises. In this connection it must be remarked that it is practically impossible to deduce the actual number of poor simply on the basis of support lists. Such counts give, at most, an impression of their distribution through the town and their susceptibility to certain diseases. One example will clarify this. In 1570 Norwich registered 2,342 poor, with some 1,335 adults. Of these, only 237 received regular support, scarcely 18 per cent of the adults currently deemed as poor. Five years later, their number mounted to 390 or nearly 30 per cent of the poor men and women recorded in the census. For the same reasons, assistance lists serve even less well for study of the demographic characteristics of poor families. The frequent incidence of widows or couples with numerous children do not necessarily indicate that these categories formed the bulk of the poor; in most cases their large number mirrored only the criteria employed by officialdom. Composition of the assisted group depended on factors which in general had little to do with the real needs of the lower classes. According to the financial means over which the institution disposed, the rising or falling demand for labour, the socio-political situation in the affected town (such as fear of revolt), and other 'external' factors, some groups were accepted,

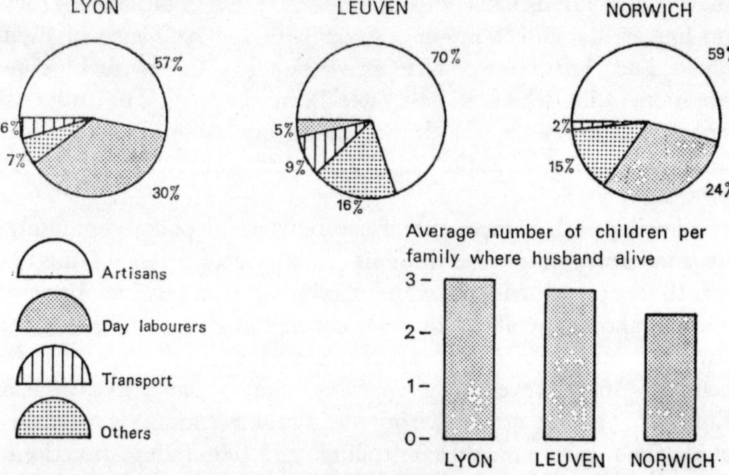

Fig. 9 Occupational and demographic characteristics of the poor listed in censuses carried out in Lyon (1534–39), Leuven (1546) and Norwich (1570).

Note. From these data it can be seen that poverty in the three towns studied cannot be ascribed to lack of training or exceptional family size.

Sources: Calculated from N. Z. Davis, 'Poor relief, Humanism and Heresy: The Case of Lyon', *Studies in Medieval and Renaissance History*, V, (1968), pp. 222–3; J. Cuvelier, 'Documents concernant la réforme de la bienfaisance à Louvain au XVIe siècle', *Bulletin de la Commission royale d'histoire de Belgique*, 105 (1940), pp. 48–55, 101–15; J. F. Pound, 'An Elisabethan Census of the Poor', *Univ. of Birmingham Historical Journal, 8* (1962), pp. 141–2, 152–5.

some rejected. Hence, the aged and lame poor predominated at some times, while the majority of the assisted at other times consisted of young and able poor.

Institution of a *gemene beurs* indicated that the authorities wished to endow their new social policy with a permanent character. In England and the French towns the continuity of the system was best guaranteed; tax assessment largely eliminated fluctuations in the receipts of the centralized relief fund. It scarcely needs to be said that the creation of a 'common box' proceeded without great enthusiasm. Since the rich handed over their contributions henceforth to an impersonal organization, they no longer had direct moral contact with the recipients of their alms. The charitable gesture as a result lost the symbolic connotations with which it had once been charged. The order to siphon all assistance via the 'common box' sometimes aroused heavy resistance – apparently more often in catholic than in protestant areas.[16]

Viewing each component of the new social policy separately, its 'modernity' might be dubious. In the second half of the fifteenth century measures were regularly taken against beggars and vagabonds, while traditional conceptions concerning charity survived until late in the sixteenth and even the seventeenth century. If, however, one considers that some sixty western European towns created, roughly simultaneously, a coordinated alms system with controlling and regulating functions, then one detects a turning-point. The connection between the triumph of commercial capitalism and the genesis of the new social policy appears undeniable. In all centres where industrial production was dominated by commercial capital, poor relief evolved from discontinuous and undifferentiated assistance, chiefly disbursed as voluntary private charity, into a continuous and selective system, in large measure applied by public bodies, which often exercised powers to secure the requisite funds. We do not mean that private charity no longer played an important role in the sixteenth century, quite the reverse; but reorganization of poor relief did imply that most alms would thereafter be distributed to the poor through a public institution in which only the most important burghers participated.

The decisive impact of commercial capitalism was also to be seen in the fact that comparable social policies were never effected in eastern Europe during this period. Certainly, measures were taken in the fifteenth and sixteenth centuries for suppression of begging and vagabondage in several trans-Elbian countries. The Polish theologian André Fricius Modrevius even published a treatise in 1551 in which he heartily condemned idleness: beggars ought to be severely punished, because they contravened Christian morality and endangered public order; he judged that only the 'deserving' poor ought to be supported and that such support ought to be strictly limited to the subsistence minimum. However, the actual stimulus to carry out a radical reorganization of traditional poor relief was missing in eastern Europe. Feudal lords, true enough, wanted to counter vagabondage as a hindrance to the effective operation of the seigneurial economy, but they had no interest in the realization of a coordinated system of relief with controlling and regulating functions, because they were not dependent on a labour market in the true sense. Hence, a 'rational' social policy failed to emerge in eastern Europe.

The connection between charity, social control, and labour regulation is strikingly illustrated by the *Aumône générale* of Lyon. In April 1529 a serious disturbance took place in the Rhône town: 1,000 to 1,200 hungry paupers stormed cloisters and the homes of prominent burghers, plundered grain cellars and split up the 'booty'. Although the *Grande Rebeyne* was quickly and mercilessly suppressed, the magistrates feared new outbursts. When grain prices rose again in May 1531, they took no more risks, instituting an *Aumône générale*: poor relief was centralized, collections organized, lists of the poor taken, etc. The programme was a complete success. Lyon was spared rebellion and even hunger riots. Although initially intended to be a temporary measure to meet a short-term need, the body achieved formal institutional character in 1534. The merchants, the most important pillars of the *Aumône*, clearly saw the great services which centralized poor relief could provide as an instrument of social control and labour regulation. The rich Piedmontese merchant Étienne Turquet, one of the co-founders of the *Aumône* and rector of the institution in 1535–36, proposed to the magistrates in 1536 to introduce the silk industry to Lyon. The authorities looked favourably on his request and donated 500 crowns. The *Aumône* hired several houses, set them up as workshops, and paid the wages of Italian silk specialists whom Turquet recruited to train the children of maintained poor. From the moment the children were sufficiently schooled, they had to go into the service of craftsmen installed at Lyon by Turquet and his associates. In the following decades, the merchant-rectors of the *Aumône* systematically carried out this policy.

Although the ulterior motive of regulating labour behind sixteenth-century poor relief seldom expressed itself as blatantly as at Lyon, identical motives clearly moved the overwhelming majority of local governments. From 1529, sturdy beggars in Venice were put to the galleys, at half the usual wage. The English poor law of 1536 determined that poor children from five to fourteen might be placed by the Justices of the Peace with craftsmen or farmers, for whom they had to work without pay. In Leuven, from 1541, the unemployed were obliged to gather twice daily before the town hall with their tools; on pain of being stricken from the poor list, they could not object to their working conditions nor desert their employers. In Troyes, an important industrial town, the magistrates stipulated in 1545 that poor youths, on reaching their ninth year, had to go into service of an artisan.

Why did increased poverty not lead universally to reorganization of poor relief? While introduction of the new dispensation depended on the specific development of different countries, provinces, and towns, economic factors appear to have been the greatest determinants. Everywhere the burghers expected that social control could be combined with labour regulation (in other words, where they expected economic expansion or recovery) they rendered assistance to the formation of the new social policy. We do not maintain that religious or humanistic impulses played no role. In some small towns, the ideas of the reformers presumably had a certain influence, as in Wittenberg and Leisnig, but as with poverty itself, such motives were not sufficient to create a coordinated alms system. The ideals of humanists and religious reformers were only put into practice by secular authorities when they could be 'translated' into economic terms, that is, when the trinity charity – control – labour duty coincided with the real or imagined interests of the merchant entrepreneurs. In Spain, for example, emphasis on the work ethic or centralization of poor relief was absent, because the country had few industrial centres of significance. Little could be done with the labour of paupers – the need was for skilled craftsmen. The Iberian Peninsula experienced in the sixteenth century an apparent paradox: on one side, an extraordinary increase in the number of *pícaros*, the economically 'redundant'; on the other, a severe shortage of qualified workers. Hence stimulus was lacking to bring into being a new welfare system.

The absence of a radical reorganization of poor relief in Spain cannot be ascribed to the 'laziness' of the population. Scotland's experience was much the same. The temporary Act of 1574, perpetuated in 1579, was a detailed copy of most of the provisions of the English poor law. In contrast to England, however, no measures were taken to put sturdy beggars to work; parishes were not compelled to provide raw materials nor to erect workhouses 'for setting the poor on work and for avoiding of idleness'. A poor tax was, it is true, instituted, to be paid by well-to-do burghers, but the authorities appear only sporadically and for short periods to have collected it. The explanation must be sought in the undeveloped and unindustrialized character of sixteenth-century Scotland. Wage labour provided only a small part of national income, and non-agrarian labour was limited to urban craftsmen, protected by hereditary privileges. Measures aimed at a more efficient constitution of the labour force were considered senseless by the Scottish upper classes. In other western European towns traditional charity was not reformed due to the drastic decline of population, the irreversible decline of local industry, or other factors which made such an effort superfluous for the elite. In Leyden no new poor laws were proclaimed in the sixteenth century because the cloth industry experienced a serious structural crisis; numerous entrepreneurs went bankrupt, and the number of looms declined by half. For like reasons the northern Italian towns, excepting Venice and Verona, decided not to reorganize poor relief. In 1540 scarcely 1,000 pieces of cloth were manufactured in Brescia, compared to around 8,000 in the early sixteenth century. In Milan members of the cloth guild dropped from 158 around 1515 to 59 in the thirties. The population of Pavia declined as a result of war and epidemics from 16,000 around 1500 to scarcely 7,000 in 1535. Two years later, Florence counted a mere 63 cloth workshops versus 270 in 1480; moreover, the population of the town diminished between 1510 and 1530 by 20 per cent.

Economic changes also explain why a new welfare system was given up in other places after a while. The *gemene beurs* in Ieper, once a shining example for the Netherlands, was degraded at the end of the sixteenth century to a foundlings' home. The explanation: the old cloth industry was entirely dismantled, while an attempt to initiate serge manufacturing never took off. Around 1600 the economy of Ieper consisted of only a few marginal industries, small concerns with only local significance.

The authorities consequently saw no particular reason to continue to carry out a coordinated social policy.

In Venice and Geneva the reverse was the case. The population of Venice, where poor relief was reorganized in 1528–29, rose from *c.* 115,000 in 1509 to *c.* 168,000 in the 1560s. Parallel to demographic expansion, demands for labour rose. In contrast to the other northern Italian towns, the Venetian textile industry grew rapidly: manufacture of cloth rose from around 1,000 pieces before 1520 to *c.* 10,000 around 1550 and an average of 20,000 pieces per annum in the last quarter of the century. The shipbuilding industry also grew, requiring an increased workforce; the arsenal put 1,000 to work in 1493, around 2,000 in the 1530s, and 3,400 to 4,000 in the following decades. The same holds for Geneva. Three waves of immigration (1549–60, 1572–74, and 1585–87) brought thousands of protestant refugees to the town, where capital, technical knowhow, and labour forces were optimally united. Encouraged by the secular authorities and the Church, with Calvin at the head, numerous entrepreneurs created new industries; since they were predominantly finishing industries and given the abundance of cheap labour, Genevan entrepreneurs could make large profits. In these circumstances the poor law published in 1541 remained in force.

Finally, it must be noted that the new social policy was nowhere so efficiently applied as in England. The statute of 1597–98 was the synthesis of all earlier dispositions concerning poor relief. The essential outlines of this Act, issued anew with slight modifications in 1601, remained in effect for nearly 250 years. Strict prohibition of begging, the duty of all sturdy poor to work, centralization of poor relief, and collection of a poor tax payable by the parishes were fixed upon the 'Untroubled Island'. The unique continuity of the English poor law indicates that economic growth sustained itself in the long-term as the country slowly but surely gained an edge over the Continent.

Chapter 4

CHANGING ECONOMIC PATTERNS AND THE UTILITY OF POVERTY (*c.1630–c.1750*)

BETWEEN 1600 (in the Mediterranean) and 1660 (in the North), the expansion which characterized 'the long sixteenth century' gradually came to a halt. Economically, socially and demographically, many countries faced severe dislocation, and the repercussions continued to be felt until the second quarter of the eighteenth century. This long depression was, however, scarcely comparable to the crisis of the late Middle Ages: certainly several areas suffered severe human and material losses in the seventeenth century, yet there was no question of a catastrophic and ubiquitous collapse, nullifying the achievements of the preceding expansion. Furthermore, in this period England created the preconditions essential for the definitive breakthrough of the capitalist mode of production. Therefore, the question, 'Is the term "general crisis" applicable to the seventeenth century?' appears less relevant than 'Why did the lines of development of western European countries diverge so markedly in this period?' This problem demands a thorough investigation of the factors which retarded or, alternatively, stimulated economic growth. Evidently, growing regional differences cannot be systematically investigated, compared, and explained within the scope of this essay. Instead, the focus will be socio-economic changes in England and France, because the divergent paths followed by these two countries clearly show the inherent possibilities and limitations of specific relations of production.

1. France and England: diverging agrarian structures

In his classic monograph *Les Paysans de Languedoc (The Peasants of Languedoc)*, Emmanuel Le Roy Ladurie viewed the crisis of seventeenth-century France as the unavoidable result of growing disproportion between population and food supply: since agricultural production did not follow the expansive demographic trend, a subsistence crisis was inevitable. He ascribed this 'Malthusian check' to technological stagnation, *immobilisme*, in turn due to 'cultural blockages'. To explain the miscarriage of agrarian capitalism in France, Le Roy Ladurie falls back in the last instance on 'invisible mental barriers', which were 'the most constraining of all' on the economy. A similar line of thought was developed by Hugues Neveux, who emphasized the absence of a 'capitalist spirit' among the richer leaseholders of sixteenth-century France: 'The *censier* strove not for maximum profits but for a substantial social and political position. In these circumstances, it was not at all necessary to increase the grain harvest . . . There, undoubtedly, lay the answer of the paradox of stagnating production alongside rising demand.' In short, both authors explained the seventeenth century crisis in the same way that the great depression of the late Middle Ages has been explained. Prodigal feudal landlords were replaced by equally unenterprising proprietors, who sought nothing more than to squeeze the free but economically dependent peasants; this form of surplus extraction stimulated productive investment in the early modern period as little as before. The similarity between the two crises was boldly portrayed by Neveux:

> Comparable indeed were the levels of population and grain production; analogous was the threat of a malthusian dislocation; equivalent was the fragmentation of peasant holdings, no longer able to feed a family; unavoidable was the need to seek supplementary income; all that against a background of stagnating technology, of which the potential, whether for economic or mental reasons, was not always utilized to the full.

The German historian Wilhelm Abel similarly intepreted the whole of European history from the thirteenth to the nineteenth century. Just as Le Roy Ladurie and Neveux, he postulated the structural impotence of the *ancien régime*'s economy to raise agrarian productivity substantially and accepted the natural tendency of the population to increase without restraint despite a restricted supply of land. These assumptions led him to characterize the recurrent subsistence crises in pre-industrial Europe as Malthusian 'bottle-necks': each phase of expansion must lead to an insupportable tension between size of population and food supply, which necessarily resulted in demographic decline or collapse. Abel considered poverty in the *ancien régime* to be a result not of a specific social organization of production, but as a 'natural' phenomenon, inherent in a 'society of scarcity', determined by technological backwardness and a tendency towards uninhibited demographic growth.[1]

Detailed demographic, ecological, and ethnological studies have brought to light how far the latter premise strays from reality. Malthus's theory that growth of population would only be inhibited by dearth and death, is contradicted by numerous observations; both human and animal populations appear to keep their size more or less limited by means of self-regulating mechanisms. Above all, fertility is highly sensitive to socio-economic factors. From the early Middle Ages on, patterns of behaviour can be recognized in various European regions at various times, consistent with the application of conscious family planning through increased age of women at marriage and extended celibacy. Hence demographic changes in pre-industrial Europe were dependent in large measure on specific agrarian structures, particularly surplus extraction relations. This explains why the Malthusian cycle of long-term stagnation persisted in some seventeenth-century western European countries, while it was gradually disrupted in other areas. The divergent agrarian structures of France and England illustrate this point.

The preceding chapter established that the demographic recovery under way from the mid-fifteenth century led to a far-reaching fragmentation of peasant holdings and dwindling agricultural productivity in France, but exactly the reverse in England. This opposite outcome of comparable population growth can only be explained by the different ways in which the relationships among landlords, monarchy, and peasants evolved in the two countries after the fifteenth century.

Protection of small peasant proprietors by the French monarchy with an eye on its fiscal interests led to agrarian stagnation in the long run. In order to cover the steeply rising costs of its foreign and internal policies, the absolutist state proceeded to squeeze the poor unmercifully. Tax collections rose from an annual average of 345 tons of fine silver in 1600–10 to 700 tons in 1641, an amount equal to 10.5 million hectolitres of wheat, enough to feed 15 per cent of the population of France throughout the year. The burden of this extraordinary fiscal exaction was borne chiefly by the rural masses: in the middle of the seventeenth century, the monarchy seized 12 to 13 per cent of gross annual agrarian income, twice as much as in *c.* 1600. The economic position of the peasantry was also undermined by the 'second-best strategy' of the French nobility. Since most landlords due to the combined opposition of the peasantry and the absolutist state failed to create large, consolidated farms, they chose the only way still open to them, namely, maximum exploitation of the peasantry. As Jan de Vries recently noted:

> both to keep up with the level of expenditure required by residence in Paris and Versailles and to secure a measure of independence from a fickle crown, noble landowners pressed their agents and lawyers to increase their incomes. With agricultural reorganization ruled out by the policies of absolutism, the next best method was to squeeze more income from the peasantry through sharecropping tenures and the revival of feudal obligations.

This development hindered agricultural investment and, consequently, technological improvement. For exactly those reasons, the needs of the populace for grain and of the state for taxes were never adequately met under the *ancien régime*, due to the extreme exploitation of the peasantry. In other words, subsistence crises were unavoidable in France because the forms of surplus extraction in an absolutist state which was based on the small peasant proprietor excluded any possibility of increased production. The old mode of production was simply 'sucked dry'; it was in no sense altered.[2]

In contrast, a nearly unique structure emerged in England, based on landlords, capitalist tenants, and wage labourers, which led to a radical transformation of agrarian production. We referred earlier to the success with which many landowners from the fifteenth century on created large estates to the cost of small peasant proprietors. During the Civil War the Crown definitively lost the power to stop the advance of large estates, and by the end of the seventeenth century landlords controlled no less than 70 to 75 per cent of cultivated land. The great landowners exploited their estates by renting them out to capitalist tenants, who retained a decent portion of the proceeds. This symbiotic relationship between landlord and tenant was the indispensable condition for agrarian improvement. Capitalist tenants, who drew upon a free labour market for their requisite labour force, did not see their capital investment creamed off by concomitant increases in rent, so that they were encouraged to introduce technological improvements which raised agricultural productivity. Hence, from the 1660s on, the island remained, in contrast to most other western European countries, in large part spared from major price fluctuations and subsistence crises, simultaneously able to react more adequately to the challenge created by declining grain prices; large tenants disposed of sufficient means to put part of their arable into pasture in order to profit from the more favourable price structure of meat and dairy products. In short, 'it was the transformation of the agrarian class structure which had taken place over the period since the later fourteenth century that allowed England to increase substantially its agricultural productivity and thus to avoid a repetition of the previous crisis'.[3] This development not only allowed some 40 per cent of the English population to abandon the land by the end of the seventeenth century, mainly to enter into industrial activities, but also favoured the growth of the domestic market, which in turn allowed continuing industrial expansion.

The impoverishment processes which had attained such enormous proportions in the sixteenth century remained at work in the seventeenth, but as socio-economic differentiation between France and England grew, the causes of poverty in the two countries increasingly diverged. The crisis of agrarian productivity which France, like most other European countries, experienced in the seventeenth century had catastrophic results. The economic position of the bulk of French peasants worsened from around 1630 at an accelerating rate. The 'second-best strategy' of landlords and the crushing taxation of the absolutist state, which placed the weight of its enormous military efforts on the rural population, drove innumerable peasants steadily deeper into debt. The old, complex, but purposeful mechanisms worked infallibly: unable to repay usurious loans taken out after harvest failure, during tax collection, or due to a family misfortune, the peasant had to burden his few possessions with fresh debts or surrender his goods to his creditors. Gradual dispossession advanced inexorably during the seventeenth century. While every villager of the Hurepoix, south of Paris, still owned at least a dwelling and a few morsels of land around 1550, a quarter to one-third of the inhabitants in the time of Colbert possessed no property, not even a home for their family. In the relatively prosperous Beauvaisis, the situation around 1700 was not much more favourable: 90 per cent of the peasants were *manouvriers* or *haricotiers*, who seldom owned their home, never enough land to provide for themselves, always turning to other activities to make ends meet. The century after 1630 was a scarcely interrupted series of subsistence crises in France. Dearth and plague visited each generation with the regularity of a clock, thinning out its members. Peasant revolts inflamed extensive areas of the kingdom and at times even threatened the further development of the absolutist monarchy, indicative that the impoverished peasants were conscious of their social degradation. All movements of protest were doomed to failure, however, basically because the rebels did not question the socio-economic system that lay at the root of their sorrows: some exceptions aside, the extraordinary financial demands of the Crown, the most visible agent of surplus extraction, formed the most significant grievance, since it hit the whole peasantry simultaneously. The anti-fiscal struggle, in other words, functioned simultaneously as trigger and as catalyst.

Seventeenth-century English agricultural authorities, such as Walter Blyth, were convinced 'that the new gospel of increased productivity which they preached would, by itself, cure all human ills'.[4] Research shows that nothing was farther from the truth. Development of agrarian capitalism worked hand in glove with the impoverishment process in rural England. Until the end of the sixteenth century the English monarchy, though with increasingly less success, strove to hinder enclosure since it led to eviction of tenants and rural depopulation. The dearth year 1597 saw the last Act against depopulating; in 1608 the first, limited pro-Enclosure Act was published; in 1621 the first general Enclosure Bill followed; three years later all statutes against enclosure were repealed. Despite repeated revolts, the English peasantry could not stop the rising tide. During the revolutionary period their lot was sealed. With the defeat of the Levellers and Diggers, the last checks to the triumph of agrarian capitalism fell aside. The pleas of Gerrard Winstanley for 'a free commonwealth', in which 'all the poor commoners have a free use and benefit of the land', belonged to the past by 1660. Along with the restoration of Charles II, the House of Commons confirmed the abolition of feudal tenures and the Court of Wards, liberating forever landlords from dependence on the Crown. Landlords gained absolute ownership of their estates. However, since only those feudal tenures were abolished which bound landowner and Crown, copyholders remained subject to arbitrary death duties, which could be collected by landlords as a means to evict recalcitrant peasants. This policy was confirmed in 1677, when an Act stipulated that the possession of small freeholders should be no less insecure than that of copyholders unless supported by written, legal titles. The main concern of the government was in the future to stimulate production and to protect producers: consumers and subsistence farmers were no longer secure. After 1670, grain export, regardless of price levels, was approved, and imports virtually forbidden; only in times of extreme dearth were exceptions made.

The social consequences of all these changes, conducive to a 'rational' approach to economic problems, were predictable: ever more land came into the hands of ever fewer men. Confiscated lands were sold by Parliament in large blocks, so that only the rich could buy them. Large clearances, financed by local landlords, London capitalists, and foreign entrepreneurs, increased arable but limited communal rights. Changes in the interpretation of the law weakened the position of tenant versus landlord, in favour of enclosers and landowners with minerals under their ground. Since copyholders had no absolute property rights to their holding and the Parliament of 1656 refused to specify maximum entry fines, the number of copyhold tenancies sank visibly. Moreover, abolition of the Court of Wards was not compensated by a land tax, but by an assize, paid primarily by the poorer consumers. In short, 'the century after the failure of the radicals to win legal security for the small men is the century in which many small landowners were forced to sell out in consequence of rack-renting, heavy fines, taxation and lack of resources to compete with capitalist farmers'.[5]

The triumph of agrarian capitalism thus made possible increased productivity and laid the basis for England's generally successful economic development. This implied, however, the proletarianization of broad strata of the populace. Two historians have recently noted,

> that enclosures lead to highly complex economic changes – changes that are technically progressive, since they give rise to greater efficiency and specialization, but are simultaneously socially disastrous to labor, since in themselves they produce, by inexorable economic logic, an initial and appreciable decline in the standard of living of peasants and so of the working population as a whole.[6]

This conclusion may be extended to the rise of new capitalist relations in agriculture, only one facet of which was enclosure.

2. The restructuring of industry

The seventeenth century witnessed major changes in the most important and widespread industry of the *ancien régime*'s economy, textile manufacture. Italian cloth nearly disappeared from the export market, the rural as well as urban expansion of the Flemish wool industry was cut short and settled into long-term contraction, and the cloth industry in the old French centres, such as Amiens, Reims, Rouen, and Beauvais stagnated or even declined despite the protectionist measures of the Crown; conversely, the textile industry in Holland and England entered a phase of spectacular growth. Flemish refugees, especially from Hondschoote, introduced in both countries the so-called 'new draperies', lighter and cheaper cloth made from coarse, stringy wool. Leyden soon developed into one of the most important industrial centres of Europe. From around 12,000 inhabitants in 1582, the population rose to nearly 70,000 in the middle of the seventeenth century. In 1671 total production of all types of cloth amounted to not less than 139,000 pieces. The rise of the new draperies in England was in large part an answer to the stagnation of traditional wool manufacturers and the commercial crisis of the early seventeenth century. The transition to production of lighter, cheaper, and more colourful fabrics opened up the Iberian peninsula and the Mediterranean to the English textile industry, centred in East Anglia, the West Riding, and the south-western counties, above all Devon and western Somerset. From Exeter alone, 119,000 pieces of perpetuana and serge were exported in 1680. Thanks to the economic freedom which they gained, the low price which they paid for raw materials and labour, and the reorganization of foreign trade supported by the government,

English entrepreneurs lowered their prices after the Restoration to a point where Holland and most other continental producers could no longer compete. By the end of the seventeenth century, England had conquered the dynamic market for new draperies.

While thus in some areas of Europe more employment was created, thousands of craftsmen and workers in other regions lost their livelihoods for ever. Northern Italy was the most striking example in this period of total socio-economic dislocation. Since the drastic collapse of the cloth industry was not compensated by the growth of other industries, a prolonged process of disinvestment in manufacturing occurred, causing massive unemployment. By 1700 the number of wool weavers in Venice, Milan, and Como dropped to scarcely 5 per cent of their sixteenth-century total. Although the silk industry offered somewhat better resistance, the gradual decline of this once blooming sector had fatal results. In 1675 the silk industry of Genoa numbered only 2,500 looms, as against some 10,000 in 1565. And in Venice total production of silks was reduced to less than one-third between the early seventeenth century and 1695. Italy, in the words of C. M. Cipolla, had begun her career as an underdeveloped area within Europe.

A second important change was the displacement of industry to the countryside. The advantages of rural labour spoke for themselves and were long known to entrepreneurs. It was not enough, however, for there to be a demand for rural labour – the supply had to be assured as well. Both conditions were amply satisfied in the seventeenth century. Growing relative overpopulation, mostly destitute of any alternative, formed an inexhaustible reservoir of cheap and willing labour during a period when urban wages were kept high by rising assizes and competition for labour by the tertiary sector. In these circumstances, the textile industry continued to move from town to countryside: in the early eighteenth century the bulk of all wool, linen, cotton, and blended cloth in Europe was produced in the great rural districts of England, France, Germany, the Low Countries, and Switzerland.

In both town and country, industrial organization underwent profound, albeit gradual transformations. The competition of rural industry and the attempts of merchants to adapt textile manufacturing to the changing needs of the market undermined the stabilizing functions of guilds. Capitalist undertakings, employing large numbers of workers, became increasingly more numerous. However, centralized production remained the exception. Transition towards factory production was not cleared by the great *manufactures*, those 'fortunate accidents' chartered and subsidized by the Crown, but by the proliferation of proto-industries, the first phase of industrialization. Merchants generally preferred the putting-out system, which demanded hardly any fixed capital and offered the possibility to employ rural labourers on a large scale. The generalization of the putting-out system in the seventeenth century implied growing concentration of commercial and financial control. In 1676 fourteen traders, representing scarcely 10 per cent of the total number of merchants, exported from Exeter not less than 70 per cent of all the serges manufactured in Devon. In Amiens the sale of serges produced in the town and the surrounding countryside was in the hands of eight or nine *négociants*, all interrelated. This development resulted in the complete economic dependence of both rural labourers and the bulk of urban artisans. The former lived in permanent insecurity: their labour was barely if at all regulated, so that they could be exploited to the extreme. Opportunities for work depended on putting-out merchants, who could easily withdraw their circulating capital and invest elsewhere. Urban textile workers were not much better off. Since the guilds gradually lost their significance and were increasingly controlled by the richest producers, the smaller masters and the journeymen could less and less resist underpayment, covert use of the truck system, payment in debased currency, and other abuses.

Strikes and disturbances, though numerous, seldom accomplished anything. Employers, supported by local and central authorities, played off one professional category against another and made use of the distrust of craftsmen for 'unfree' labourers to sow divisiveness among recalcitrant workers. Only the generally secret associations of highly skilled journeymen, *compagnonnages* in France, improved working conditions. However, these foreshadowings of the trade unions of the future were in the seventeenth century mere islands in a sea of casual labourers, who, due to wide distribution, mutual competition, ignorance and moral distress, were in no state to take purposeful action. No wonder then that in all centres with an important textile industry the vast majority of those receiving poor relief con-

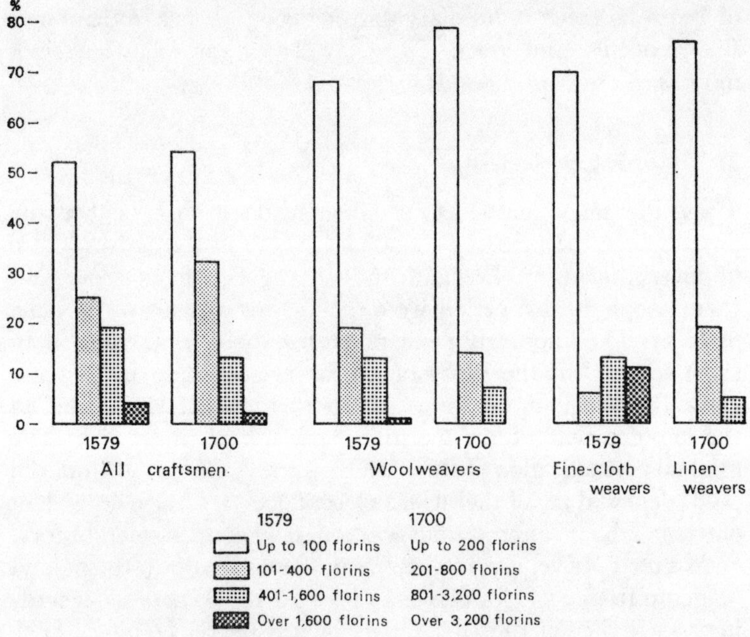

Fig. 10 Percentage distribution of estimated wealth among the textile producers at Nördlingen, in 1579 and 1700.

This comparison shows that the proportion of textile producers to be found in the wealthiest brackets had sharply contracted by 1700.

Source: based on Friedrichs, 'Class Formation', pp. 30, 39.

Note. The interval represented by each wealth category has been doubled in size, to counterbalance a decline of almost 50 per cent in the value of the florin between 1579 and 1700.

sisted of journeymen, apprentices, and casual labourers. These weavers and spinners owned nothing besides some few simple utensils and depended completely on minute fluctuations of the price of bread and level of employment. If the former rose and the latter fell, their misery grew unspeakable. In December 1693, as a subsistence crisis began, 3,584 poor were censused in Beauvais, or 38 per cent of the urban population; 80 per cent of those on relief whose occupation is known were unemployed textile workers. In April 1694 the special commissioner of the Bishop of Beauvais noted in his diary that the poor ate cats, rotten horse flesh, entrails, and grass. To no avail: in the following eight months, more than 3,000 starved.

3. Towards a proletariat

Thus, the seventeenth century demonstrated that neither the progress nor the arrest of economic growth in themselves retard impoverishment. In England and on the Continent more and more people in this period were the victims of downward social mobility. The impoverishment process probably slackened off in some senses, but the ranks of the impoverished in every sense grew. Furthermore, the industrial restructuring of Europe led to the proliferation of an agrarian and urban proletariat. The gradual crystallization of this class of workers, dislodged from the land, deprived of all the means of production, totally dependent on wage labour, unprotected, was a new phenomenon in history.

As noted above, rural labourers in Tudor and Stuart England made up from 25 to 35 per cent of the rural population. According to a writer of the 1640s, they owned nearly nothing: 'The fourth part of the inhabitants of the parishes of England are miserable people, and (harvest time excepted) without any subsistence'. Half a century later, the social situation had worsened. A fairly reliable source, Gregory King, classified 24 per cent of the national population during the 1680s and 1690s as 'cottagers and paupers' – a telling identification – and a further 23 per cent as 'labouring people and out servants'. Both groups, representing some 47 per cent of Englishmen, earned too little, according to King, to supply their daily needs. Regional studies have largely confirmed these grim estimates. During the 1660s, 31 per cent of the Kentish rural population was exempted from taxation due to poverty. In the Lake District, the situation was not much more favourable: in southern Westmorland 385 out of 1,570 households paid no hearthtax in 1669–72, and in northern Westmorland 825 out of 2,791, or 24 to 30 per cent respectively. In Devon and Leicestershire, finally, approximately one-third of the households were exempted from the hearthtax in 1670 and 1674. The national extent of the rural proletariat after the Restoration may thus be estimated at a quarter to a half the population.[7]

In France the proportion of landless labourers was undoubtedly much smaller. *Manouvriers*, the majority of every village, still owned a scrap of land at the end of the seventeenth century, with a cottage and small garden, even a cow, some sheep and poultry. Their 'ownership', however, failed to provide a family's living. Pierre Goubert reckoned that, to be economically independent, a peasant had to farm a minimum of twelve hectares in years of plenty, twenty-seven in years of want. Reckoned thus, no *manouvrier*, no *haricotier*, not even an average *laboureur* (freeholder) maintained his independence. Only the greatest *laboureurs*, owners of at least twenty-seven hectares, were in a position to feed their families properly in all circumstances, but this group comprised scarcely one-tenth of the peasantry. Contemporaries were thoroughly aware of the need of the *manouvriers.* In a Parisian memoire we read that they 'were compelled to labor from morning till evening, without having anything more than a morsel of dark bread and some water, considering themselves fortunate once or twice a year when they have some lard to put on their bread, and never have a taste of wine'.[8] Vauban, a well-informed witness, endorsed that verdict. He classified 10 per cent of the French population as 'beggars' and another 30 per cent as 'near beggars'. Whatever way he reckoned the budget of *manouvriers*, he too concluded that they could only make ends meet by working at least 180 days per annum, receiving a 'fair' wage, having a wife who earned a supplementary income from industrial activities, having no more than two children, and hoping that grain prices stayed at 'normal' levels. Consequently it can be no surprise that the numerous harvest failures, epidemics, and swarms of plundering soldiers forced increasingly more families to beg. In Alsace, in the region of Alençon, their number was as high as 12 per cent, certainly a debatable estimate, yet indicative in any case of the structural character of begging and vagabondage in seventeenth-century France.

In Electoral Saxony, the number of *Gärtner* and *Häusler*, small cottagers with a bit of land, rose spectacularly between 1550 and 1750. In the middle of the sixteenth century both groups comprised a mere 7 per cent of the agrarian population. Two centuries later they formed some 48 per cent of the peasantry. Most of them were by then dependent for their livelihood on the rural textile industry, widespread in south-western Saxony and southern Upper Lusatia.

Rural Overijssel showed that even in the 'Golden Age', not all of the United Provinces prospered. In Salland and Twente, the two most thickly populated regions of the province, the proportion of cottagers in the rural population between 1602 and 1720 rose from 22 to 45 per cent and 44 to 49 per cent respectively. The concentration of wealth in the countryside and small towns, altogether some 51,000 inhabitants, was overwhelming, for 6 per cent in 1675 held nearly 87 per cent of the total wealth, while 71 per cent had to satisfy themselves with 13 per cent. The lowest 23 per cent owned nothing, absolutely nothing.

Worsening living conditions in many rural areas obliged large numbers of the inhabitants to find subsistence elsewhere. Although quantitative data over the overall extent of horizontal mobility in the seventeenth century is lacking, undoubtedly a steadily increasing number of people were on the road. An example is provided by Paul A. Slack, who studied the geographic mobility among the lower strata of English society between 1598 and 1664. According to the statute of 1597 each parish had to keep its own register of 'rogues' whipped and returned to their place of birth or residence. Of 2,651 vagrants whose place of origin could be determined, 50 per cent had travelled more than 60 km and 28 per cent had gone more than 120 km.

Table 8.

Distances between places of origin and punishment of English vagrants, 1598–1664.

Distance to place of origin (kilometres)	*Number of vagrants*	*Per cent of total*
Up to 30	694	26
31–60	617	23
61–90	365	14
91–120	234	9
121–240	435	16.5
Over 240	306	11.5
Total	2,651	100

Source: recalculated from P. A. Slack, 'Vagrants and vagrancy in England 1598–1664', *The Economic History Review*, 2nd ser., 27 (1974), p. 369.

Another example comes from Clayworth, a village in Nottinghamshire, where a survey of the surnames of residents suggests that between 1676 and 1688 not less than 37 per cent moved. An investigation into the origins of the 540 migrants who passed by the hospital of Montpellier during 1696 to 1699 shows that about 83 per cent of them were rural labourers who trekked from the north to the south of France to seek work.

Some uprooted peasants settled in thinly populated areas: forest clearings, heath, fens. The majority, however, forsook the country and melted into the urban proletariat. Although townsmen in most European countries were no more numerous than before, they concentrated in fewer centres. While around 1600 barely 4 per cent of the north-east European population had lived in towns of more than 20,000 nearly 8 per cent did so in the middle of the eighteenth century. Explosive demographic growth characterized Paris, London and the *Randstad*, a group of neighbouring towns in the Netherlands, including Amsterdam, Haarlem, Leyden, The Hague, Delft, and Rotterdam; their aggregate population rose from 370,000 in the 1570s to 1,500,000 by 1700, by which time Londoners represented no less than 10 per cent of the national population, as against only 5 per cent a century before. These colossal cities literally devoured people. According to Gregory King, the death-rate of villages stood at 29 per 1,000, of small towns 33, of London 42. This discrepancy comes as no surprise: nowhere were living conditions among the lower classes so pitiful as in the densely populated centres. In the countryside the poor could often increase their meagre incomes with wages in kind, homegrown vegetables, wood gathered on the commons, and small game poached in neighbouring woods. In the towns, in contrast, they were completely dependent on money wages and the market. Throw in their miserable dwelling and it becomes clear why mortality among the urban poor was frightfully high. One striking example: in 1693 to 1694, the population of Lyon suffered dearth and a severe crisis in the silk industry simultaneously. In comparison to the normal death rate for 1688 to 1692, the number of deaths in 1693 and 1694 jumped respectively by fifty-seven to 163 per cent in the parish of St George, nineteen and 115 per cent in St Paul, and sixteen and 97 per cent in St Vincent. The professional composition of the three parishes brings to light that the hierarchy of death corresponded to the hierarchy of wealth: while the silk workers formed some 70 per cent of the population in the parish of St George, they represented in the other parishes only 30 to 40 per cent.

Without a continuing flood of uprooted countrymen, urban population could not grow, let alone maintain itself. The English historian E. A. Wrigley has tried to evaluate the demographic impact of London after 1650, taking into account the growing population and the excessive mortality of the metropolis. Supposing that the average age of immigrants was about twenty, and that all children born in London stayed there, then it seems that the survivors of nearly one-sixth of all British births would have lived in London twenty years after their birth. Including temporary immigrants, the number of adult Englishmen who at some stage of their life had direct contact with London life rises even higher.

Continuous immigration of the dispossessed, living off casual labour, undermined the already precarious socio-economic position of the vast majority of town-dwellers. In all centres where an important export industry was established, the status of 'craftsman'. 'wage labourer', and 'poor' became more or less indistinguishable. In Leyden, half of all houses in the seventeenth century were occupied by textile workers living on the edge of poverty, or even in chronic need. In Beauvais 54 per cent of the hearths were taxed in 1696 at less than two *livres tournois*, less than three or four days' wages. Nearly all textile workers belonged to this group: all weavers, 91 per cent of serge weavers, 90 per cent of wool carders, all spinners; 80 per cent of these last could not raise even a single *livre*. In Exeter the social situation was even more sombre: 80 per cent of those assessed – those on relief not included – lived at or below the threshold of poverty. In Granada, Spain's greatest industrial centre, the authorities estimated in 1679 the number of poor, dependent for their daily bread on the silk industry, at half the urban population.

Although exploitation of children existed earlier, it took on greater proportions than ever before in the seventeenth century. Child labour was even one of the competitive advantages on which the Leyden cloth industry depended. From the end of the sixteenth century, dozens of boys and girls between six and eighteen were placed by orphanages and poorhouses with Leyden cloth-makers.

Since recruiting centres could not cover the demand for cheap and docile textile workers, from around 1630 hundreds of children were imported yearly from the regions of Liège, Aachen, Julich, and elsewhere. There was even a transport service organized for the children under the watch of a special official. Between 1638 and 1671, some 8,000 young workers were borne off to Leyden. For the children themselves and for numerous adults, unskilled men and working women, this had disastrous results. The latter were no match for the 'competition' of the former and were pushed out of the labour market. As for the children, most were so young that the long and hard workdays undermined their physical and mental health; they were so badly paid that their wages can only with difficulty be considered 'remuneration'; and they had to carry out such simple tasks that they had no chance to practise a trade later on. Yet no protest rose from the authorities or the ministers of religion against such inhuman practices. 'Good' Calvinists that they were, they ascribed an uplifting value to work. The controllers appointed by the town authorities around the middle of the seventeenth century helped to prevent the most serious abuses, such as maltreatment and retention of wages, yet nothing touched the heart of the matter. However, together with the entrepreneurs, the authorities cared well for the spirits of the children: three schoolmasters were commissioned to bring to them the 'true Christian reformed religion'.

The evolution of diet indicates that a significant portion of the urban population was impoverished, both absolutely and relatively, during the seventeenth century. In Rome, annual grain consumption *per capita* dwindled from 290 kg around 1600 to 203 around 1700, or a decline of 30 per cent. In the early eighteenth century, moreover, the inhabitants of the papal town consumed 15 to 25 per cent less meat than a century earlier. In Toulouse the decline was even steeper: in 1707–09, the average yearly consumption of beef and mutton amounted to a mere 10 kg *per capita* versus 30 kg in 1655–59. Admittedly 1709 was a disastrous year, but that in no way alters the general tendency, for average consumption of beef diminished in the long term from around 15 kg *per capita per annum* in 1655–59 to scarcely 7 kg by 1750.

Clearly, *average* food consumption does not reflect the full picture. Urban assizes, however, provide no information concern-

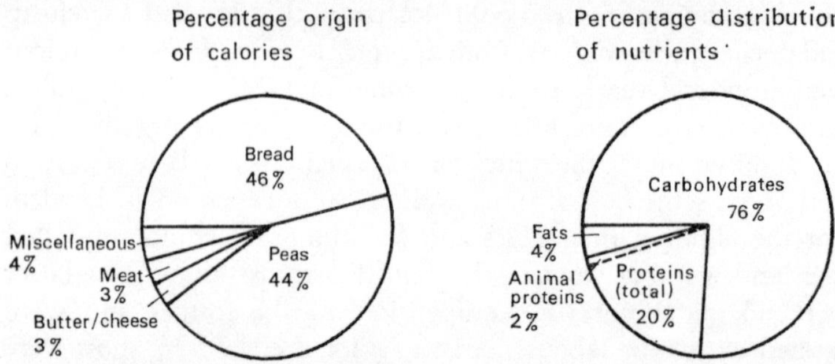

Fig. 11 Average diet, *per capita* and per day, of the poor in the *Hôpital Général* of Caen (Normandy) about 1725.

Source: based on M.–J. Villemon, 'L'alimentation du pauvre de l'hôpital général de Caen au début du XVIIIe siècle', *Annales de Normandie* (1971), pp. 254–7.

ing the diet of the different social classes. The only possible way to know the food basket of the poor is through analysis of the accounts of a charitable institution such as the archives of the *hôpital général* of Caen, Normandy. The 500 to 600 poor who were sealed up in this institution around 1700 were undoubtedly better fed than the 'free' poor. But, from the qualitative perspective, the food baskets of the two groups obviously were not much different. Bread and peas provided in the *hôpital* nearly 90 per cent of total calories, some 3,000 *per capita* daily; the diet consisted thus of an excess of vegetable proteins and a gross deficiency of fats. Moreover, two vitamins in particular were lacking. The diet as a whole provided scarcely half the required amount of vitamin D. This serious deficiency had fatal consequences because it encouraged rickets, skeletal calcification with associated deformities. Above all, the children and adolescents who had to work so young suffered. Eventually their spinal columns were completely bent, their slender bones grew curved, and they had bony joints. Even worse was the near total absence of vitamin C. This explains the vulnerability of the poor to scurvy, as well as their low resistance when faced with heavy exertion, cold, or infection.

Chronic unemployment obliged many urban poor to roam from one place to another in search of subsistence. More than forty per cent of all vagrants apprehended in Salisbury between

1598 and 1638 were born in or had lived in other towns. Everywhere the authorities fulminated against this 'riff-raff, ordinarily composed of people who are godless, who are without religion, and without instruction; who live in licence and dissoluteness and in a shameful and even horrible way, without the distinction of sex, kinship, or relationships, like animals'.[9]

The permanent confrontation with the migrating possessionless became an obsession for the 'right-minded' European. Some continued to give charity without distinction, but the great majority of the propertied considered the wandering poor to be a threat to law and order, evidently damned by their impiety and ignorance. In innumerable seventeenth-century paintings, vagabonds, beggars, rogues and street musicians were painted in feverish colours. Sympathy for the lower classes was, however, not the chief theme; apart from some exceptions, such as Rembrandt and Louis le Nain, painters degraded the poor to picturesque or even repulsive creatures, scarcely human. The recurrent theme of the beggars' duel was only a pretext to depict the anxieties and horror of the upper classes for the 'scum' of society. One looks in vain for some trace of understanding, some vague feeling of sympathy.

From the end of the sixteenth century, projects were brought forth in England and France to purge the country regularly of its vagabonds. Some authors considered that the most suitable means was deportation to the colonies. Richard Eburne, a Somerset preacher, proposed in 1624 to transport each year at least 16,000 poor, two per parish, to the other side of the Atlantic. Both the French and English colonies fulfilled to a limited degree the function of a safety valve. Numerous uprooted and declassed people abandoned the Old World, compelled by the authorities or attracted by castles in the air dangled before their eyes by promoters. Between 1620 and 1640, some 80,000 Englishmen emigrated to North America and the West Indies. Many French rural labourers engaged themselves to journey to the Antilles. From La Rochelle alone, more than 6,000 departed between 1634 and 1715. Yet this movement should not be exaggerated: in the period 1650 to 1800 at the most 100,000 Frenchmen emigrated to the colonies, whether voluntarily or forced. Obviously, such a policy was merely a palliative. Poverty as a social problem demanded other solutions.

4. The great confinement: a uniform solution for the same problems?

The English preacher William Perkins expounded a common point of view when he said: 'rogues, beggars, vagabonds . . . commonly are of no civil societies or corporation, nor of any particular Church: and are as rotten legges, and armes, that droppe from the body. . . . To wander up and downe from yeare to yeare to this ende, to seeke and procure bodily maintenance, is no calling, but the life of a beast.' Their sole hope for salvation was to be put to work, so that they could perhaps be restored to a disciplined community through diligence in a calling. Work, the curse of man after the Fall, was a religious duty, a means to worship God.[10] Similar ideas gained ground in catholic lands. In France, for example, work came to be portrayed as a form of asceticism, as a spiritual exercise, even as a prayer. A Lyonese catechism gave three reasons for the duty of work: to earn bread, to avoid idleness, but also 'to do penance and to earn heaven'. The mystique of work was no new phenomenon. Religious reformers in the sixteenth century condemned idleness, and work was sanctified, but in the course of the seventeenth century the exaltation of work assumed previously unknown proportions in both protestant and catholic countries, and this moralizing attitude characterized both laity and clergy. The English scientific reformer Samuel Hartlib and the French merchant J. Albo agreed that the labours of the poor followed the law of God.

This point of view was strengthened by the emergent idea that poverty was not only useful but even essential to the welfare of the state. Horizontal redistribution of wealth, the rise of the nation-state, long-term changes in the structure of international trade, repeated disruptions of important foreign markets, and internal problems caused by violent short-term fluctuations brought governments to an economic policy directed towards encouragement of national production and export and, concomitantly, towards undermining foreign competition. Few of the methods employed to influence the economy were novel to this period, but gradually there arose a more coherent body of thought over ways in which state power could be applied to achieve economic goals and, conversely, over ways by which economic power could be used to attain political goals. However little consistent their principles were and however much their intentions differed over the nature and the implications of the required measures, most mercantilist writers recognized that the problems of national prosperity, employment, and poverty were interrelated. In general, they considered labour as the source of all wealth, or even wealth itself. Hence they advocated not only demographic measures but considered it necessary to force the labouring masses to serve the nationalistic interests of the state. Deemed crude, ignorant, depraved, rebellious and, above all, lazy, the wages of the lower classes had to be held as low as possible. Thus were the poor kept industrious, while the country gained a competitive advantage in international commerce. The national interest required, in other words, that the masses be held in a permanent state of poverty.

The 'doctrine of the utility of poverty' justified strong measures against the needy. Cardinal Richelieu compared humanity to 'mules, accustomed to heavy burdens and more easily ruined by long rests than by work'. Sir William Petty even suggested that it would be better 'to burn a thousand men's labour for a time, than let those thousand men by nonemployment lose their faculty of labouring'. Though such ideas were not new, emphasis fell more than ever before on the potential gains to be drawn from employing paupers. *Tuchthuizen, hôpitaux généraux*, workhouses, and *Zuchthäusern* sprouted up. These institutions, part houses of correction, part locations for centralized handicraft production, had as their goal to separate all those groups of society supposed to be most inclined towards laziness and disorder, especially beggars and vagabonds, to discipline them with a strict regimen of work and moral instruction, to turn them into a docile and profitable labour force. Certainly, not all the unemployed could be locked up in such institutions. As 'houses of terror', however, they offered the possibility for indirect savings in poor relief and stimulation of the labour market. One might expect that the overwhelming majority of the poor remaining at large would be so terrorized by the prospect of landing in a sort of 'concentration camp' that they would be prepared to work for the least possible wage. As an English landowner expressed it: the advantage of the workhouse

> does not arise from what the poor people can do towards their own subsistence, but from the apprehensions the poor have of it. These prompt them to exert and do their utmost to keep themselves off the parish, and render them exceedingly averse to submit to come into the house until extreme necessity compels them.[11]

Since the publication of a fascinating study by Michel Foucault on the history of mental illness, various historians have labelled the seventeenth century as the time of the 'Great Confinement', identified with a purely repressive policy. Although this generalization has since been disputed, in our minds insufficient attention has been focused on the different functions fulfilled by the workhouse vis-à-vis time and place. The following concise survey is an attempt to clarify the changing goals of this particular social policy.

In some countries, attempts were made in the second half of the sixteenth century to shut away in special institutions those groups seen to be socially marginal and potentially dangerous. In 1552–53 Edward VI, influenced by Bishop Nicolas Ridley, put at the disposal of London authorities an old, decayed palace, the Bridewell, for that purpose. Though work was provided for the inmates, emphasis lay upon disciplining the 'sturdy beggars'. The same held true for the houses of correction erected in succeeding decades in some other English towns, patterned on the London example. Also, the 'hospitals' founded by the Pope in the last quarter of the sixteenth century sought to punish beggars and vagabonds, to discipline them rather than to set them to work.

The Dutch humanist Dirck Volckertsz Coornhert was the first to launch the idea that the idle poor be educated by forced labour to be useful members of society. In his *Boeventucht* (Discipline of Knaves), written in 1567 (but first published in 1587), he proposed not only to hold sharper surveillance over poor relief but also opposed existing patterns of punishment. He argued that corporal punishment completely failed to solve the social problem, because it encouraged delinquents instead of putting them on the straight and narrow path; protection of society should characterize punishment. According to Coornhert, efficient social control had to rest on two principles: loss of freedom and forced labour, in order to end through discipline and exercise the idleness which was the mother of all impiety. The ideas of

Coornhert were carried on by his follower Hendrik Laurensz Spiegel and by the physician Sebastian Egbertsz, who filled various high offices in the Amsterdam magistracy. Their plans were soon brought into practice. In 1589 the magistrates decided to establish a *tuchthuis* for men, and in 1596 followed a like institution for women. Idealistic notions of improvement and education for the 'delinquents' soon fell into the background. The pursuit of profitable employment of the poor became the chief concern, so that education in one or another handicraft came to nothing. The men almost exclusively chopped and rasped Brazilian dyewood. This simple but laborious task appeared especially lucrative: one disposed of a cheap work force unable to protest against their living conditions and thus open to maximum exploitation. The same held for women and young children, who had to spin, knit or sew. Thus, the original plan was reduced to a reassuring spectacle for the well-to-do burghers, who, on payment of an entrance-fee, could ascertain for themselves the useful and, above all, profitable work done by the 'dregs' of society.

No less than twenty-six Dutch towns imitated the example of Amsterdam during the seventeenth century. As indicated by their names, the accent in nearly all rasp-houses and spinning-houses fell on the employment of the idle poor. That economic motives played a prominent, if not decisive role appears from the locations of the *tuchthuizen*: more than half were set up in the county of Holland, the commercial and industrial heart of the Republic. That all institutions except six were founded in the first half of the seventeenth century likewise testified to the close bond between economic development and social policy: from around 1650, the first signs appeared of economic stagnation and even decline.

The Dutch *tuchthuizen* directly or indirectly provided examples for the southern Netherlands, Germany, and Scandinavia. In 1613 the plague-house at Antwerp was rebuilt as a house of correction, where beggars and vagabonds were locked up and put to work. Some years later, similar houses were created in Brugge, Brussels, Ghent, Ieper, and Mechelen. The system had nonetheless little chance of success. All attempts to put the poor to work in centralized institutions were abandoned after a while. This failure is not surprising: the Flemish towns were confronted with the decline of their traditional wool industry, while Antwerp and Brussels specialized in the manufacture of luxury goods, in which the need for unskilled workers was extremely limited.

As for Germany and central Europe, in only four towns were *Zuchthäusern* founded in the early seventeenth century, namely in Bremen (1609 to 1613), Lübeck (1613), Hamburg (1614 to 1622), and Danzig (1629). All these institutions fulfilled from the beginning the combined functions of Bridewell and workhouse. Why did the other German and central European towns not create similar foundations in this period? The explanation in our opinion is that Bremen, Hamburg and Danzig were the only centres which flourished amidst general decline, while Lübeck, though declining in relation to Hamburg, held its ground better than most other German towns. Then, towards the end of the seventeenth century, *Zuchthäusern* arose in Breslau, Nuremberg, and Vienna (1670), Leipzig (1671), Luneburg (1676), Brunswick (1678), Frankfurt-am-Main (1679), Munich (1682), Magdeburg and Spandau near Berlin (1687), and finally Königsberg (1691). These foundations possibly were related to the slow and limited yet undeniable economic recovery and relative scarcity of cheap labour which followed the Thirty Years War.

Inasmuch as we can follow affairs in Scandinavia, only two houses of correction were set up, both provided with workshops. It was certainly no mere accident that they were in Copenhagen, the most important trade centre in Scandinavia, and in Stockholm, the port controlling the bulk of Swedish imports and exports, nor that both institutions were created in the period which witnessed the spectacular economic, political, and cultural awakening of northern Europe.

The example of France is particularly interesting, because it indicates that political as well as economic factors could bring about the movement 'to lock up the poor'. Until the 1640s, mercantilist principles lay at the heart of French social policy. At the end of the sixteenth century Barthélemy de Laffemas, Chamberlain of Henry IV, published two booklets in which he advocated the establishment of *manufactures* in order to put the poor to work. Moreover, for every trade, a bureau was to be created to oppose the associations of journeymen and to ensure that all able beggars did useful labour; the recalcitrant were to be coerced by confinement in a public institution. Some years later, he added further details to his programme, proposing to establish two workhouses in the principal towns of the kingdom, one for unmarried women, one for needy men fit for heavy labour. The institutions were to be financed by the merchants and entrepreneurs established in the centres concerned. De Laffemas's ideas were revived and elaborated in the early seventeenth century by numerous French writers, who all drew connections among the meagre industrial capacity of France, unrestrained imports of foreign manufactures, massive unemployment, and alarming poverty. At the assembly of the Estates-General in 1614, various schemes were brought forward to encourage profitable employment for the poor. The economist du Noyer de Saint-Martin as well turned his attention between 1614 and 1639 to the problem of poverty. He defended among other things the creation of a national registration service responsible for regulation of the available labour force. This service would distribute work tickets which allowed the unemployed to find a job via employment bureaus; anyone without a ticket would be shut away in a workhouse. In his famous *Traité de l'Oeconomie politique,* Antoine de Montchrestien publicized similar notions. He advised the Crown to order a census of all its subjects in order to regulate the labour market. If, moreover, several central workshops were set up in every province, then there would be no more excuse for idleness. From that moment, beggars and vagabonds would no longer deserve their liberty and might straight away be put to useful work. Mercantilist schemes corresponded completely with practical realities; when the city fathers of Lyon, one of the foremost industrial centres of France, founded in 1614 a *hôpital général,* their intentions were, in essence, to employ the poor profitably. Hence the magistrates limited poor relief to those physically incapable of working and forbade burghers on pain of fine to give alms. The healthy poor were set to work in the numerous workshops of the *hôpital général;* the men rasped dye-wood, the women and children above eight spun, wound, and twisted silk thread.

After 1640, the economic arguments cited in favour of the *hôpitaux généraux* gradually gave way to political motives posing as religious and moral principles. In most towns where an *hôpital général* had been founded, the activists henceforth emphasized the disciplining of the lower classes. Their motto was 'Moral Order'. The Company of the Holy Sacrament or, according to its enemies, the *cabale des dévots* was the driving force in this field. This powerful, secret association of devout laity and clergy displayed surprising activity. In the 1650s its members, via a strictly controlled network of around sixty provincial branches, exercised influence from Paris on the whole of France. The Company carried out an unflagging, ruthless campaign for order, a rational crusade against the 'evils of the age'. It played an important role in the condemnation of Jansenism, the suppression of Tartuffe, and the growing erosion of protestant liberties after 1630. Its weight, however, fell particularly hard on popular licentiousness: the rituals of the *compagnonnages* (confraternities of journeymen), profanity, drunkenness, extraordinary public amusements, casual marriages, prostitution and all other 'disorders of the poor'. Begging and vagabondage formed the select targets of the *dévots.* They elaborated plans for repression based on the idea that a proper society could only be sustained by removing its anti-social elements. Through wealth, influence and intense propaganda the *dévots* succeeded quite quickly in putting their ideas into practice. Their crowning achievement was the royal edict of June 1662 which stipulated that in every town and large village in France, *hôpitaux généraux* were to be founded, 'in order to contain beggars and to instruct them in piety and the christian religion'.

How is this radical reversal to be explained? Two factors combined. First, the French economy passed through a general recession from the end of the 1630s, which dragged on until around 1700. With textiles, nowhere were the high levels reached between 1625 and 1635 matched under Louis XIV. In these circumstances, economic arguments obviously could no longer play an effective role in the determination of social policy.[12] In the second place, the rural and urban popular rebellions which took place in the period 1623 to 1648 must be considered. No year passed without one or another province being confronted with rebellions. This wave of desperate upsurgences grew even more dangerous when the hunger and wrath of the poor, crushed by royal taxation and threatened with starvation due to successive harvest failures, combined with the war-weary revolt of *officiers* led by the *Parlement* of Paris. By 1653, Mazarin and Turenne had annihilated the last shreds of resistance; the elites had learned their lesson. As Perry Anderson has remarked, 'The very depth of the plebeian unrest revealed by the Fronde shortened the last emotional breakaway of the dissident aristocracy from the monarchy.'[13] Henceforth, both parties joined their forces in order to hold the lower classes in check.

The activities of the Company of the Holy Sacrament must be seen from this point of view. Without a doubt, large numbers of its members acted out of purely religious motives. The Company was founded between 1627 and 1630, during an expansionary phase of the French Counter-Reformation, the 'time of the saints', from 1600 to 1640–50. It was a forceful movement, characterized by large-scale projects for social discipline. Indeed, one of the results of the Counter-Reformation was 'the appearance of well-trained and educated priests and ministers, who were bent upon destroying vestigial paganism, and who imposed external, uniform standards of belief'. This evolution 'weakened one of the essential bonds that had held isolated districts together – their common cultural assumptions'.[14] Secular authorities made use of this powerful religious instrument for their own pursuits, to impose a political order on the lower classes. The social composition of the Company of the Holy Sacrament speaks for itself: the vast majority were nobles and magistrates. Since this elite, just as the monarchy, feared the recurrent wrath of the masses, they allied in the field of social policy. Nearly all prominent aristocrats and *officiers*, including Chancellor Pierre Séguier, famous and hated for his merciless action against rebels, were associated with the *cabale*. Understandably, the Company kept the names of its members and sympathizers secret: the public outside had to be kept ignorant of the real intentions hidden behind the piety. Religious arguments employed by the *dévots* thus fulfilled several functions: to guarantee the essential cooperation of the clergy, to justify harsh measures against the poor, to portray a unique body of hierarchic images by which the poor 'knew their place', and, finally, to sublimate the anxieties of the dominant groups.

One problem still needs explanation. Why did the authorities prefer such a costly 'solution', namely the construction of *hôpitaux généraux,* in place of the old system of exemplary punishment? As discussed above, begging and vagabondage reached previously unknown proportions, in seventeenth-century France. The ubiquity of paupers and, above all, their growing horizontal mobility confronted the authorities with immense problems. Proclamation of an edict against migration was pointless, since bands of soldiers and popular uprisings repeatedly ravaged the countryside. However, peasant revolts turned the balance in favour of the 'great confinement', proving that systematic, generalized terror and indoctrination were indispensable components of efficient socio-political control. All Frenchmen had to be taught that the distinction between 'masters' and 'servants' was necessary and part of divine providence. Such goals could only be attained by the creation of *hôpitaux généraux,* symbols in brick and stone of a sanctified Order. In opposition to exemplary executions, by definition irregular, limited and selective, the *hôpitaux généraux* confronted all potential lawbreakers with a permanent, ubiquitous and terrifying sanction: loss of freedom, living death. The natural fear of being locked up, so the elite reasoned, would encourage the lower classes to fulfil their duties to society; a network of *hôpitaux généraux* appeared to be the best guarantee for internal order. This policy apparently had its successes. The government managed to control in large measure the disorders of the poor. Isolated revolts still broke out after the Fronde, but for several generations general agitation belonged to the past.

All this does not signify that the economic potential of the *hôpitaux généraux* were lost from view during the reign of Louis XIV. The projects of Colbert went much further than perfecting the existing system of control. This untiring minister was convinced that it sufficed to give French industry systematic public injections and to provide an extensive, cheap and docile workforce for the nation's wealth to be used to the full. Hence, his outspoken preference for public support through the provision of work. In 1667 he wrote to the Aldermen of Auxerre: 'Since abundance always results from labour and poverty from idleness, your most important task is to find means to restrain the poor and to set them to work.' In 1681 he congratulated the intendant of Rouen for his efforts to move the clergy of Fécamp to provide useful work to the poor, 'since nothing is so detrimental to the State as the begging of able men'.[15] Purely artificial means, such as creation of royal *manufactures* and locking up the poor with an eye towards their profitable employment, could not, however, aid French industry very much: structural obstacles limited in advance the effect of such attempts. Some exceptions aside, the *hôpitaux généraux,* either as workshops or as training centres for unskilled workers, had little significance.

In short, the numerous waverings of royal legislation concerning the control of begging and vagabondage in seventeenth-century France must be ascribed as much to stagnation in the national economy as to the intensity of the struggle among the various social groups.

Nowhere in north-western Europe was social policy dictated by economic considerations so much as in England. The Poor Law of 1601, which remained in force until its total abolition in 1834, had a three-fold target: provision of work for the unemployed, education and apprenticing of paupers' children, and support for 'the lame, the impotent, the old, the blind, and such other among them being poor and not able to work'. A dual administrative principle was asserted, by which the parish was established as the responsible unit and placed under the central supervision of the Privy Council. All with sufficient means were regularly taxed by the overseers of the poor, officials drawn from the churchwardens and four other 'substantial householders', in order to provide the raw materials on which the poor could be put to work. If a parish were in no position to assemble the necessary funds by taxation, the rates were to be distributed over the hundred. The system was controlled by the Justices of the Peace, who had to ensure that the fundamental principles of the Poor Law were strictly applied throughout the realm of England and Wales.

Until around 1660 the Elizabethan Poor Law, supplemented by two further Acts, one for the erection of workhouses and the other for the definition of the law of charitable bequests, was brought into practice in quite a flexible fashion, since, although in this period the basis was laid for the commercial and industrial expansion characteristic of the following decades, stagnation, crisis, and even partial decline dominated the English economy from the 1620s to the Restoration. The rise of new industries in no sense compensated for the collapse of old ones, while technological improvements in agriculture made extremely difficult the return to their smallholdings of part-time workers in industrial enterprises. In such circumstances strict adherence to the Poor Law was impossible. The authorities were even obliged to take action against the most severe social problems, such as evictions, massive dismissals and excessive food prices.

Economic expansion after the Civil War made an end to this more or less humane attitude towards the poor. Since an extensive supply of labour was required, poor relief, that fount of idleness and cause of 'high' wages, had to be restricted at all costs. Labour, sobriety, and discipline were now deemed the preservers of the nation. For the future, the central government devolved on the discretion of local authorities' decisions respecting administration of provisions for the poor. Until the nineteenth century every parish would be responsible for its own unemployed. This radical change was caused by the victory of the Parliamentary side against the absolutism which had advocated centralization, but it was also facilitated by growing regional economic differentiation. In a situation in which purely or dominantly rural areas lay next to relatively quickly industrializing districts, a situation in which the pace of the uprooting of the poor and their absorption into industry varied considerably, a uniform social policy was not only superfluous, but even incompatible with the national interest. The harmony between the measures taken locally and the prosperity of the 'whole' country was guaranteed by two factors. Parliament was drawn from the same classes and representative of the same propertied interests as local authorities, and the horizontal mobility of the labouring population was limited by the act of Settlement and Removal.

The Act of 1662, passed partly in order to solve the problem posed by the masses of cashiered soldiers, empowered Justices of the Peace to eject any newcomer to a parish who arrived without means of his own and send him back to his last legal residence. In 1691 settlement by residence was exchanged for settlement by merit: henceforth, a pauper had to 'deserve' his settlement, directly, or indirectly through spouse, parent or grandparent. The statute introduced, *inter alia,* two important ways to gain settlement: one was completion of an indentured apprenticeship, the settlement fixed according to the apprentice's last forty-days' residence; the other was annual hiring, if unmarried and childless. Although the extent to which this legislation was executed remains problematic, it seems indisputable that the Act of Settlement offered possibilities to the authorities to conduct the migration of labour along the desired channels.

From the 1670s, profitable employment of the poor became the common panacea of all English writers on the trade and industry of their country. Innumerable schemes were proposed to combine poor relief with economic progress. Sir Josiah Child, the chairman of the East India Company; Andrew Yarranton, a successful businessman; Sir Matthew Hale, Lord Chief Justice of England; Thomas Firmin, a rich merchant: these and many other prominent officials and entrepreneurs considered the labour of the poor as the secret but untapped weapon of the nation in the struggle for a favourable balance of trade. All protagonists of a 'constructive' social policy shared the belief of Sir Francis Brewster, Lord Mayor of Dublin, that 'the Neglect of the Poor seems the greatest mistake in our government', and drew the conclusion that it was a national disaster 'to have so many Thousand Poor, who might by their Labour Earn, and so eat our Provisions, and instead of sending them out, export Manufactures, and that would bring in double to the Nation, whatever our Provision doth'.

But how should the labour of the poor be organized? The parish seemed to be too small a unit by which to regulate rationally employment of paupers. John Cary, a rich merchant, therefore united all the parishes within Bristol by Act of Parliament in 1696. Henceforth the 'Corporation of the Poor' was responsible for the relief and employment of all the urban poor; two workhouses were opened, one for women, the other 'for receiving in the remainder of the poor, (viz.) ancient people, boys, and young children'. Two years after the start of the enterprises, Cary wrote enthusiastically; 'The success hath answered our expectations; we are freed from beggars, our old people are comfortably provided for; our boys and girls are educated to sobriety, and are brought up to delight in labour.'

The example of Bristol soon found imitators. Within two years, workhouses were established in Tiverton, Exeter, Hereford, Colchester, Kingston and Shaftesbury. Although the idea of putting the poor to useful work was not new in the decades after the Civil War, a new emphasis was laid in all these institutions on the potential social gains to be made from such employment. Yet not until 1723 was an Act passed which allowed parishes to refuse support to paupers who did not enter the workhouse voluntarily. Sir Edward Knatchbull's Act then also granted parishes the right to unite with an eye towards the creation and maintenance of such institutions. Two decades later, England counted between 100 and 200 workhouses. How is this sudden and overwhelming success to be explained? Proliferation of workhouses in the second quarter of the eighteenth century can scarcely be considered an accident of history or as a movement without a 'comprehensive purpose', as some historians have postulated. If the phenomenon is brought into relationship with the economic problems with which England was confronted in this period, it appears clear that there was no faulty insight into the economy on the part of businessmen or their representatives.

By the early eighteenth century, the textile industry faced an imbalance between spinning and weaving activities. The loom had been so improved that the work of several spinners was required to keep one weaver busy full-time. Shortage of yarn, a major bottleneck that was not overcome until James Hargreaves's spinning jenny and Richard Arkwright's water frame were introduced in the 1760s, was felt equally in the manufacture of woollens, still the foremost export item, and in the cotton hosiery industry. When the English economy decelerated in the second quarter of the eighteenth century and entrepreneurs consequently shunned risky investments, nothing else lay at hand than to make use on a large scale of the great, nearly untapped reservoir of national wealth – the profitable employment of the poor. Spinning required neither heavy outlay nor protracted training and therefore provided an extremely suitable pursuit. One might object that construction of centralized units of production absorbed large amounts of money and that even the profits made on almost free labour possibly did not counterbalance the investment of so much fixed capital. Although detailed evidence is lacking, it is indeed more than evident that numerous workhouses were in no condition to pay their own way. On the other hand, they were generally built at the cost of the community. In other words, those who drew the greatest advantages from spinning by the poor provided only a small portion of the total capital. From the point of view of businessmen, establishment of a workhouse was a highly profitable undertaking during this period. In the circumstances, Daniel Defoe's complaints carried scarcely any weight. This redoubtable critic wrote:

Suppose, now, a workhouse for employment of poor children sets them to spinning of worsted. For every skein of worsted those poor children spin, there must be a skein the less spun by some poor family or person that spun it before . . . it is only transposing manufacture from Colchester to London, and taking the bread out of the mouths of the poor in Essex to put it into the mouths of the poor in Middlesex.

Defoe was undoubtedly right, but he found no audience until the shortage of yarn was relieved by technological improvements, that is, not until the 1760s.[16]

From numerous sources we learn that the confinement of paupers seldom went like clockwork. The rounding up of beggars and vagabonds by local authorities often led to riots. Disturbances, sometimes resulting in revolts, were not only caused by the poor themselves, but also by casual observers. In September 1675, for example, four *archiers des pauvres* who attempted to bring a young beggar to the *hôpital général* of Lyon were attacked twice along the way. First they had to deal with a number of masons who attacked them with their tools, then they met a howling mob 'of both sexes and all ages', among whom were many maid-servants and even the wife of a miller, who called them torturers and pelted them with stones. Similar incidents took place elsewhere. The vast majority of the demonstrators were day labourers, servants, artisans and small shop-keepers, catholic as well as protestant. In some cases, the arrested beggars were even taken into protection by priests and lesser nobles. This opposition to the exercise of the law by large groups of the population points in part to the survival of traditional conceptions of charity, in part to the consciousness of those above the poverty line but beneath the status of large-scale employer of labour that little in fact separated them from the actual poor. Hence, as Christopher Hill has so rightly remarked, it is

easy to understand that in many areas there was considerable sympathy for sturdy beggars, and that constables had difficulty in enforcing the poor law. Few villagers, few artisans near the poverty line, would lightly believe that original sin was the sole cause of vagabondage, that men took to the road for the fun of the thing, that all beggars should be punished, that property was more important than life.[17]

Chapter 5

ECONOMIC GROWTH, PAUPERIZATION AND THE REGULATION OF THE LABOUR MARKET *(c.1750-c.1850)*

THE second half of the eighteenth century is generally considered a fundamental divide in human history. The so-called industrial revolution afforded society the opportunity to produce an unceasing stream of goods and to deliver them to a steadily growing community. For the first time cumulative economic growth and, consequently, incremental material wealth came within the realm of possibility. Many historians have proposed that this fundamental change ended poverty in every country involved. According to the German historian Wolfram Fischer, 'With industrialization, the age-old problem of poverty was solved, so that in the developed industrial societies it poses merely an exceptional social problem, impinging on small groups or individuals.' This optimistic vision is seconded by all who reduce poverty in the *ancien régime* to 'the smallness of the national income in relation to the size of the population and the slow rate of growth of production'. From such a viewpoint, industrialization and modernization are indeed the miracles which ruled out new impoverishment processes. To cite the most famous 'optimist' among historians: 'Poverty can be cured only by economic growth, not by income redistribution. It was the pervasive and powerful stimulus of wealth in privately-owned property that produced the magnificent episode of the nineteenth century'. For R. M. Hartwell, modern poverty is merely a 'residue'. Indeed,

> 'there will always be at the fringe of society, individuals who cannot come to terms with its demand, and who will need institutional or semi-institutional care'.

The 'savage prophecy of Marx' is dismissed with a stroke of the pen. Wilhelm Abel believes that the industrial revolution freed mankind from its chains. He does not deny that the living standard of a notable part of the population worsened during the first century of economic growth after 1750, but following him it is 'clear that the misery of poverty, in terms of its origin and evolution, belonged to a receding phase of Western history'.

Although investigation of the nature and causes of nineteenth- and twentieth-century poverty falls outside the scope of this essay, it is essential to ask whether or not economic growth from 1750 onwards entailed new impoverishment processes. This requires a discussion of the specific context in which various aspects of industrialization and modernization played themselves out.[1]

1. The disruption of rural society

England: agricultural progress and capitalism

By the middle of the eighteenth century, the gradual but steady spread of major improvements in husbandry technique and agrarian organization gave England a decisive advantage over other European countries. English agriculture not only provided for the needs of the nation but even produced a significant surplus for export. Favourable conditions after 1750 (with food prices increasing as a result of demographic expansion) stimulated landlords and capitalist farmers more than ever before to raise agricultural output through extension of arable and more intensive use of land already cultivated. Most estate-owners saw that their interests were best served by the large tenant's capacity to realize profits and accumulate capital. Thus the latter were stimulated to employ technical improvements to raise productivity. The growing profits of capitalist farmers allowed landowners gradually to raise rents, while tenants had the security that they would retain their tenure if they functioned efficiently, regularly devoting a part of their profits to improve stock and equipment on their farms. As the son of a landowner said in the mid nineteenth century to his model tenants: 'It is by this friendly cooperation between landlord and tenant that the successful prosecution of industry and improvement can best be attained for your benefit as well as to mine.'[2]

The other side of the coin was the systematic undermining of the traditional peasant economy. Since agrarian improvement went hand in hand with concentration and consolidation of farms, small landholders and copyholders with qualified property rights were slowly but surely eliminated. By 1790 English landlords controlled around three-quarters of all cultivated land, while occupying freeholders held only 15 to 20 per cent, and a peasantry – in any real sense of the word – no longer existed.

Parliamentary enclosure undoubtedly formed the most dramatic aspect of agrarian change in England. Between 1761 and 1815 no less than 600,000 hectares of waste and commons were enclosed by Act of Parliament. Marginal cottagers and smallholders, living on the edge of bare subsistence, were given the choice of becoming labourers on the land or abandoning agriculture when they lost their rights on the commons. Yet the importance of this movement ought not to be overestimated: enclosure only accelerated the general expropriation process which had been at work since the sixteenth century. It remains unsettled to what extent enclosure awards drove small farmers off the land, but it seems improbable that they led to the transfer on a large scale of arable to pasture and hence depopulation in a period of growing demand for grain. The available evidence on internal migration and urban expansion does not show massive rural depopulation during the second half of the eighteenth century. Enclosure, however, advanced the proletarianization of small farmers, who had to make way for the capitalist farmers associated with the landlords. Only those who could demonstrate their rights to the commons received any compensation, and in most cases the allocated land was too small to make good the loss of common land. Furthermore, smallholders were seldom in a position to pay their portion of enclosure costs, so they were obliged to sell their cattle or even their holding. Since the savings which they retained were insufficient to enable them to practice an independent trade, they soon joined the ranks of the wage labourers. The social degradation of the peasantry due to enclosure was mirrored in the evolution of expenses for the poor rates at Broughton, Hampshire: after the enclosure award of 1790, they diminished by half during the single year 1791 but thereafter skyrocketed until far into the years after the Napoleonic wars. As J. D. Chambers wrote more than half a century ago: 'The appropriation to their own exclusive use of practically the whole of the common waste by the legal owners meant that the curtain which separated the growing army of labourers from utter proletarianization was torn down.'[3]

The course of this process can be closely followed from a detailed analysis of socio-economic transformations in one Leicestershire village. In 1765, one year before the enclosure award, only three families out of ten occupied land in Wigston Magna; seven in ten supported themselves as agricultural labourers, framework-knitters, artisans, or shopkeepers. Before enclosure, two families in three were already largely divorced from the land. There was, moreover, a large range between the least and the greatest occupiers of land: the unknown but probably significant number of cottars aside, 50 per cent of the landholders cultivated less than four ha. each, while 21 per cent had more than forty ha. each. Yet, the peasant economy still rested on a solid basis. Most households disposed of a cottage, even if no land was attached; they owned a few sheep; they could hire some pasture cheaply from the greater tenants. The majority of the landowners were still peasants, even if they held among them less than 40 per cent of the total land area. Then the enclosure award gave the old system the *coup-de-grâce.* Just as in other villages of the Midland Plain, the massive shift from arable to pasture and the engrossment of manors by graziers broke down a centuries old peasant community. 'The open-field system', in the words of W. G. Hoskins,

> had been the solid dyke protecting the peasant against the powerful tide of the money-economy that had been rising in the outside world for centuries, just as manorial custom had protected his ancestors in earlier centuries. The enclosure of the fields and the extinction of the commons made the breach by which this tide was let in.

By 1795 the number of owner-occupiers had diminished by 30 per cent. Some hired their fields to capitalist tenants; others sold out. In 1831 the peasant economy had totally disappeared. Seven large landowners possessed altogether more than half of the parish, while the range of peasant proprietors had been reduced to a handful of survivors. Yet Wigston differed in one important respect from most surrounding villages: the framework-knitting industry provided many of the dispossessed, both local and immigrant, alternative employment possibilities, so that population growth continued. The results of these fundamental transformations were dramatic: expenditure on the poor rose from around £100 per annum in the 1770s to an average of £433 by 1783–85, and twenty years later that figure had doubled. In 1832, finally, 43 per cent of families had to be supported regularly, and another 31 per cent intermittently.[4]

The spectacular growth of the English economy induced structural transformations in long isolated rural areas as well. Thus the sharp rise in the price of wool between 1780 and 1820 brought about the expansion of commercial sheep-farming in the Highlands of Scotland. While the proportion of sheep to cattle had once been one to one, it became ten to one in many parishes, even twenty to one in some. This radical change made unequal the traditional struggle between the earlier users of the land and the graziers. Coexistence of the two was ruled out for technical and economic reasons. Sheep-breeders needed both hills and lower meadows in order to feed their flocks in summer and winter; consequently small tenants were obliged to hold their cattle the whole year through on the grass immediately around their settlement, which meant a drastic reduction in number. Since sheep-breeding is one of those activities which must be practised on a large scale in order to be profitable, most farmers could not enter the business because they lacked the necessary capital. The result was the gradual depopulation of numerous parishes – sheep literally replaced men.

The growth of a labour-intensive coastal economy from the end of the eighteenth century only partially and temporarily counterbalanced the sheep 'clearances'. The expansion of the Highland kelp industry, in direct response to the growth of new chemical industries in England, provided the bulk of the population few advantages. The supply of labour was so large that landlords could keep wages extremely low, and most adjusted their rents regularly in order optimally to skim off the earnings of their tenants. Moreover the kelp boom promoted population growth, since the means of subsistence were once again a bit more abundant, while the contemporaneous extension of potato cultivation allowed more food to be produced on the same surface area. Encouraged by high profits drawn from the kelp industry, some landlords accelerated this process by further division of holdings. In 1799, the Duke of Argyll wrote to his Chamberlain: 'As you inform me that small tenants can afford to pay more rent for farms in Tiry than gentlemen-farmers, owing to the manufacture of kelp, this determines me to let the farms to small tenants which have been and are at present possessed by tacksmen who reside upon farms in Mull.'

The proletarianization of innumerable cottars turned utterly tragic when kelp prices collapsed after the Napoleonic Wars. The augmented population faced chronic underemployment and periodic malnutrition. A few years later, the same lot befell the centres which had specialized in herring fishery since 1789. The general fall in prices from the 1820s on ended their short-lasting prosperity. In short, the structural transformation of the Highland economy, determined by the industrialization of England, ultimately brought only proletarianization and impoverishment to the mass of the people.[5]

Division of farms into minute parcels was not a phenomenon peculiar to Scotland. In various English regions, a similar process was underway, usually closely connected to expansion of rural industry. In Lancashire, for example, cottage workers, according to a contemporary, were generally 'willing to pay something from the labour of their looms for the convenience of having a few acres of ground upon which they may support two or three cows for the subsistence of their families'.[6] This combination of home industry and extreme fragmentation of the land raised rents and made possible low prices for industrial wares. The enclosure movement in Lancashire was directed not so much in favour of commercial cultivation of grain as towards creation of 'optimal' production units for rural weavers, as can be seen clearly in the parliamentary enclosures and enclosures-by-agreement which took place between 1710 and 1770, and were above all in districts where rural weaving developed. Master producers bought farmsteads, subdivided them, and rented out crofts to their weavers, just as owners of factories built cottages for their workers.

Agrarian capitalism undoubtedly ended dearth and starvation in England, except in a few years and in some isolated areas. Increasing agricultural production and productivity not only allowed a greater population to be fed but also fostered the growth of the internal market, a *sine qua non* of sustained industrial growth. Improvements in agricultural technique and in agrarian organization, moreover, made it possible for a growing portion of the population to be put to industrial tasks. The price of this remarkable modernization process was, however, the dislocation and the final dissolution of the old peasant culture. For the overwhelming majority of rural inhabitants, economic growth was synonymous with proletarianization. At Wigston Magna, old folks over eighty still toiled as framework-knitters, and children were already labelled 'rural labourers' by their tenth birthday. Indeed, 'every hour of work now had a money-value; unemployment became a disaster, for there was no piece of land the wage-earner could turn to'. Furthermore, for the first time in history, the landowners and great tenants joined an ideology to their interests. Not only pursuit of profit inspired the ejection of cottagers from commons and the dispossession of smallholders; they became matters of social discipline. Total economic dependence, so maintained many gentlemen, was the best guarantee of the permanent submission of the lower classes.

France: the trap of feudalism

The present state of historical knowledge does not allow a conclusive answer to be given to the question of whether the real agricultural output of eighteenth-century France grew substantially or not. Some progress was made, but from all available evidence concerning extent of land clearances, contraction of fallow, evolution of yield ratios, introduction of new agricultural techniques and changes in agrarian organization, it seems that it was a very sluggish, mediocre and limited process. There was no 'agricultural revolution'. In some areas production increased, perhaps even productivity, but this apparently only kept pace with population growth. Michel Morineau labelled the expansion of French agriculture in the eighteenth century as 'development within stagnation', the antithesis of real growth. The most important transformation was the gradual extension of 'poverty-cultures' such as buckwheat, maize and potatoes – sure signs of general impoverishment.

The causes of this relative 'backwardness', as said before, are to be found in that the old mode of production in France was simply 'sucked dry' for centuries. The *ancien régime*, forming the living and working environment of the rural masses, remained in its fundamental structures feudal and aristocratic. The economic and social organization of French agriculture was still characterized by the predominance of small, individual peasant producers and the survival of seigneurial surplus extraction applied by extra-economic coercion, so that for most peasants, the term 'feudalism', just as in earlier epochs, had a living meaning: servitude attached to the land, upon which rested seigneurial dues in money or in kind.

Due to the varying levels of surplus extraction and its complex composition, it is exceptionally difficult to determine precisely the burden of the *complexum feodale.* Although in some regions it may have diminished in relation to the increased harvest, the eighteenth-century peasantry had in any case to surrender a significant part of their net production to a small minority of feudal lords – generally 25 to 30 per cent, including tithes. From the 1730s onward, moreover, the great landowners profited from a strong upwards trend in rents. Between 1720–29 and 1780–89, the nominal rise amounted to 142 per cent, while the weighted index of agricultural prices in the same period rose only 60 per cent; on the eve of the Revolution, the adjusted land rent lay some 50 per cent higher than in the second quarter of the century. Altogether, after subtraction of seed, seigneurial dues, tithes and taxes, *manouvriers* retained half their total harvest, while *métayers* would consider themselves lucky if they held a third for their own use. The social consequences were the more serious because the vast majority of peasants disposed of very small morsels of land. In most parts of France, an average of 75 per cent of the eighteenth-century peasantry possessed less than five hectares, the minimal area required to assure the economic independence of a family, and in nearly every province at least 25 per cent were smaller than one hectare. The combination of both factors, namely the dominance of smallholding and the pressure of surplus extraction, hindered the introduction of technical improvements designed to raise productivity.

The precarious situation of the peasantry was worsened by the tendency towards concentration which took place gradually from the 1730s on. In order to profit from the growing demand for foodstuffs, a minority of capitalist *fermiers* attempted to lay their hands on more and more farms. By renting *en bloc* extensive properties, they obtained far better terms of tenancy than other producers. Moreover, these *fermiers* did all they could to appropriate the holdings of the subsistence peasants. Among other things, they demanded exorbitant fees to plough a small parcel of ground. Thus, many *manouvriers* were forced to put their holdings at the disposal of a capitalist tenant and to sell him their labour. In 1768 a high official spoke plainly: 'The tyranny of the great occupiers over lesser folk should receive the immediate attention of the ministry . . . If one resists the occupiers, he can be sure that he shall no longer have work at harvest-time and that, on their side, they shall refuse to plough the land of him who does not submit blindly.'[7]

Another important change with far reaching consequences for the peasantry was the rise of professional 'managers', the *fermiers généraux,* who rented all the estates of one or more landlords and hired them out in turn for their own profit. These capitalists, who often functioned as collectors of seigneurial dues and ecclesiastical tithes as well, sometimes controlled the disposable produce of ten or even twenty estates.

The tendency towards concentration, bound to a substantial raising of surplus extraction, reached its zenith during the period 1763 to 1775. The so-called 'physiocratic offensive' was not only characterized by the encouragement of reclamation and the free circulation of grain, but in some provinces it was paired to a 'seigneurial reaction' and a systematic assault on common lands. In Burgundy, Brittany and Normandy, old unused exactions were enforced anew, back payments demanded at once, and vast commons re-allocated. This last approach signalled the ruin of many subsistence farmers, unable to lay claims at law. As the procurer-general of the Parliament of Rouen clearly expounded in 1766: 'Common pasture of any kind belongs to the landowners, and not to the poor, that is to say not to those who have no property . . . The real patrimony of these small occupiers who are all day-labourers are the wages which successful farming enables large farmers to pay for their labour.'[8]

The triumph of 'agrarian individualism' (the expression of Marc Bloch) quickened the proletarianization of the lower classes. It was certainly no accident that the government in the 1760s and 70s proclaimed a number of edicts which guaranteed complete freedom for rural industry. Yet, in the end, the physiocratic movement led to nothing besides intensification of social tensions. The favourable evolution of prices put landlords and, above all, the capitalist *fermiers* in a position to book significant profits. Most, however, made little or no attempt to raise the productivity of land and labour by employing new key techniques or investing extensive capital in essential farm facilities. Augmented incomes were generally wasted on luxuries and services or turned towards the purchase of more land. The physiocratic boom undoubtedly spurred development, but only in the restrictive sense of the term: the rise of production was chiefly the result of expansion (enlargement of cultivated area and input of more labour), caused by the 'widening of capital' directed towards the realization of speculative profits. It was not the result of real growth, which required 'deepening of capital' in order to raise the efficiency of a given unit of capital and labour input. The question of how far the absolutist state assisted in the maintenance of feudal structures cannot be handled here, but it seems incontestable that the specific nature of surplus extraction in France formed nearly insurmountable blockages to successful economic growth.

When by 1775 grain harvests seemed to suffice for internal demand and prices stagnated, speculative capital soon shifted away from agriculture. To make matters worse, rentals, taxes and feudal dues were not diminished during the economic malaise, so that small producers were less than ever before in a position to employ technical innovations. When Arnoult, a member of the *Constituante,* in his *Manuel Champêtre* reviewed the activities of the physiocrats, he upbraided all enlightened agrarian reformers of his time, and those of the future, too:

> Oh, you who complain over the recalcitrance of the peasant who refuses to introduce your new plow, your new sowing-machine, your crossed or diagonally plowed field, your repeatedly dug-up furrows, your masses of manure which are four times what he can afford—before tripling his expenses for the uncertain hope of a tripled harvest, begin by putting him in a position to provide clogs for his children.[9]

Although total figures are lacking, without a doubt the ranks of the rural proletariat and semi-proletariat in eighteenth-century France were markedly extended. In the region of Andance (between Lyon and Valence), the number of rural day-labourers without property rose from scarcely 12 per cent in 1696 to around 33 per cent in 1789. Every regional investigation shows that by 1790 at least half of the rural population wholly or partially depended on wages and that their purchasing power had fallen by 25 per cent. It is possible that individual employment opportunities grew in the long run, compensating for the decline of real wages, but this optimistic thesis, for which there is no evidence, in no sense alters the heart of the matter, namely the absolute and relative impoverishment of the rural labour force. Admittedly the poor no longer starved, as in the past. Cyclical variations in agricultural prices abated, thanks to rising grain production, improvements in transport, more efficient measures on the part of the authorities during dearth and the expansion of 'poverty cultures'. But 'proletarianization replaced the graveyard', to cite Le Roy Ladurie.[10] Not surprisingly, delayed marriage for women in the eighteenth century reached its nadir.

The Revolution delivered very little to the *manouvriers.* Neither the confiscation and sale of the property of the Church and *émigrés*, nor the numerous agrarian decrees proclaimed by National Assembly, Convention, and Jacobins brought structural changes. In some provinces a large part of the land may have concentrated in the hands of the peasantry, but this profited mainly the rich *laboureurs* and *fermiers.* Small landholders gained only from the abolition of ecclesiastical tithes and seigneurial dues, while the subsistence peasantry and the landless profited only from the disappearance of personal dues. The division of commons, provided for in the law of 10 June 1793, offered the *manouvriers* no relief, because more radical measures were not taken. What could poor peasants do with extra slivers of land, that no more than before enabled them to support their families? Fragmentation only increased their structural difficulties. The danger existed that more important cultivators would subsequently buy up the bulk of the parcels distributed. Many village communities saw this clearly and refused to surrender collective pasturing rights. Although much land changed hands during and after the Revolution, the economic and social organization of French agriculture remained fairly unaltered. The stiff-necked resistance of the feudal aristocracy against the Revolution obliged the bourgeoisie to spare the peasantry for a long time. Until far into the nineteenth century no actions at law could be taken which would have favoured a rapid capitalistic transformation of agriculture. Hence, around 1820, more than 80 per cent of the national population still worked, full or part-time, in agriculture, as compared with barely 35 per cent in England.

Flanders: peasant industry and land fragmentation

Every foreign agronomist from the seventeenth century on viewed the Southern Netherlands as the Mecca of agriculture. Nowhere else in Europe attained such high yield ratios as Flanders and Brabant: around twenty hectolitres of rye or wheat per hectare at the end of the *ancien régime*. These achievements resulted from highly labour-intensive farming, characterized by progressive fertilization techniques, sophisticated crop rotation, and the cultivation of fodder and industrial crops. Farmsteads of three ha. could produce a surplus for the market and thus support demographic expansion. By the mid eighteenth century, the Southern Netherlands exported a yearly average of 5 per cent of the total grain harvest. This accomplishment was the more remarkable because Flanders was noted for its extreme fragmentation of land and high population density; the number of inhabitants per square kilometre in the countryside amounted to at least 100 and in some districts rose to more than 200. The sole exceptions were the sparsely settled coastal regions, where the technical and financial demands of reclamation of heavy, loamy soil encouraged the development of large farms.

In the course of the eighteenth century the proliferation of tiny holdings in the interior of Flanders went further than ever before. In the villages of Schorisse and Sint-Kornelis-Horebeke in 1711 the proportion of farms smaller than one hectare was 49 and 44 per cent respectively; by 1790 these figures had risen to 66 and 58 per cent. In Lede, east of Ghent, the number of holdings less than 0.3 ha. tripled in the period 1701 to 1791, and in the neighbouring Sint-Gillis, those under 0.6 quintupled between 1691 and 1797.

The spectacular increase of mini-holdings cannot be explained by a simple demographic-economic supply and demand model. Although the population of the interior doubled, not all areas witnessed such extreme fragmentation. In many villages, on the other hand, the number of farmsteads less than one hectare rose out of all relation to population growth. Nor can the phenomenon be ascribed to the influence of an egalitarian system of inheritance customs, since tenancy in most of Flanders was the usual form of landholding; peasant proprietors dominated only along the eastern edge of the interior. Given that real rents nearly quintupled in the eighteenth century, one is inclined to recognize this factor as conclusive. Rents, however, were generally higher for smaller farms; hence fragmentation led to increased rents, not the reverse. The explanation must be sought in a shift of the economic centre of gravity: while manufacture of nearly all varieties of textiles in the towns Lille, Kortrijk, Ghent, and Brugge stagnated or declined from the 1720s on, the total production of linen in the countryside doubled between 1700 and 1790.

This expansion initially allowed many cottars to make ends meet, but it simultaneously stimulated investment in the land. The urban middle class discerned quite soon the profits to be had from the symbiosis of peasant production and linen manufacture. Their interests in landed property was perhaps awakened by a negative factor as well, namely declining opportunities for profitable capital investments within the great towns. In any case, merchants, manufacturers and bureaucrats snapped up large amounts of land. This can be deduced from the powerful upward movement of land prices and the contemporaneous fall in mortgage rates. If peasants had been the major engrossers the demand for loans would have risen quicker than the supply, since peasants would have had to borrow money to buy land, but as matters turned out exactly the opposite there can be no doubt that the bourgeoisie was fully responsible for the rising price of land. Equally beyond doubt, landowners encouraged the multiplication of smallholdings. Cottars, turning to domestic industry voluntarily or through necessity, could sustain themselves on far less arable than full-time peasants, so that it became possible to garner even higher rents from miniscule crofts. Some merchants and manufacturers built whole series of small houses on their lands in order to increase the dependence of their tenant-workers and thus to drive up rents to the limit. In the second half of the eighteenth century, such houses with gardens of 0.2 hectares brought an average profit of 7 per cent per annum on invested capital, 50 per cent more than the rent from one ha. of arable law.

The close connection between proto-industry and land speculation appeared in the evolution of land prices during the economic crisis of the 1840s: in all rural areas where linen manufacture dominated, land prices dropped, while in the polders they held to their old levels or moderately increased. Why did landowners provide rural textile workers with a croft, no matter how small? Simply because if unable to harvest any foodstuffs, cottage-workers lost their competitive advantage: low wages. For all landowners, this came down to killing the hen that laid the golden egg; with wages equal in town and country, merchants and manufacturers chose an urban workforce.

Two factors promoted even more the tendency towards fragmentation of the land. First, expansion of proto-industry led to population growth. Disposing of a source of supplementary income, more cottars could marry, and do so earlier. Hence, the reproduction rate and the consequent demand for parcels of land rose steadily; rural areas where linen production extended furthest were also characterized by the greatest number of rented farmsteads and the strongest population increase. Second, the potato. Its cultivation in the Southern Netherlands in the eighteenth century spread prodigiously (see below). Since two-thirds of an hectare then sufficed to maintain a family of four, fragmentation could proceed to previously unknown levels. Yet, one quarter to one-third of the households in many Flemish villages at the end of the *ancien régime* had no potato patch; they disposed of a cottage and garden only, so that they were completely dependent on wage labour.

Domestic industry and potatoes saved the eighteenth-century Flemish cottars from starvation, but already strong demographic pressures were pushed to extremes. This enabled merchants and manufacturers to hold wages low, while landowners, often the same people, systematically raised rents, not in relation to the agricultural yield of small tenancies, but in relation to the overall incomes of their tenants, including wages earned from linen manufacture. This led to greater dependence on cottage industry. In most Flemish districts the traditional peasant community was totally disrupted. By 1800, 25 per cent of all inhabitants earned their daily bread exclusively from spinning or weaving. In the most industrialized areas, this figure leapt to 50 per cent. The bulk of cottage-workers were, as the bailiffs and aldermen of the Land van Waas recognized, not much more than the slaves of putting-out merchants, who arbitrarily set the rates of 'sweated labour', 'without any other guidelines than covetous self-interest and avid greed, closing their eyes to all laws, divine and human'.[11]

2. The breakthrough of industrial capitalism

Proto-industrialization

The connection between fragmentation of the land, proto-industrialization and population growth was in no sense peculiar to Flanders. In numerous parts of Europe, socio-economic polarization of the peasantry during the Middle Ages and after had led to the rise and extension of an underemployed mass of landless or nearly landless country dwellers. The availability of this large, cheap workforce formed an essential precondition for the development of rural domestic industries. When in the eighteenth century the progressive impoverishment of the peasantry coincided with a rapidly rising demand for manufactured goods, this process reached greater proportions than ever before. Although in many European countries a growing tendency towards concentration of labour was to be seen, the growth of industrial output was primarily caused by the expansion of rural manufacture within the social formation of the family economy.

The French textile industry put increasingly more *manouvriers* to work. In Languedoc manufacture of woollens spread out into hundreds of villages from the Cévennes to the Pyrenees. In Champagne the number of rural woollen weavers mounted to more than 30,000 by the end of the *ancien régime*. Between 1700 and 1790, textile production rose in both areas 143 and 127 per cent, respectively. The silk industry also called on rural workers more than ever before. During the second half of the eighteenth century some 100,000 villagers in Forez and in the Lyonnais prepared raw silk for the neighbouring metropolis. But it was above all the rapidly growing linen industry which provided impoverished peasants with a source of supplementary income. In the *généralité* of Rouen, the number of men, women and children engaged in linen manufacture shot up from scarcely 43,000 around 1730 to 188,000 on the eve of the Revolution, an increase of 337 per cent. By 1790 nearly three in four villagers in the (present) *département du Nord* were employed in cottage industry. Not for nothing was this area, in which linen production tripled between 1746 and 1788, the most thickly populated of all French provinces, with 70 to 80 per square km, or nearly twice the national average. In the essentially rural province of Maine the number of women and children spinning flax into yarn by 1790 was estimated at 150,000, presumably four or five times more than half a century earlier. Rural cotton-spinning developed just as spectacularly. In the 1780s 25,000 workers in Alsace alone were engaged in this trade. Although centralized production seemingly made quicker progress in metallurgy than in textiles, the rural labour force in this sector expanded too. Significantly, the number of pin-makers in the Pays d'Ouche multiplied tenfold between 1700 and 1789, and the number of pieceworkers employed in manufacturing small ironware in the region of St Etienne jumped in the same period from 1,500 to 8,000.

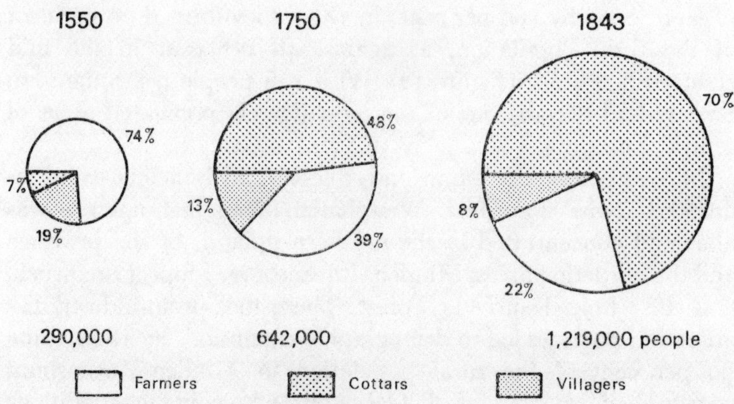

Fig. 12 Cottars as percentage of rural population in Saxony, 1550–1843.

Source: based on K. Blaschke, *Bevölkerungsgeschichte von Sachsen bis zum industriellen Revolution* (Weimar, 1967), p. 190.

In central Europe, the revival of international trade spurred on urban merchants and great landlords to make use of the growing mass of poor cottars as an industrial workforce. In Saxony, where the linen industry had flourished since the fifteenth century, processes similar to those in Flanders took place. Growing demand for industrial wares brought about expansion of commercial flax farming and rural linen production, creating new means of subsistence. The sharp rise of agricultural prices after the Seven Years War, moreover, favoured more intensive farming methods and the introduction of new types of animal fodder, especially clover. Thanks to these improvements, grain production doubled between 1750 and 1800. Another important factor conducive to the multiplication of tiny holdings was the spread of potatoes: arable planted with this crop increased twelvefold between 1800 and 1830. The combination of growing productivity and proto-industrialization resulted in significant population growth. In 1843 Saxony had twice as many inhabitants as one hundred years earlier. Demographic expansion, however, was not paired to urbanization; the proportion of townsmen to countrymen remained roughly unchanged. Radical changes did take place in the countryside, nonetheless. The number of *Gärtner* and *Häusler*, cottagers holding only a miniscule parcel of land, grew by 160 per cent; in 1843, they formed 70 per cent of the rural population, as against 48 per cent in the mid eighteenth century (Figure 12). With 136 people per square km Saxony had become one of the most densely populated areas of central Europe.

In Westphalia, the Rhineland, Silesia, and Bohemia, rural industry likewise flourished. Westphalian linen manufacture was above all concentrated in the northern uplands of the province and the bordering areas, Minden, Ravensburg, Lippe, Osnabrück, and the whole Teutoburg Forest. There too, proto-industrialization and potatoes led to demographic expansion. By 1800, some 70 per cent of the rural population in Minden–Ravensburg consisted of cottars and day-labourers whose living conditions were greatly determined by fluctuations in the international linen market. In the first half of the nineteenth century this figure leapt up to 90 per cent. The Rhineland, where both textile industry and metallurgy were favoured by natural resources, also developed impressively. At the end of the eighteenth century most villages in this area had become true hives of industry. Some localities produced 50 per cent more manufactured goods than during the 1750s. However, economic expansion was surpassed by population growth. In the Duchy of Berg, for example, the number of inhabitants rose from 140,000 in 1730 to 260,000 in 1792, an increase of 80 per cent. Where, according to contemporaries, one hundred years earlier peasant holdings had predominated, rows and rows of small houses now stood, each with its small garden, and often a croft. In Bohemia, linen manufacturing spread out mainly in the hilly and least fertile parts of the country. Official reports estimated the number of rural flax spinners in 1772 at 230,000 – a figure bound to rise in the succeeding years. By 1793, in one part of northern Bohemia alone, some 500,000 earned their living exclusively from spinning and weaving.

Meanwhile, the population density for the whole country rose from 37 per square km. in 1764 to 55 in 1789. That this demographic pressure increased above all in the linen districts of northern Bohemia – from 48 to 82 inhabitants per square km. – indicates the close connection between proto-industrialization and population growth. Silesia witnessed the same scenario. The expansion of linen production in hundreds of mountain villages and the growth of a prospering export trade made Silesia one of the 'richest' areas of central Europe. This development was yet again responsible for the substantial population growth which took place between 1741 and 1791, from a million to around 1.7 million inhabitants.

In northern and eastern Switzerland, cottage industries in the course of the eighteenth century developed into an essential part of the rural economy. In the mountainous Oberland and the lake area of Zürich canton, cotton manufacture expanded rapidly from around 1700 on. The flatter centreland, in contrast, remained purely agrarian. This divergent development was the result of the socio-economic differentiation of the peasantry inherited from the preceding centuries. In the fertile valley, village communities, with the aid of municipal authorities, strove to protect commons from poor newcomers. The regular raising of entry fines imposed by the more well-to-do landowners drove the possessionless slowly but surely to Oberland, where a reservoir of cheap labour was created. Hence the textile industry took hold primarily in the uplands. By the end of the eighteenth century, only one-third of the villagers of Oberland still belonged to the peasantry in the proper sense; the rest consisted of poor spinners, weavers, and day-labourers, who had only a cottage and parcel of land. Immigration and industrialization brought about spectacular demographic growth. Between 1634 and 1792 the population of the canton of Zürich nearly tripled, while the number of townsmen grew by less than 80 per cent and the number of villagers in the neighbouring valleys by no more than 60 per cent. In the east of Switzerland rural textile production developed at a similarly quick tempo, particularly after 1750. In the region of St Gall, the number of men, women, and children engaged in cotton-spinning and embroidery in the last quarter of the century is estimated at 80 per cent of the population.

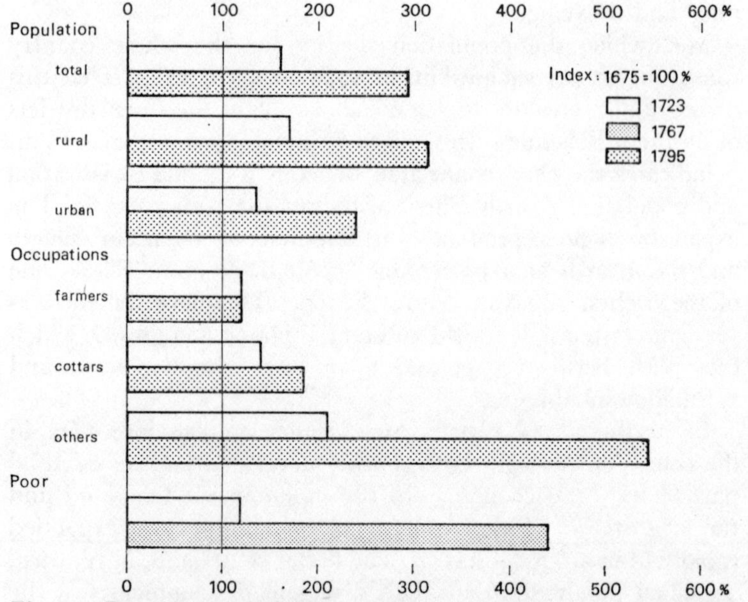

Fig. 13 Proto-industrialization, population growth and impoverishment in Twente (Overijssel) 1675–1795.

Source: based on B. H. Slicher van Bath, *Een Samenleving onder spanning. Geschiedenis van het platteland van Overijssel* (Assen, 1957), pp. 58–61, 334–5, 457–65.

In the province of Overijssel, to give a last example, linen manufacture took off in the countryside from the late seventeenth century on. It was no accident that it concentrated overwhelmingly in Twente, the district counting the greatest number of poor in 1675, some 27.5 per cent, compared with 13 and 16 per cent in Salland and Vollenhove. Nearly half the population of Twente consisted of cottars averaging one hectare of land. Since the number of peasants in the proper sense remained practically unaltered between 1675 and 1723, the accelerated population growth of this period – 61 per cent plus – must be ascribed to the spread of proto-industry. Rural demographic expansion in Twente exceeded by 30 to 40 per cent the growth of neighbouring districts. By the early eighteenth century, the arable could no longer be increased, while the multiplication of smallholdings had reached its absolute limits. An increasing number of rural inhabitants were obliged to rely exclusively on industrial activities. Hence the proportion of peasants and cottars in the fifty years after 1675 dropped from 75 per cent to 65 per cent, although the portion of townsmen remained constant. These changes had dramatic results when the textile industry, from around 1750 onwards, was no longer a match for growing foreign competition. The economic crisis, involving massive unemployment and a total wage freeze, was further aggravated by rising grain prices. In nearly twenty years, real wages fell by 40 per cent. Innumerable cottage workers were brought to begging. Between 1723 and 1767 the number of needy nearly trebled to no less than 50 per cent of the population.

These examples show that the poverty of the peasantry was a major precondition for the expansion of cottage industry. In every rural area in which textile manufacture or metallurgy emerged on a large scale, an extensive part of the population consisted of cottars living on the edge of subsistence, or even below. The availability of a large and cheap labour force was the critical factor in proto-industrialization. It seems equally undeniable that demographic growth in such areas attained far greater proportions than in places without cottage industry. Economic changes largely undermined the influence of traditional social control, which in the past had maintained a demographic balance, as appears from a family reconstitution study of Shepshed, Leicestershire, between 1600 and 1851. During the eighteenth century, Shepshed became the most industrialized village of the shire: in 1812, there were more than 1,000 knitting-frames for a total population of just over 3,000. The transformation of peasants and craftsmen into an agrarian and industrial proletariat was paired to a radical deviation from customary pattern of marriage. By the second quarter of the nineteenth century, men and women alike married nearly five years earlier than their predecessors in the pre-industrial village.

Ready to work for wages, they could reach their maximum productivity at an earlier age, so that there was no longer any reason to delay marriage. Since exactly these extra five years of married life correspond to maximum female fertility, the fall in age at marriage led to a substantial increase of completed family size. This growth was of such dimension that it even exceeded the 'positive check' of high mortality levels among the infants and children of proto-industrial families. Moreover, the interval between generations shortened, so that more children were born per unit of time. The net rate of reproduction (i.e. the generational replacement rate) rose from 1.10 to 1.57. Hence the population of Shepshed quintupled in less than two centuries.

The German historian Hans Medick has remarked: 'The conditions shaping household and family . . . were based on an increasing exploitation [*Verwertung*] of the *total* family labour force.' The labour of women, children, and the aged became common. It was this internal dynamic, resulting in self-exploitation, which made possible the quick growth of the proto-industrial system. This special case of 'economic development with unlimited supplies of labour'[12] enabled employers to realize enormous profits. They could subtract the foodstuffs raised by rural industrial families from their labour costs. Moreover, the self-regulating system of the family economy proved effective for the transition to proto-industrialization, due to 'the inclination of the poor, landless producers to fall back on "self-exploitation" in the production of craft goods, if this was necessary to ensure customary family subsistence and economic self-sufficiency'. Finally, competition among cottage workers grew progressively greater through the relatively constant process of demographic expansion inherent to proto-industrialization.[13]

Not surprisingly, the accelerated growth of the world economy, dominated by merchant capital, resulted in the expansion of industrial mass production in the countryside. Although artisans in some rural areas were men of small capital, owning their own raw materials and equipment and even selling their own fabrics at the nearest market, the overwhelming majority of eighteenth-century proto-industrial workers directly or indirectly were dependent on putting-out merchants or manufacturers. Often hundreds or even thousands of cottage workers drew their raw materials from a single capitalist businessman, to whom they had to surrender their entire production. In 1711, 140 great manufacturers from Roubaix, besides 10,000 weavers in the town and its surroundings, employed around 30,000 spinners dispersed throughout Artois and Picardy. About the same time, a single *négociant,* one Poupart, controlled 4,000 full and part-time textile producers in the countryside of Sedan. By 1762, more than 6,000 rural spinners and weavers in the Limburg region worked for the famous merchant-entrepreneur Bernard Scheibler of Monschau. The number of cottage spinners dependent on the great Linz Manufactory in Upper Austria at the end of the *ancien régime* amounted to no less than 16,000. And, the cotton magnate, J. J. Leitenberger, owner of several large mills in Bohemia, employed some 5,000 rural spinners in 1791.

In all areas where employment opportunities depended on the circulating capital of putting-out businessmen, the society created by proto-industrialization was characterized by structural insecurity and poverty. Availability of crofts planted with foodstuffs; continuing population growth; excessive dispersal of the labour force; complete lack of legal protection: all these factors worked together to hold wages at extremely low levels. In Flanders, for example, the daily income of a family of five engaged in rural linen production by 1792 was less than the wages of two unskilled labourers. Professional skill offered no particular defence against the sharp fluctuations of the market. Employers had no fixed expenses, so that they could transfer the shock of a depression largely on to their workers, and periods of enforced idleness were numerous, as a result of repeated disruption of international trade, the many difficulties in the supply of raw materials, random changes of fashion, and the like. Cottage workers were seldom paid weekly, because most employers only balanced their accounts at the end of a production cycle, which could last up to two or three months. This occasioned a spiral of debts, which in turn facilitated application of the truck system. Other misuses flourished, such as payment in bad coin and delivery of inferior raw materials. Since rural spinners and weavers of even a single employer were widely scattered, they could not easily undertake collective actions. Their opposition in general remained limited to individual protests, especially the embezzlement of raw materials. Needless to say, the law protected the employer. In England, for example, an Act of

1703 relating to the wool, linen, fustian, cotton, and iron industries, stipulated that a worker found guilty of theft of property entrusted to him be fined twice its value. In 1746 the costs of prosecution were added to this penalty. Nine years later, matters previously considered breach of contract were henceforth to be considered criminal offences, punishable by two weeks imprisonment. In 1777 this term was lengthened to three months.

The precarious situation of cottage workers was not only caused by specific relations of production inherent to the proto-industrial system; it was also generated by the life-cycle of the family. Before children could contribute to the household economy they hindered its production possibilities, because successive births prevented the mother from working full-time. The subsistence margin of the family was narrowed therefore during just that period in which its requirements grew. As Medick wrote: 'It was precisely this temporal disjunction between production and reproduction within the proto-industrial family which trapped it between the Scylla of "primary misery" (arising from the conditions of the proto-industrial system) and the Charybdis of "secondary poverty" (brought on by the family life-cycle).' In short, proto-industrialization inexorably led to the proletarianization and improverishment of a steady growing part of the rural population. There is no lack of contemporary witnesses portraying the living conditions of this mass of unorganized sweated labour in the most sombre of colours, but perhaps it will suffice to cite three witnesses who only with difficulty could be suspected of bias. In 1765 the *Keure* of Ghent, the agency charged with quality control of linens, sketched the situation of Flemish cottage workers:

> More than half of the producers and weavers of linen cloth live in cottages and huts in the countryside where they are occupied in weaving, especially in wintertime by lamplight. The women and children prepare and spin the flax. . . . They subsist on rye bread, potatoes, buttermilk, a little bacon on Sundays and water. That is all their food. There is no one more wretched than them in the whole world.

Tournai, industrial inspector in the province of Maine, wrote in 1780:

> There may be no more grinding poverty than that of the weavers in the district of Le Mans; presumably not even one in four there can say that he owns the piece being worked on his loom, despite its minimal value. Hardly any one weaver or very few at most can read and write.

A rich farmer and village officer in Zürich canton tersely summarized in 1793 the results of proto-industrialization:

> The cotton industry, like a foul pile of dung, has produced and given birth to all this vermin, the crawling and proud beggar pack.[14]

The transition to the factory system

After 1750 England experienced a gradual but irrevocable transition from proto-industry, based on the family economy, to the factory system, characterized by concentration of labour and mechanization of production. The question why this decisive transformation took place exactly then and there is still one of the most controversial themes of socio-economic history. Without searching for a 'Holy Grail of explanation', it is necessary to shed some light on several aspects of this complex problem which are closely connected to new impoverishment processes.

From the point of view of employers, domestic industry offered certain competitive advantages, particularly cheap labour and the ease with which workers could be laid off, thus allowing minimal investment of fixed capital. Yet the proto-industrial system contained the seeds of its own ruin. The excessive geographic dispersal of workshops entailed considerable loss of time and problems of control, giving an opening to embezzlement of stock and to delivery of inferior produce. Even more important, the rural workforce, partially engaged in agriculture, was not inclined towards continuous industrial employment. During harvest season many cottage workers simply abandoned manufacturing. The most serious implication of the family economy for employers, however, was that cottagers were not ruled by the goal of a monetary surplus or a net profit. Indeed, 'the object of its productive labour, rather, was to bring into equilibrium, into a "labour–consumer balance", the basic necessities of economic, social and cultural subsistence on the one side, and the expenditure of labour by the family on the other'.

If its income rose as a result of favourable economic conditions, then the family was not encouraged to increase its effort proportionally beyond a certain point; cottage workers chose consumption and free time instead of extra wages, leading to a 'backward-sloping supply-of-labour curve'. Within this context applied the well-known maxim of William Temple, a cloth manufacturer from Gloucester, that the sole means to bring workers to greater efforts was 'to lay them under the necessity of labouring all the time they can spare from rest and sleep, in order to procure the common necessaries of life'.

Hence enclosure seemed more than desirable to entrepreneurs, if for no other reason than that rights to the commons favoured the irregularity of rural industrial labour. Also, the subsidy for export of grain came to be considered favourably, because it raised the price of bread and consequently forced the poor to work harder. Since it generally seemed impossible to draw sufficient labour from the already engaged cottage workers, merchants and manufacturers who wished to profit from growing demand for industrial products could do little else than successively broaden their operational zone. This, however, sharpened precisely those structural difficulties *vis-à-vis* distribution and control which gradually drove upwards the price of finished goods. Sooner or later, most employers were trapped in a 'cost cage', so that they had to search for means which allowed greater production within their radius of action.[15]

During the second half of the eighteenth century, the pressure on the proto-industrial system in England grew steadily heavier. Opportunities for geographic expansion were by this time largely exhausted. The growth of capitalist agriculture created an extensive rural proletariat which no longer held land and depended totally on wage labour for its subsistence; thus, either proto-industrialization would limit itself to areas where cottage workers could draw supplementary income from agriculture, or more landless people had to be engaged, which meant paying higher wages. Evidently neither of the two policies offered a viable solution. Even less, since the growth of international trade had encouraged the development of proto-industry on the continent, where the geographic expansion of the system hardly encountered serious obstacles. The traditional peasantry was gradually disrupted in these countries, it is true, but this process was characterized above all by the further multiplication of numerous smallholdings, which formed precisely the fertile soil necessary for the rise of cottage industry. Although documentary material is fragmentary, it appears from the available information that the wages of industrial workers in France, Flanders and central Europe were lower than in England, so that these areas had a competitive advantage which could only be overcome by structural innovation – mechanization.

Technological changes are largely dependent on organizational factors. The switch from cottage industry to the factory system does not seem to have taken place in regions where putting-out merchants predominated. Since these merchants engaged in manufacture only within the borders of their commercial horizons, they were not readily inclined to raise their fixed costs substantially. Besides, if putters-out wished to assure their domination of direct producers, then they had every interest in maintaining traditional conditions of production. Otherwise the danger arose that the more important manufactures in the course of time would set themselves up as competitors and free themselves from commercial capital. As Takahashi has written: 'This cutting off of the small producers from the market, this monopoly of the market by the putters-out, clearly had the effect of blocking the road on which the direct producers were independently rising as commodity producers, and becoming capitalists.'[16]

The example of England shows how far industrial growth could depend on specific production relationships. After 1700 textile manufacture expanded in the West Riding, to the cost of the West Country and East Anglia. Various factors were responsible for this important shift. Yorkshire, specializing in cheap fabrics, disposed of numerous natural resources and sufficient labour; in this area of smallholders and cottagers, land and loom were easily joined together so that wages were lower than elsewhere. Nonetheless, these favourable conditions do not adequately explain the spectacular growth of the textile industry in Yorkshire, where wages rose more quickly during the eighteenth century than in England generally. And as for physical advantages, coal was extensively employed only in dyeing and finishing processes before the steam-engine (post–1800), while the supply of water to drive mills can scarcely be considered the most critical factor. The explanation must be sought in the organization of production and marketing. In the West Country and in East Anglia manufacturing was dominated by great clothiers, who dispensed wool to artisans and their families. In the West Riding, in contrast, the producer of broadcloth was nearly always a man of small capital, who acted as a purchaser of raw materials and a seller of finished material. Josiah Tucker, future Dean of Gloucester, clearly recognized in 1757 the favourable entrepreneurial climate of the West Riding:

> Though in fact the spinner, weaver, millman, dyer, dresser, etc., are all of them the journeymen of the agent or commissioner, who stands in the stead of him who is the clothier in other places, yet by acting thus upon a distinct footing they conceive themselves as far independent of him, and of each other, as any buyer or seller whatever. And being thus independent, they are all rivals, all animated with the same desire of bringing their goods to market upon the cheapest terms and of excelling one another.

Moreover, cloth exports from Yorkshire were not monopolized by London wholesale dealers, as in the West Country and East Anglia. Production in the West Riding was handled increasingly by an active group of merchants, often drawn from the ranks of cloth manufacturers, from Leeds, Wakefield and Halifax. Since these merchants, unlike their London counterparts, were totally engaged in the cloth market, they did not strive for strict distinction between commercial and industrial activities. This holds for Lancashire as well, where many capitalist employers dealt not only with financing the cloth industry but also appeared as merchants and vice versa.[17]

In short, the rise of independent entrepreneurs was not hindered in the Midland Counties by putting-out merchants who wanted to maintain traditional production conditions at any price. Landowners, middlemen and weavers with a small amount of capital could work their way up to become petty industrial capitalists and could employ technological improvements. This more or less symbiotic relationship between merchant and manufacturer helped clear the path for the eventual breakthrough of the capitalist mode of production.

Things differed on the Continent. Certainly, there were areas in which industrial production was controlled increasingly by independent manufacturers and emancipated 'middlemen', who displayed entrepreneurial initiative and promoted mechanization. In most regions the urban trading houses nevertheless had a monopoly position: they alone bought raw materials, dispensed them to cottage workers, and dealt with the finished or semi-finished goods. The restraining influence of commercial capital delayed the transition from cottage industry to mechanized production in nearly all these regions – sometimes it awaited the twentieth century before the factory system arose. Furthermore, in some regions characterized by an advanced stage of proto-industrial expansion, the total dependence of the direct producers on putting-out merchants in the long run led to de-industrialization. Flanders was a striking example of such a cul-de-sac.

We have already noted that Flemish spinners in the eighteenth century were completely in the grip of putting-out merchants; the same was true for most weavers. Some employed a few wage labourers in addition to their family, but they were the exception to the rule. Capitalist wholesale dealers of flax and linen defended with tooth and claw this organization of production, because the turnover period of their circulating capital could in this way be reduced to the minimum. The availability of an extensive and impotent workforce, reproducing itself quickly and without cost, allowed urban trading houses to pay low wages. The more so, because population growth by far exceeded demand for linen. Great landowners and rich peasants alike had an interest in the expansion of proto-industry: one could drive up rents; the other could profit from low wages. Finally, the role of the Church must be taken into account; in Flanders it held extensive estates and consequently drew profits from the proliferation of cottage industry. Perhaps even more important was the care of the Church for the salvation of rural labourers. So long as the family remained the dominant unit of production, spiritual authority was questioned only by marginal individuals. Concentration of labour, in contrast, increased the danger of a break with traditional values and norms, which could in turn lead to growing irreligious behaviour. It was probably chiefly the fear that cottage workers would be submerged 'morally' into the ranks of the manufacturing proletariat which moved the Church to advocate the maintenance of the proto-industrial system in Flanders. In any case, the community of interest uniting commercial capital and landed property was responsible for the growing technological backwardness of the Flemish linen industry. Even after the catastrophic crisis of the 1840s, during which many cottage workers ended more than a century of twofold exploitation with starvation, capitalist merchants in the province of West Flanders did not establish flax-mills. The transition to the factory system was ultimately stimulated by the government, which furnished special allowances to small entrepreneurs to buy machines.

Although the socio-economic and the political context differed completely, Silesia experienced the same sort of vicious circle described as 'involution'.[18] The creation and subsequent expansion of proto-industry were closely bound to feudalism in this region. Landlords considered cultivation of flax and rural linen manufacture as the pre-eminent means to draw greater incomes from their serfs and, simultaneously, to raise the value of their estates. The serf-weaver was not only subject to the traditional feudal dues, but at the same time he had to pay a tax in order to practise his trade, a further sum for commutation of his labour services, and an amount to exempt his wife and children, needed as ancillary labour, from service on the land or in the house of their lord. Feudal dues had to be paid in kind (flax, yarn or linen) or in cash (earned by linen weaving). Urban guilds, seeing clearly that the expansion of rural industry threatened their economic position, tried to hinder this development. They did not succeed against the powerful Junkers, who were initially supported by the Habsburg authorities, and when the latter realized that they had made a fundamental mistake the tide could no longer be turned. In the struggle between local and foreign merchants for control of the export of manufacturers, the Junkers chose the side of English and Dutch merchants, because the rise of an internal bourgeoisie would endanger their political prerogatives. The alliance of feudal lords and foreign merchants excluded all technological innovations: the former realized that mechanization would provide them only few advantages and would in the long run even undermine their power; the latter, for obvious reasons, did not wish to invest extensive amounts of capital in plant and equipment. Rural spinners and weavers, on their part, were so exploited by both the dominant groups that they could barely sustain their families, let alone save anything to display entrepreneurial initiatives. Besides, landlords systematically opposed the introduction of labour-saving techniques, which would have caused unemployment among serfs and thus a decline of feudal incomes while promoting the emergence of industrial entrepreneurs.

The measures taken by Frederick the Great after the incorporation of Silesia into Prussia changed nothing in the basic structure of industrial organization. On the contrary, the Junkers received extra capital in the form of royal grants and loans from the mortgage bank, known as the *Landschaft*. The King even proclaimed an ordinance which stipulated that all dwellers could be compelled to spin flax and that their children could not marry unless able to attest that they supported themselves by spinning. However, from the moment that English manufactures flooded the international market, the Silesian proto-industry was consigned to death. Technological backwardness, favoured by landlords and capitalist wholesellers, literally strangled the once flourishing cottage industry. By the 1820s export of yarn had halted completely, defeated by the murderous competition of English mechanized spinning mills; within the following twenty years, linen export too dropped to nearly nothing. Utterly destitute, cottage workers died by the thousands during the 1840s, just as in Ireland.

The rise of a new working class

In those regions where proto-industrialization did lead to mechanized production the social changes due to this transformation were limited until far into the nineteenth century. By 1850, the total number of factory workers amounted to not much more than 5 per cent in England, barely 4 per cent in Belgium, around 3 per cent in France, and less than 2 per cent in Switzerland and Prussia. The domestic system appeared to be more tenacious than on first sight might have been expected. As D. S. Landes has remarked: 'It dragged on unconscionably in those trades where the technological advantage of power machinery was still small . . . or where the home artisan could build himself a rudimentary device.'[19] The rise of the factory system certainly signified the end of numerous small workshops but in the initial stages favoured concomitant expansion of domestic industries.

In England the multiplication of mechanized spinning mills

resulted in an enormous extension of handloom weaving. Precisely the cheapness and superfluity of labour due to the disruption of rural society and large-scale immigration out of Ireland retarded the introduction of labour-saving devices in this important industrial task. The number of handloom weavers jumped from 50,000 around 1770 to more than 240,000 in the earlier 1820s. This development put employers in a position to depress wages systematically: the weekly earnings of a weaver declined from *c.* 25 shillings at the end of the eighteenth century to *c.* 9 shillings in 1817. The social degradation of handloom weavers thus long preceded the mechanization of production. It was only after the collapse of the 1825 boom that introduction of the power loom accelerated and the long death struggle of the handloom weavers began. By 1840 the number had diminished by more than 100,000, and in 1856 only 23,000 remained. This tragedy is dismissed by some historians with the pronouncement that

> every new fashion, every new machine, and every new process has a tendency to render more useful the service of one class of artisans and less useful those of another; and consequently to lower the wages of one class, and raise those of the other. The natural remedy is that the workmen, the demand for whose services has ceased or diminished should betake themselves to the new sources of employment which almost always accompany, and generally have, in fact, occasioned the change.[20]

Apparently they presuppose that the replacement of workers by machines released a proportional amount of capital to provide the same workers with new employment opportunities. However, they fail to take into account that in the meantime, numerous persons were impoverished and that many others flooded these industries which were still easily entered, with the result that the mechanization was hindered or even postponed indefinitely. Moreover, such processes as a rule advanced the social degradation of the workers who were already engaged in the 'compensatory' industries. The British silk industry, for example, which during the eighteenth century recorded remarkable gains, became in the following century an asylum, as it were, for weavers from the cotton and woollen industries. Although only a minority of highly skilled workers, such as the weavers of nanking, gingang, and mousseline, could switch from cotton to silk, the retraining of those people caused a gradual displacement of the silk industry to the areas around Manchester and Macclesfield. Silk workers in the older centres, such as Spitalfields, could not compete with the extremely low wages paid to the former cotton weavers, and they were gradually driven out. Increasingly cheap labour thus delayed technical improvements. The change from hand to power loom did not take place in the British silk industry, outside of a limited line of goods, before the end of the nineteenth century.

The impoverishment of English framework knitters likewise preceded the mechanization of their trade. Framework knitting like handloom weaving, was characterized until the early nineteenth century by organizational and technological stagnation due to the growing supply of cheap labour. By 1811 the total number of stockingers employed on a domestic basis was estimated at more than 50,000. Needless to say, the more important masters took advantage of the situation, lowering wages and raising frame-rents. When the trade encountered serious difficulties as a result of the Napoleonic Wars and the collapse of the South American market, the capitalist hosiers alone could hold their heads above water. They tried as much as possible to depress wages by manufacturing 'cut-ups', cheap stockings of low quality, and by hiring 'colts', unskilled workers. Both small masters and skilled workers reacted strongly against this policy: the former because their economic position was undermined; the latter because wages were drastically lowered. The subsequent destruction of machines ought not to be misinterpreted: the Luddites smashed only the equipment – which was not new at all – of those hosiers who underpaid their workers, employed unskilled labour, or produced 'cut-ups'.

Because the transition from cottage industry to factory labour ended an age-old pattern of family and community life, most artisans preferred underpaid labour in 'honourable' trades, that is industries still dominated by handicrafts, in place of the iron world of the factory. Only severe need could move craftsmen to submit to the factory system. Agriculture and cottage industry in this period still provided too many chances for employment, even if steadily more poorly paid, for an adult male to be driven to the 'dark, Satanic mills'. Early factory owners, therefore, could not count on a ready supply of working men. Hence they turned to women and children, who could not otherwise make a living after the mechanization of spinning. Since the new working methods of the factories required little muscular strength, both women and children could be employed on a large scale. They offered two further advantages: they were an extremely good bargain and, accustomed to do as they were told at home, they were open to the strict discipline of the factory. In the early nineteenth century, no less than 70 per cent of the labour force of the Ghent cotton industry consisted of women and children aged from six to sixteen. In the cotton factories of the United Kingdom the figure leapt to some 75 per cent.

From the viewpoint of employers, widows with numerous children formed the ideal workforce. The owners of cotton mills in New Lanark and Catrine in Scotland recruited dozens of such households, and they were not the only ones who openly announced how gladly they would welcome more. Supply, however, fell short of demand. Other sources of willing labour had to be tapped. Many entrepreneurs besieged orphanages and poorhouses in order to gather the 'cheapest raw material in the market'. One anonymous writer declared in 1824:

> There is scarcely a single manufacturer who has set up in Potsdam or Berlin since the mid eighteenth century without claiming children from the orphanage for his enterprise. The conditions stipulated are always alike and boil down to the orphanage's provision for the children on its own cost joined to the manufacturers' endeavouring to train the children – out of patriotism – in the required skill, without wages, save for lodging and fuel.

In 1781 Antwerp textile manufacturers labelled the local orphanage for boys a 'training school for the factories'. When David Dale set up his cotton mills at New Lanark, he brought along a youthful work-force from the poorhouses of Edinburgh and Glasgow; in 1799, Robert Owen encountered around 500 such child paupers there. Samuel Oldknow, another famous cotton manufacturer, found apprentices for his mills at Mellor in a number of London parishes and institutions, such as the Duke of York's Orphanage in Chelsea and the Foundling Hospital. At Belfast, finally, the cotton industry, which developed from 1790 onwards, received its most notable initial support from the 'Charitable Society', which sent numerous child paupers to the factories.

These practices grew so famous that 'factory labour' began to signify 'child slavery' in the public's mind. In 1817 Robert Dale Owen accompanied his father on a trip to the foremost cotton mills of northern England. When he recalled in his memoirs the impression this had made on him, he wrote:

> The facts we collected seemed to me terrible almost beyond belief. Not in exceptional cases, but as a rule, we found children of ten years worked regularly fourteen hours a day, with but half an hour's interval for the midday meal, which was eaten in the factory. In the fine yarn cotton mills they were subjected to this labour in a temperature usually exceeding seventy-five degrees; and in all the cotton factories they breathed an atmosphere more or less injurious to the lungs, because of the dust and minute cotton fibres that pervaded it. In some cases we found that greed of gain had impelled the mill-owners to still greater extremes of inhumanity utterly disgraceful, indeed, to a civilized nation.

Certainly, there was nothing new about child labour; it is also true that it was an essential component of the family economy and that adult attitudes to children were often extremely harsh. Men who struggled for existence could not spare the least of their earnings and had, consequently, little opportunity to entertain feelings like compassion, the luxury of the rich. There can be little doubt that sadistic factory owners and foremen were the exception, not the rule, but that is neither here nor there. 'The crime of the factory system', to cite E. P. Thompson, 'was to inherit the worst features of the domestic system in a context which had none of the domestic compensations.' Indeed, 'in the mill, the machinery dictated environment, discipline, speed and regularity of work and working hours, for the delicate and the strong alike'. Either to perform manual labour or to become an extension of the machine, submitting to the unchanging regularity of the automaton: it made a world of a difference.[21]

Some twenty years ago the Belgian historian Jan Dhondt demonstrated that early factory workers largely originated among the 'ranks of the have-nots and the hungry, who had neither skill nor work, who lived from hand to mouth'.[22] The large-scale employment of child paupers by many industrial capitalists in late eighteenth- and early nineteenth-century Europe supports this conclusion. And it is striking how the regulation of the labour market in nearly every city which experienced quick industrial growth in the century after 1750 became the foremost purpose of poor-law administration. A single example: within two months after the reorganization of poor relief at Antwerp in July 1779, no less than eighteen textile manufacturers turned to the poor-law administration with a request for healthy workers; the request was promptly fulfilled, and nearly 400 adult poor had to apply to the entrepreneurs. As we shall see, such massive provision was rather exceptional, because it was superfluous. As industrialization advanced, manufacturers had less and less often to make their wishes known to the poor-law administration. In time, the wheels of social control turned so smoothly that the poor had no other choice than to enter the factories if they wished to 'enjoy' public support.

In order to convey to the 'transient, marginal and deviant' the essential principle of work discipline, a whole series of coercive measures unfolded. Any means which tied workers to the factory were seen to be good. Although the tending of a spinning machine required not much more than a month's training, factory owners usually hired no one unless he bound himself to work for an apprentice's wages for eleven or twelve months; the precise terms depended on national laws regarding apprenticeship. Employers loaned their workers such large advances on their wages that they could seldom redeem their debts and were consequently tied hand and foot to their patrons. In France and Belgium the law specified that a labourer be returned his *livret,* a workbook without which he could not be hired, only when he had paid off his debts. Entrepreneurs, finally, had the right to set up regulations for internal order, at their discretion. They had only one purpose: to impose strict work discipline by a complex system of fines, subtracted at the end of the week from wages. Late arrival, lingering at meal time, smoking, singing, swearing, brawling: for every non-productive activity or gesture, a fine. In many towns, the authorities lent a hand. At Ghent, for example, a worker found during working hours in a public place was considered a vagrant and arrested. At Antwerp, at the end of the eighteenth century, the magistracy even proclaimed an ordinance stipulating that, in the future, the police would use strong measures against poor children who played in the street during working hours.

The disintegration of the guild system

Expansion of rural industry often brought about the collapse of urban production; one needs only to think of the irreversible displacement of hosiery from London to the Midlands, the decline of fine cloth manufacture in Aachen in favour of the surrounding countryside, the flight of *bonneterie* from Orléans to the Beauce, and the fall of Haarlem's linen bleaching as a result of competition of capitalist manufacturers in the Wuppertal. Leyden offers perhaps the most tragic example of a flourishing urban economy ruined by the rise of rural industry. From the last quarter of the seventeenth century on, Leyden's cloth producers, faced with growing English competition and loss of the French market, encountered serious difficulties. Between 1671 and 1725 production nearly halved, from 139,000 pieces to 72,000. A drastic fall in wages enabled the more important entrepreneurs to survive, but spectacular development of cloth manufacture in the region of Verviers administered the *coup-de-grâce*. Although the workers of Leyden by 1725 scarcely earned enough to live, their wages exceeded by a factor of three those of the rural labour force near Verviers, which disposed of small parcels of land and paid no significant excises or taxes. Leyden was no match for this unequal competition. In 1795 production amounted to only 28,000 pieces, one-fifth of the seventeenth-century high point. The 'happy few' who remained at work received starvation wages and were subjected to the truck system by their employers. In the 1740s around one-third of the total population was continually on poor relief. For most, emigration was the only answer. At the end of the century, Leyden numbered scarcely 30,000, reduced from 72,000 one hundred years earlier.

Still, the eighteenth century witnessed the Golden Age of many towns. This was particularly true with centres specializing in luxury goods or the preparatory and finishing processes of textiles and metallurgy. The expansion of urban industries, however, paired itself to the disintegration of the guild system and the proletarianization of most artisans. Although the guilds survived in many countries to the end of the *ancien régime,* their influence on economic life grew less and less. Even in places where they retained their old authority in law, they stood powerless against capitalist merchants and entrepreneurs. Opposition between capital and labour was centuries old, but never before had it been so pronounced. Everywhere the more important employers, to whom commercial and industrial growth offered previously unknown opportunities for accumulation of capital, tightened their grip on small producers.

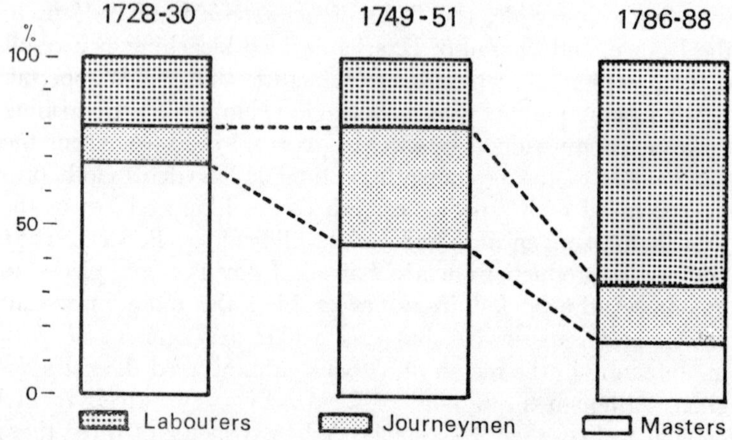

Fig. 14 Professional classification of the Lyonese silkweavers, according to their marriage contracts, by percentages, 1728–88.

Note. As the actual number of masters more than doubled between 1739 and 1786, the declining percentage of master silkweavers registering themselves at marriage as such reflects a growing consciousness of socio-economic degradation.

Source: based on M. Garden, *Lyon et les Lyonnais au XVIIIe siècle* (Paris, 1970), pp. 282–3.

In the Lyonese silk industry the old opposition between merchants and guildsmen was settled in the course of the eighteenth century completely in favour of the former. At the end of the *ancien régime*, the top of urban society consisted of some 350 merchant-manufacturers, who provided work for some 6,000 *façonniers*, or master silkweavers, who, although they bore the title 'master' and often owned the means of production, were completely controlled by the former. The *façonniers*, in turn employed 12,000 apprentices, journeymen, and their womenfolk, along with some 10,000 unskilled day-labourers, who made up no part of the guild. Socio-economic differences between the master silkweavers and their journeymen by this time had become minimal; both groups had in fact been degraded to wage labourers employed by the capitalist merchants. The fundamental dividing line was no longer between *façonniers* and dependent workers, but the opposition between capital and labour. The 'middle class' was eliminated: two-thirds of all guildsmen, regardless of their legal status, had been reduced to a common position, somewhere between poverty and middling status. The proportion of 'masters' registering themselves at marriage as such declined from 69 per cent in 1728–30 to 17 per cent in 1786–88 (Figure 14). Around 1780 the guildsmen thought of themselves as 'slaves' of the wholesale dealers, who remunerated them almost arbitrarily. Subsequent wage disputes united all silk workers – masters, journeymen, apprentices, and the unskilled – against the 'despotic' capitalists. When the master silk-weaver Denis Monnet looked back in 1791 at the strike of 1786, he wrote:

> The shameful avarice or, better said, the greed of the merchant-manufacturers of this town finally brought the *master craftsmen* to despair; unable to support themselves even by toiling night and day, they turned to the authorities; but they were one and all merchants and rejected petitions and protests. The workers decided to produce material at a price which they themselves would set, *in order to make a living from their labour.*

The movement accomplished nothing. Government troops restored order, and five days after the outbreak of trouble the foremost 'mischief-makers' were hanged. The Revolution changed little or nothing. In contrast, merchant-manufacturers profited from the economic slump to strengthen their 'tyranny'.

Brugge fustian weavers were allotted a like fate. Only a small number of merchants were in a state to buy large quantities of cotton on the international market. When profits on the sale of fustians began to fall as a result of English and northern German competition, the merchants tried to gain control of the manufacturing process in order to ensure their profitable trade in cotton. With the *baratto* system – sale of cotton for delivery of fustians at a future date – and the establishment of maximum prices for finished fabrics, they succeeded. The once independent manufacturers were slowly but surely reduced to wage labourers. By 1779, more than 70 per cent of master fustian weavers had to be supported regularly by the poor-law administration. Most serious of all, the dominance of commercial capital blocked the rise of a cotton industry at Brugge, since the merchants employed no technological innovations.

In other urban industries, the guild system was attacked from the inside, often with the support of the authorities. At Brugge, for example, social differentiation among linen weavers was initially fostered by the lax attitude of the magistracy in respect of adherence to guild regulations. When the magistrates allowed manufacturers to use an unlimited number of looms during the 1750s there was anarchy. In 1734 two-thirds of the master linen weavers declared that their apprentices had defected to better-off employers; small producers were forced either to fill their orders or to perform wage labour. Although the town government later revised its attitude and limited the number of looms per master to ten, the tendency was not to be reversed. The new ordinance was easily evaded: poor masters, seemingly independent manufacturers, in reality worked for large employers, to whom they surrendered their entire production. At the end of the century, twenty capitalists dominated the Brugge linen weavers; some of them owned more than fifty looms. This development brought apprentices no relief. Certainly, the larger employers paid higher wages initially than did smaller ones, but from the moment the former excluded the latter, they could do as they chose with their labour force. The answer henceforth to wage demands was the lockout.

Nor did Antwerp's linen weavers escape proletarianization. In 1725 they declared that some of them, despite all guild regulations, owned more than ten looms, so that the rest were left behind. Although the magistracy determined in the following year that any one linen weaver might dispose of at most six looms, small masters in fact lost the battle. The new ordinance had no bearing on the producers of mixed fabrics. Jan van der Smissen, dean of the linen weavers, could actually extend his business without limits: he manufactured material made of cotton and linen. In 1761 he employed in his workshop forty-two labourers and placed orders with 341 domestic workers. Three years later he and five other capitalists together owned 350 looms; around 3,000 workers depended on them. Meanwhile, most small producers had given up their trades. In 1764 Antwerp numbered only twenty master linen weavers, employing 250 workers, whereas in 1738 there had been 64 masters, 140 journeymen, 15 apprentices and 500 unskilled workers. Other Antwerp industries underwent similar developments. The final result was always the same: proletarianization and impoverishment. At the end of the century, the deans of the cloth dressers' guild summarized the consequences of industrial concentration: 'The

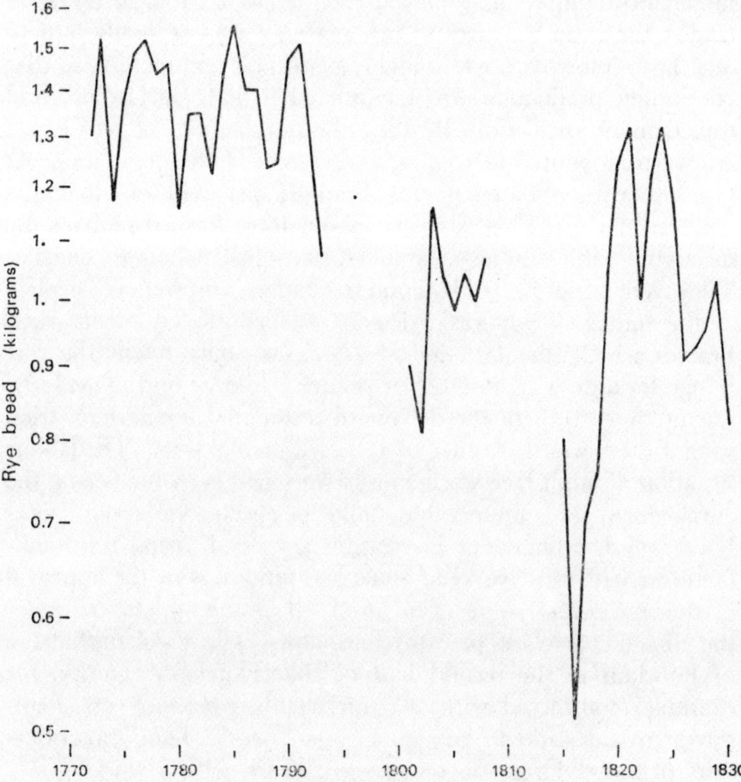

Fig. 15 Average daily wages, converted into kilograms of rye bread, of laceworkers in Antwerp, 1772–1830.

Source: calculated from C. Lis, *Verarmingsprocessen te Antwerpen, 1750–1850* (4 vols, unpublished Ph.D. thesis, Brussels, 1975), III, pp. 110–16.

Note. In 1795–96, laceworkers represented 40 per cent of the total number of employed women; in 1830, the proportion had declined to 20 per cent.

factories of this town accomplish nothing other than enrichment of a few and impoverishment of innumerable widows and children.'[23]

It was no accident that the lace industry gained in importance during the eighteenth century: no other activity seemed more suited to women and children. The circulating capital of the merchant-manufacturers played such a crucial role in no other trade: the ratio of wages to raw material was generally four to one. Lace, moreover, was a highly perishable commodity, so that continuing production was guaranteed so long as fashion, and thus demand, held firm. By 1750 the number of lace workers at Antwerp amounted to 10,000, 25 per cent of the population. At Caen they represented no less than 84 per cent of all textile workers in 1792. This extensive labour force formed perhaps the most vulnerable and most exploited part of the whole proletariat. They were not protected by guild regulations and were completely at the mercy of wholesale dealers who controlled the market. Besides which, the lace industry was in many towns the sole refuge for a growing number of women, children and the elderly, unemployed through the decline of traditional textile industries, so that there was no chance to get a reasonable wage. The labour situation of adult lace workers was worsened even further by the employment of innumerable child paupers. Numerous poorhouses and orphanages incessantly provided merchant-manufacturers with new workers. Some institutions, with the approval of the authorities, were even fitted up as *manufactures*, under the direct control of private contractors. The girls' orphanage of Potsdam in the second half of the eighteenth century, for example, contracted with two merchants who took on themselves to train 200 to 300 girls in lace work. The 'apprenticeship' of the children was set at seven years, with a working day of nine hours. For five years they had to work without pay; thereafter they received one-sixth of the usual wage. No wonder that profits were particularly high! In the *dépôt de mendicité* of Beaulieu in France, where women and children continuously made lace for merchant-manufacturers, net monthly profits amounted to an average of 138 per cent in the years 1773–75. All these factors reduced the price of 'free' labour to essentially nil. By 1800, daily wages of skilled lace workers at Antwerp (Figure 15) equalled a single kilogram of ryebread, and, not surprisingly, more than half of the women supported by the Antwerp poor-law administration were lace workers.

3. Pauperization and migrations

The labouring poor

Although reliable statistical information is scarce, there can be no doubt that poverty in eighteenth-century European towns and country rose to levels previously unknown. Based on the *enquêtes* of the *Comité de Mendicité* and on Lavoisier's *De la richesse territoriale du Royaume de France*, Alfred Soboul estimated the extent of the proletariat and semi-proletariat in rural France around 1790 at about 40 per cent, all of whom can be considered poor, most destitute. They had no land, or too little to support a family, and their meagre incomes depended on numerous uncertainties. A poor harvest chased food prices sky high and diminished the demand for agricultural labour, so that their budget was doubly affected. In most cases serious dearth caused the collapse of textile manufacture, with the result that all those living off cottage industry encountered underemployment or even total unemployment. Numerous monographs show that the transition from poverty to destitution was only a single step for rural labourers and *manouvriers*. In the (later) *département du Nord*, around 1790, the indigent comprised some 20 per cent of the population; in Brittany, it was in the order of 20 to 25 per cent; in the mountain communities of the Pyrenees, even 30 to 40 per cent.

The urban proletariat expanded just as strongly. In Strasbourg, the proportion of wage labourers rose from 29 per cent at the end of the seventeenth century to 45 per cent in 1784, and in Sedan, where linen manufacturing was characterized by guild organization until the early eighteenth century, they made up no less than 46 per cent of the total population by 1789. Other centres witnessed a similar proletarianization process. On the eve of the Revolution, wage labourers represented 48 per cent of the inhabitants of Troyes, 50 per cent in Nantes, and 60 per cent in Elbeuf. The poverty of this social category is hardly contestable. At Elbeuf in the 1790s wage labourers made up only 8 per cent of all landowners and controlled scarcely 4 per cent of total wealth. Around the same time, nearly half of the population of Toulouse owned nothing at marriage besides some furniture and other household goods of little value. Their inheritances indicate that the married lives of the lower classes seldom or never allowed them to improve their situation. On the contrary, most wage labourers and servants left only debts behind, and those who surprised their heirs with a surplus disposed of less than 1 per cent of urban wealth. How could it be otherwise? The increasingly dominant role played by capital in manufacturing, by the disintegration of the guild system, and by the uninterrupted flood of uprooted country dwellers, worsened systematically the vulnerability and the dependence of urban workers. Those employed in important export industries, moreover, were at the mercy of the smallest oscillations of the market as international competition grew increasingly sharper. As the ecclesiastics of Lyon said in May 1789:

> The prosperity of our silk industry, famed throughout Europe, depends upon a thousand circumstances. Now a royal mourning, then the prince who forbids imports, or the war or disorder which diminishes demand; or, lack of silk and other raw materials halts production. Today, 60,000 workers do not suffice, tomorrow 20,000 are too many.

They knew of what they spoke: from 1689 to 1791, the Lyonese silk industry passed through seventeen crises, combining generalized unemployment and severe destitution. These crises verify that the poor must be defined as those without savings. During the dearth of 1709, for example, the magistracy of Lyon was obliged to support 67,160 citizens, 77 per cent of the inhabitants. The more the craftsmen were dominated by capitalists, the more vulnerable they were. By 1790, around 39 per cent of adult workers in France, according to the *Comité de Mendicité*, earned just enough during 'normal' years to cover their needs. For a family of five, this signified a daily ration of bread of no more than three kilograms.

In the course of the eighteenth century the French elite began to equate wage labour and poverty. Following Linguet, lawyer and publicist, the people consisted of 'all those without property, fixed income, rents, or salaries, living from wages when they suffice or suffering when wages are too small; they starve when wages are lacking'. Clicquot de Blervache gave the succinct formula: 'labour is the sole inheritance of the people. They must work or beg'. The most penetrating analysis was made by Necker: 'That group within society whose lot seems to be perpetuated by the effect of social laws is composed of all those who, living off hand labour, submit to the imperative law of the owners and are compelled to satisfy themselves with a wage commensurate with the bare necessities of life.'

These witnesses were not mistaken. Systematic study of marriage contracts in the *Faubourg* Saint-Antoine of Paris shows 30 per cent of a total population estimated at 43,000 were not able to conclude a contract and that 56 per cent of those contracting were wage labourers, plus some artisans. Forty years later, one in three in this ward had to be supported, three times more than the average for Paris as a whole. Another example: by 1776, wage labourers, servants excluded, formed 31 per cent of the population of Amiens, all exempt from taxation on account of their poverty. One must consider this an underestimate, since numerous seasonal labourers and unmarried and unemployed immigrants remained unregistered. In Lyon, finally, eighteenth-century silk workers represented no less than 65 to 70 per cent of the poor receiving relief.[24]

In central Europe, poverty grew to be a mass phenomenon. It has recently been demonstrated that by the end of the eighteenth century more than 80 per cent of rural inhabitants in western Germany and 60 per cent east of the Elbe had to earn a living by wage labour or domestic industry, due to the minimal extent of their holdings and the enormous weight of surplus extraction – often as high as 40 per cent of gross production. Although the poverty of the masses cannot yet be quantitatively measured, numerous contemporary witnesses indicate that the vast majority permanently lived at subsistence minima. So long as grain prices stayed low and employment was not threatened, most landless or nearly landless could more or less make ends meet, but a bad harvest or temporary unemployment automatically led to hopeless misery. When both came together death followed. During the famine of 1771–73, around 60,000 starved to death in Saxony, some 6 per cent of the population. Areas with the greatest concentrations of proto-industrial workers were the most severely affected: in mountainous areas 8 to 9 per cent of the inhabitants, compared with 2.5 per cent in Lower Lusatia, where a peasantry in the real sense still dominated. At the same time, in the countryside around Zürich no less than 42,000, 31 per cent of the population, lived in extreme need, not counting supported needy. In the mountainous Oberland, where linen manufacture formed the sole means of existence for the bulk of the population, misery was even more pronounced. By 1790, around 40 per cent of villagers in this proto-industrial area were considered poor by the authorities. The urban population was little better off. During the last quarter of the eighteenth century, the *Unterschichten* – wage labourers, servants, and small craftsmen living at or under the poverty line – represented 30 to 40 per cent of the population of Bonn, Coblenz, and Mainz and even 50 per cent of Basel. Everywhere, total destitution was the lot of one in two of the poor. The large towns numbered even more destitute families: in Cologne 24 per cent of the inhabitants were beggars, and in Berlin one-third regularly called on public support.[25]

Statistical information on poverty in the Southern Netherlands in the second half of the eighteenth century scarcely exists, but some figures illustrate the rural situation. In two Brabant villages, Overijse and Bierges, 23.5 per cent and 41.5 per cent of the families around 1750 received relief. According to contemporaries, misery in other rural areas was at least as great as in Brabant. In 1762 the Estates of Limburg declared that innumerable weavers were compelled to abandon the countryside or to beg. Four years later, the government allowed rural labourers in Luxemburg to emigrate, since they could not find means of subsistance in their homeland. In 1765, the authorities of the Land van Waas complained in despair of the growing number of 'deserving' poor. Taking account of the extreme fragmentation of landholdings and the near total dependence of country-dwellers on cottage industry in many districts, these verdicts seem in no sense exaggerated.

There is no lack of reliable data on the urban indigent. With two exceptions, however, they all relate to people being supported, so that they are of limited use. Such evidence shows that one part of the population was in such distress that it could not live without public assistance (Table 9). The cases of Antwerp

Table 9.

The supported needy as percentage of total population in selected cities of the Southern Netherlands, 1755–94.

Town	*Year*	*Supported needy* *% of the total population*	*Needy*
Antwerp	1755	7–8	
	1773	11	
	1787–9	13	20–22
Brussels	1755	7	
Leuven	1755	22	
Ath	1772	8	
Mons	1794	12–13	
Tournai	1794	12–13	
Mechelen	1794	13	26

Sources: calculated from Lis, *Verarmingsprocessen*, III, pp. 39–40; L. van Buyten, 'De ellendingen in de moderne bronnen der Zuidelijke Nederlanden', *Tijdschrift voor Geschiedenis, 88* (1975), p. 540; M. van der Auwera, *Funkties en implikaties van openbare ondersteuningsmechanismen te Mechelen, 16e–18e eeuw* (unpublished M.A. thesis, Ghent, 1976), pp. 82–6.

and Mechelen show that the total number of needy lay much higher than the number of those on relief. In the late 1780s only 13 per cent of the population of Antwerp received support, although the poor-law administration estimated the number of needy at 20 to 22 per cent, and at Mechelen in 1794 only 2,810 of the 21,557 inhabitants were registered for public maintenance, although the town government counted 5,543 'poor'. How can this discrepancy be explained? Restricted by chronic lack of funds, the poor relief had to make a choice. The structural imbalance between the number of those seeking relief on one side and the finances available obliged charitable institutions either to assist properly a few needy or to give many a mere pittance. Usually the poor-law administration opted for the second 'remedy', but if the number of needy continued to rise, this policy became insupportable. At Antwerp in the 1780s, for example, an aged person without means of subsistence received the monetary equivalent of 2 to 2.5 kg of rye bread. After subtraction of necessary expenditures for rent and fuel, the beneficiary during normal years could buy less than 1½ kg of rye bread per day. Any further diminution of this mercy ration was out of the question. Hence, the poor-law administration of Antwerp turned to the other 'remedy': stricter selection. Until 1798 a needy family with two children could lodge a claim for public support. In 1799 the minimum number of children was raised to three, in 1823 to four, and in 1837 to five, when it was further stipulated that all children had to be younger than twelve and that the head of household could earn no more than 1.65 francs a day, the equivalent of 6 to 7 kg rye bread. This did not imply that all other needy families were left to their fates; it signified, however, that they were transferred by the poor-law administration to the *secours casuel* or to the *secours accidentel.* In the former, they still received support during the winter, in the latter, only during exceptional circumstances such as famine. In short, increasingly more needy were struck off official poor lists, and a sort of 'recruitment reserve' arose.

Does the number of *needy* registered by the poor-law administration correspond to the number of *poor*? The answer depends on the definition of poverty: yes, if one labelled a person as poor who could not cover the most essential daily needs; no, if one applied the concept to all who disposed of nothing more than their labour. The latter implied that the poor at the end of the *ancien régime* represented no less than two-thirds of the Antwerp population; this figure closely mirrors reality, for more than half of the inhabitants during the last quarter of the eighteenth century were engaged in textile manufacturing, and nearly 79 per cent of these textile workers were totally propertyless; they formed the greatest part of the population on relief: 40 to 50 per cent of adult men, 69 per cent of adult women, 90 per cent of children. The family's life-cycle determined whether or not the wage labourer at any one moment was eligible for public support. The number of children, their age and their health were of crucial importance, not poverty as such, since the majority were poor. Hence the bulk of the supported needy nearly everywhere consisted of children, widows, and the aged, ill, and infirm, individuals who due to their sex or weak physical condition could not earn the wages of a healthy, adult worker or who could not work at all. As E. Buret asked rhetorically in the Paris of 1836: 'Must they, before registration on the poor list, be in such need that they be in utter distress, in a horrifying state where one more privation, no matter how small, would send them beyond the limits of physical and emotional endurance?'[26]

The same was true in England. The only reasonably detailed data on the number of assisted paupers available are those in the *Abstract of Returns Relative to the Relief of the Poor* of 1802–03, following which one million persons, or 11 per cent of the total population of England and Wales, received public support. Although this census was as incomplete as it was inaccurate – paupers *inside* local poorhouses were not counted, while those who petitioned two or three times a year for support were probably registered more than once – two important conclusions emerge. First, the number of *supported needy* in England and Wales in 'ordinary' years was of the same order as in other western European countries. Second, this specific category was predominently composed of the physically weak, just as on the Continent: roughly 50 per cent of all those regularly receiving outdoor relief were children under fifteen, and 9 to 20 per cent aged, sick, and lame. The actual number of needy may thus perhaps be doubled. In any case, pauperism here too took on greater proportions in the course of the eighteenth century. Approximate expenses for poor relief *per capita* of the population rose from scarcely two shillings around 1700 to nine or ten shillings in 1802–03; the latter amount was just sufficient to support a family of four or five for one month. Since the cost of living during this period only doubled, it does not seem absurd to suppose that the needy as a percentage of the total population in the early nineteenth century lay two to three times higher than one hundred years earlier. Besides, it is truly remarkable that the English intelligentsia, just as their French counterparts, ever more frequently used the term 'poor' to describe someone who owned only his labour. Patrick Colquhoun, a friend of Adam Smith, was not alone in drawing that sharp distinction between poverty, 'the state of everyone who must labour for his subsistence', and need, the state of everyone whose labour fell short of his maintenance. Coleridge further emphasized the close relationship between the poor and the workers, 'whom by an ominous but too appropriate change in our phraseology, we are now accustomed to call the labouring poor'.[27]

To calculate levels of impoverishment during the *ancien régime* and the nineteenth century, many historians employ wage series and cost-of-living indices. This method provides indisputably valuable indications of changes in the maximum real incomes to be earned by particular categories, chiefly adult men employed full-time, but it does not allow study of their actual living standards, let alone the budget of their family or the average earnings of the working population as a whole. As T. S. Ashton wrote: 'We require not a single index but many, each derived from retail prices, each confined to a short run of years, each relating to a single area, perhaps to a single social or occupational group within an area.' Even then, the problems are not solved. It does not suffice to know the wage of the head of the household; one must also be informed of the wages of wife and children. Further, it is absolutely necessary to dispose of information concerning underemployment, since these variables can make theoretically acceptable incomes a mere caricature. Finally, attention must be given to long-term changes in the structure of expenditures. Gradual transition to other types of food and clothing, use of new fuels, and changes in housing conditions can deeply influence the cost-of-living index. If these conditions are not fulfilled there is a real danger that wage data will be completely misinterpreted. The example of Antwerp indicates this sufficiently. By 1850 real wages of adult males averaged only 5 to 10 per cent lower than around 1780, yet a massive impoverishment process took place in this period: *per capita* consumption of grain, meat, salted fish, and beer dropped by 20 per cent, 22 per cent, 49 per cent, and 57 per cent respectively. The explanation must be sought in a combination of two factors. First, the collapse of the traditional textile industry condemned thousands of women and children to unemployment. In the second quarter of the nineteenth century Antwerp counted only 37 per cent of women employed in one or another industry, compared with 56 per cent at the end of the *ancien régime*. Dwindling demand for women's labour in turn resulted in a sharp diminution of wages: in the 1850s, real wages amounted at most to 70 per cent of earlier levels. Simultaneously the need for child labour disappeared; children under fourteen could earn a living in just a few economic sectors after 1820. Secondly, rents rose between 1780 and 1850 by no less than 135 per cent. Although the poor attempted to cope with this dramatic price rise by moving to the cheapest possible housing, they were obliged to devote a steadily greater part of their budget for rent: 30 per cent around 1850, where seventy years earlier it had been 14 per cent. In conclusion, according to the composition of the family, the real incomes of the working population dropped by 10 to 30 per cent, while twice as much had to be expended for rent.[28]

The quantity and the kinds of food consumed are perhaps the best criteria by which to measure objectively the standard of living of a pre-industrial population; statistical data on long-term changes in the *per capita* food basket during the eighteenth century and first half of the nineteenth are still too fragmentary, however, to draw decisive conclusions. The large-scale expansion of 'poverty-cultures' indicates, nonetheless, massive

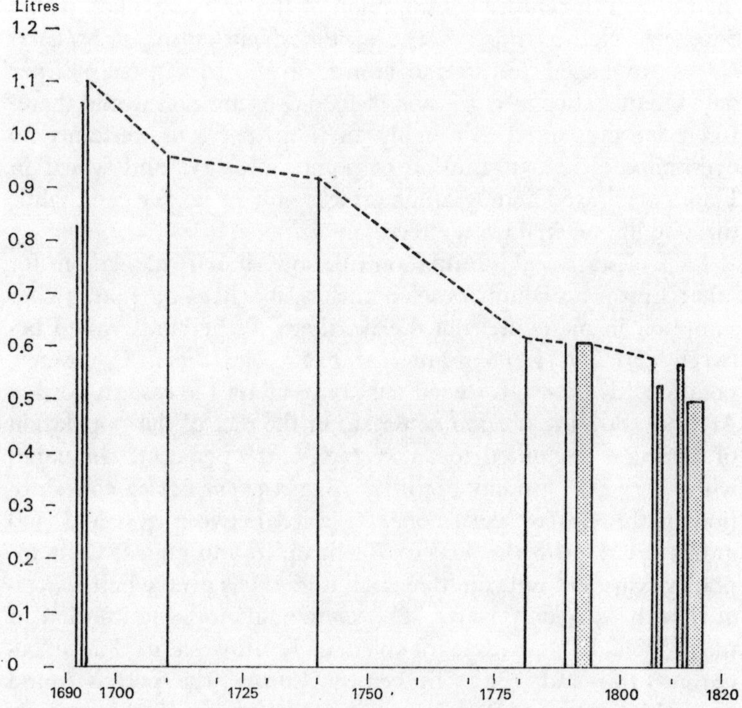

Fig. 16 The decline of average *per capita* grain consumption in rural Flanders, 1692–1816.

Source: based on C. Vandenbroeke, *Agriculture et alimentation dans les Pays-Bas autrichiens* (Ghent and Leuven, 1975), p. 257.

impoverishment, for, as Michel Morineau remarked, 'to be forced to feed on maize instead of wheat, on potatoes instead of rye or, in some areas like Brittany, buckwheat signified a loss of standing, a loss to be delayed as long as possible.'

In every country of western and central Europe, potato cultivation expanded impressively in the century after 1750. Until around 1740, *per capita* grain consumption in the Southern Netherlands varied between 0.9 and 1 litre *per diem*. Thereafter, a spectacular decrease took hold: nearly 40 per cent between 1740 and 1790, and another 10 per cent in the period 1790 to 1814. This implied a diminution of 650 to 800 calories per person per day. Concomitant extension of potato cultivation, however, offered partial compensation. By the second decade of the nineteenth century consumption of the 'miracle tuber' in the Southern Netherlands, excepting the *département des Deux-Nèthes*, averaged 700 to 750 grams, or 490 to 525 calories per day. Quantitative retrogression of food consumption would therefore have amounted to roughly 20 to 40 per cent, certainly no overestimate, for substitution of potatoes for rye and wheat in Flanders allowed demographic growth only of 30 per cent, while the population in fact doubled.

Lack of statistical information rules out similar calculations for other European countries. Nonetheless, in 1812–13, potato consumption in many areas of the Northern Netherlands varied between 500 and 1,200 grams *per capita per diem*. In France, potato cultivation broadened out above all on the eastern border. Around 1801 the portion of potato in the diet of the population of Lorraine amounted to an average of 18 per cent, compared with 5 per cent around 1750. By 1812–13, *per capita* consumption in the eastern *départements* varied between 300 and 500 grams per day; in the Vosges, it ran up to 700 grams. Contemporary witnesses indicate that such a diet was everywhere associated with extreme poverty. The same holds for consumption of maize, which more than doubled in south-western France between 1750 and 1840. In central Europe the potato found general acceptance after the catastrophic famine of 1771–73. By the early nineteenth century, 300,000 ha. were already planted with potatoes, some 1.5 per cent of total arable of Germany, yielding a daily *per capita* 200 grams. In the following decades, total production quintupled. Potatoes grew to be the pre-eminent food of the lower classes. Friedrich List, the famous political economist, wrote in 1844: 'Among the most basic necessities are included in many areas of Germany potatoes without salt, a soup with black bread . . ., oatmeal porridge, and, here and there, dark dumplings . . . I have seen areas where one herring . . . during the meal went from hand to hand to give everyone . . . a bit of flavour for his potatoes.'

In Ireland, the Hebrides and the Scottish Highlands, bread corn had been totally exchanged for potatoes by the early nineteenth century. According to some authors, daily consumption of this 'wholesome root' reached ten to twelve pounds *per capita* in Ireland. The extraordinary significance of the potato for the poor cannot be doubted in these areas. Sir John Sinclair, Scots agronomist and writer, voiced a general opinion when he noted in 1812: 'It is difficult to conceive how the people of this country could have subsisted had it not been for the fortunate introduction and extensive cultivation of this most valuable plant.' In England, finally, the potato ration rose between 1775 and 1795 from 200 to 400 grams daily *per capita*. During the first half of the nineteenth century, 'the lowest species of human food', as Caird later described it, increased its importance. G. R. Porter, declared in 1851: 'Unless in years of scarcity no part of the inhabitants of England except perhaps in the extreme north, and there only partially, have no recourse to rye or barley bread, but a larger and increasing number are in a great measure fed upon potatoes.'[29]

Some estimates of average *per capita* food consumption at the end of the *ancien régime* are available. Though they are too scarce to allow generalizations, these data show the great handicap of all 'averages': they tell us nothing about the actual food basket of different social classes. Yet, even such abstractions can be instructive.

Around 1800 every inhabitant of the Southern Netherlands theoretically disposed of the daily rations shown in Table 10. From the quantitative perspective this diet would suffice. The daily needs of a family of five (two labouring adults and three children of three, six and twelve) may be estimated at 10,900 to 12,200 calories, or 2,180 to 2,440 per person. However, it is not enough merely to consider the proper amount of calories; account must also be taken of the chemical composition of foods. Most specialists agree that a balanced diet consists of 15 per cent proteins, 25 to 30 per cent fats, and 55 to 60 per cent carbohydrates; moreover, they emphasize the essential importance of animal proteins, which contain every necessary amino acid. In general, it is accepted that for adults at least one-third of proteins

Table 10.

Average Diet in Southern Netherlands, *c.* 1800.

Foodstuffs	*Consumption per capita and per diem*				
	Quantity	*Number of calories*	*Constituents (in grams)*		
			Proteins	*Fats*	*Carbohydrates*
Bread*	500 grams	1,250	35.3	14.6	257.9
Potatoes	700 grams	490	11.4	0.5	106
Meat	27 grams	60	5.0	4.5	–
Butter	27 grams	205	0.1	22.7	–
Cheese	1 gram	3	0.2	0.1	–
Fish	6 grams	13	2.5	1.1	–
Sugar	5 grams	17	–	–	4.4
Syrup	3 grams	7	–	–	–
Rice	1 gram	3	–	–	–
Eggs	0.137	10	0.8	0.7	–
Milk	0.082 litres	5	2.7	3	3.8
Buttermilk	0.411 litres	122	12.2	1.5	14.0
Vegetables	0.030 litres	45	3.0	0.2	7.5
Total		2,230	73.2	48.9	393.6
Beer	0.500 litres	225	or	or	or
Gin	0.016 litres	45			
Wine	0.012 litres	8	14%	10%	76%
Grand Total		2,508			

Source: based on the table in Vandenbroeke, *Agriculture*, p. 593.
* Mixed loaves consisting of 2/3 rye and 1/3 wheat.

must be of animal origins, and for children more than half. Keeping these proportions in mind, it is clear that the average diet in the Southern Netherlands at the end of the *ancien régime* was in large measure deficient. The consumption of animal proteins amounted to scarcely twenty-four grams, or one-third of the total, and the number of calories provided by fats was completely insufficient. Add the imbalance of calcium and phosphates, the near total absence of vitamin A, and the gross shortage of vitamin D, and it becomes clear why so many children died between nine months and three years, why the bone structure of innumerable survivors was malformed, and why numerous adults suffered from serious eye diseases. Just as in some of the developing countries today, people in the eighteenth century died not so much directly from hunger as from illness due to malnutrition.

The fundamental question remains unanswered: how many inhabitants of the Southern Netherlands 'enjoyed' this average food basket around 1800? Some approximations show that the lower classes were in no state to provide for themselves the bulk of the indicated foods. Taking Antwerp's labouring poor as an example, Table 11 shows the wages of two families of five, earning nineteen and eleven stivers per day respectively.

Table 11

Wages of two Antwerp families, earning respectively 19 and 11 stivers per day, *c.* 1800.

Family members	Type one		Type two	
	Occupation	Daily wage (stivers)	Occupation	Daily wage (stivers)
Father	Masons' labourer	12	Textile worker	6
Mother	Seamstress	4	Lace-maker	2
1st child	Textile worker	2	Textile worker	2
2nd child	Textile worker	1	Textile worker	1
3rd child	–	–	–	–
Total		19		11

Source: Lis, *Verarmingsprocessen*, III, pp. 100–18; IV, pp. 215–19.

These wages represent the common level of remuneration at Antwerp during the last quarter of the eighteenth century. Optimistically supposing that each family member could find work 270 days a year, their joint incomes amounted to 5,130 and 2,970 stivers per year. Incidentally, from an analysis of the Antwerp 'poor lists', it appears that an 'average' working family of five had an income around 1780 of 3,460 stivers per year, including possible support from poor relief. Since expenses for rent and fuel took at least 20 per cent of their budgets, the two 'typical families' of Table 11 could devote some 4,100 and 2,380 stivers to foodstuffs, whereas to feed them the whole year through with the 'average' food basket (without alcoholic drink) some 5,500 stivers were required. Even in the most favourable circumstances (low prices and full employment), the incomes of both 'typical families' fell far short of the sum necessary to purchase all mentioned foodstuffs, type one by 25 per cent, type two by no less than 57 per cent. How was the diet of the labouring poor in fact constituted? Table 12 gives the answer, showing what foodstuffs, plus calorie equivalents, each 'typical family' could purchase after subtraction of daily expenses.

Table 12

Purchasing power of two Antwerp families, *c.* 1800.

Food stuffs	Type one		Type two	
	Quantity (in grams)	Number of calories	Quantity (in grams)	Number of calories
Ryebread	7,640	14,590	4,440	8,480
Potatoes	20,740	14,520	12,040	8,425
Meat	1,210	2,730	700	1,585
Butter	1,100	8,240	640	4,785
Cheese	1,575	4,410	915	2,560
Fish	3,025	7,045	1,755	4,090

Clearly, the lower classes depended almost exclusively on rye bread and potatoes. A mason's labourer's family could buy some meat or cheese in addition to this poverty diet, but only on condition that all members of the family worked 270 days a year and that food prices stayed low. As for the textile worker, he was never able to provide his family a proper quantity of rye bread or potatoes; their *per capita* subsistence ration consisted of scarcely 1,700 calories. The validity of this figure is beyond dispute: in 1814, the Antwerp poor-law administration decided that a poor widower with three children to support must be able to make do with something more than a half kg of potatoes, exactly a half kg of rye bread, and 22 g of fat per person per day, the equivalent of 1,510 calories in all. But misery had not yet reached its zenith. The alarming way in which the living standards of the poorest part of the population of Antwerp were affected during the first half of the nineteenth century appears clearly from a comparison of the average *per capita* consumption of calories of regularly supported families in 1780 and 1850, two years of low prices. The methods used were as follows. The wages of all family members were combined and supplemented with the aid provided by poor relief. The families and their total incomes were then divided according to the number of family members. Subsequently the average amount paid for rent was subtracted

Table 13
Average calorie intake *per capita* and *per diem* of supported Antwerp poor, 1780 and 1850.

Number of Family members	Number of Calories *per capita* and *per diem* 1780	1850	Percentage shift
1	3,765	1,863	− 50.5
2	3,342	1,863	− 44.2
3	2,365	1,806	− 23.8
4	2,145	1,503	− 28.7
5	2,106	1,177	− 44.1
6	1,819	1,385	− 23.9
7	1,883	1,653	− 12.2
8	1,641	1,530	− 6.8
9	1,886	1,560	− 17.3
10	1,594	1,395	− 12.5

Source: C. Lis and H. Soly, 'Food Consumption', *loc. cit.*, p. 479.

from average family income, relief included, after which the remaining sum was converted to the food that provided the highest number of calories per price unit, namely rye bread in 1780 and potatoes in 1850. Quite simply, in the mid nineteenth century Antwerp's paupers lived on the edge of starvation. Even if they did not spend a single penny on fuel and clothing they still went hungry, and a diet of potatoes meant a severe lack of animal proteins, fats, and vitamins A and D. No wonder the medical commission appointed by the authorities in 1844 noted that 'many workers are below normal height and have bones not of the usual rectitude'. Similar declarations were lodged in many Belgian towns, irrespective of their specific economic functions. In Ghent, an important industrial town, and in Brussels, a centre of handicraft production and administration, the decline of *per capita* grain, meat, and beer consumption was of the same order as in Antwerp. In short, potatoes, coffee and other marginal food-stuffs seem to have represented the limited gains which the labouring poor drew from economic growth during the first half of the nineteenth century.

How did they survive? Statistics cannot solve this problem; too many details are lacking, while the sources for others are incomplete or untrustworthy. Moreover, numerous phenomena escape us because they left no visible traces. One needs only to think of mutual assistance. Some aspects of this important remedy can actually be measured, such as the dwelling together of the aged or widows, or of parents with their married children, but most cannot be quantified for the simple reason that they were unregistered. If one wants to form an idea of the daily struggle of the lower classes simply to exist, then one must call on qualitative source materials. Besides the famous reports of such observers as Henry Mayhew, L. R. Villermé, and Eduard Ducpétiaux, letters written by paupers themselves provide invaluable information. They reveal that help from family or neighbours preceded by far any call on the poor relief, and that public institutions were petitioned only in extreme need. Reading these poignant sketches, written almost phonetically, is of the greatest importance in gaining any insight into the 'humiliation-consciousness' of the lower classes. Again and again one notes how much they were ashamed of their destitution. Often they avoided going to church or sending their children to school because they, lacking 'acceptable' clothing, could not be seen as 'human beings'. Many felt that they lived like pigs, for, as one Antwerp pauper expressed it, 'with six in a bed, it looks that way'. Let us give the last word to the Lyonese silk workers of 1780, who exclaimed desperately:

> How did we survive? Ask the many masters who *have* emigrated or were reduced to beggars. Ask in the hospitals where our abandoned children piled up day after day, despite the protests of nature. Ask those who lost savings and inheritance. And if you want an even better understanding of how we managed to eke out our wretched lives until today, come into our workshops. You'll see workers exerting themselves for eighteen or nineteen hours a day, working continuously, without breaking for holidays of Sundays. You'll see them exhausted refusing food or revelling in the rich man's garbage and forever economizing on even the least needs. You'll see them clothed in rags, living in decaying slums. *That* is how so many of us have survived.[30]

Simply rhetoric? All available evidence points to the opposite. The *Hôpital des Enfants-Trouvés* of Paris in the early 1770s received nearly twenty-five times as many abandoned infants than one hundred years earlier: in 1670, 312; in 1772, 7,676 (Figure 17). Other French towns witnessed the same tragedy. In 1790 the number of foundlings at Clermont was two and a half times higher than in the 1740s, and the hospital of Rennes took in three times more abandoned children in 1782 than in 1774. Most

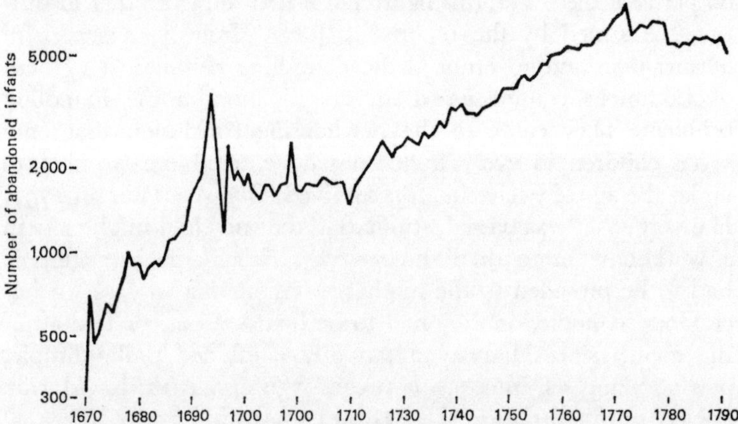

Fig. 17 Number of abandoned infants admitted into the *Hôpital des Enfants-Trouvés* of Paris, 1670–1791.

Source: C. Delasselle, 'Les enfants abandonnés à Paris au XVIIIe siècle', *Annales. Economies. Sociétés. Civilisations*, 30 (1975), p. 189.

provincial institutions were no match for the continuing increase of foundlings, due to their limited finances. They refused to lodge children, or they transported them to Paris in groups. Many parents even paid the transporters who made their living off this traffic to bring babies to the capital. Hence, an average of 20 to 30 per cent of the children received by the Foundling Hospital of Paris came from the provinces. From numerous witnesses it appears that some parents lived in such misery that they had to relieve themselves once and for all of their new, unbearable burden. Others apparently cherished the hope of taking back their children after a few years – presumably from the moment that these burdens would be able to earn their daily bread. They deluded themselves over the protection offered by this 'temporary *dépôt*'. Altogether, nine out of ten children died during the journey to the capital or within three months after reception into the hospital, while the *survivors* had only one chance in ten of reaching an age of ten to twelve.

In England there was no difference. In 1756 the authorities concluded that the London Foundling Hospital could no longer refuse any children under two months. Within forty-six months, around 15,000 babies were brought to the Hospital; more than 68 per cent died. Yet, this figure paralleled those of other institutions. Alarmed by the reports of Jonas Hanway, a successful businessman and governor of the Foundling Hospital, the House of Commons commissioned an investigation of the foundling problem. They came to the bewildering conclusion that only seven children in every hundred who entered the workhouses under the age of twelve months survived. One year later, in 1757, Hanway's Act was passed, stipulating that no child might stay in a workhouse more than three weeks; either sufficient support had to be provided to the mother to enable her to care for her children at home, or they had to be boarded out, preferably in the countryside. Hanway apparently combined philanthropic, patriotic, and self-interest: between 1756 and 1815, his Marine Society outfitted no less than 31,000 youths for service at sea.

Uprooted people

The absolute impoverishment of the lower classes, finally, can be deduced from the growing extent and intensity of migratory movements. Certainly, the man who abandoned his birthplace in the hope of finding means of subsistence elsewhere was no new phenomenon in European history: since the late Middle Ages, the number of needy seeking work had steadily grown. In the course of the eighteenth century, however, physical mobility became the allotted life of great masses whose last resources were exhausted. Migration could take three forms: seasonal movements, by which the pauper left home only a few months a year; temporary moves, by which he left for several years and then returned to the parish of his birth; and emigration proper, usually from countryside to town, but even to other countries and other continents.

The first variety of mobility was, as Olwen Hufton demonstrated in a magisterial synthesis, predominant in eighteenth-century France. For innumerable *manouvriers*, seasonal migration became the sole means to retain their parcel of land and thus avoid complete proletarianization. Absence of the head of household allowed wife and children to make ends meet with the little food produced by the holding. If the migrant were lucky, he could even collect some money to pay his taxes. '*Manger hors de la région*' without further gains was for many pitiful cottars a sufficient incitement to go wandering nine months a year. Estimates, though based on incomplete information, support the notion that around 1800 at least 200,000 engaged in seasonal migration in France, and that the subsistence of about one million people, or 3 per cent of the national population, depended on it. It was chiefly a north–south movement. The great regions of rejection were above all the Massif Central, the Auvergne, the Marche, Limousin, Rouergue, Gévaudan, Pays de Velay, then the Alps, Dauphiné, Franche-Comté, and the Pyrenees, in short, mountainous areas. Regions of reception were above all Languedoc, Roussillon, and parts of Provence and Aquitaine, in the great Mediterranean zone of viniculture. In some districts, no less than 20 to 30 per cent of all heads of family depended on this 'economy of make-shifts', to use Hufton's expression. Villages where all able-bodied men and boys for months on end begged or provided seasonal labour in often far away places were not exceptional. Travellers, such as Arthur Young, who were surprised by the apparent absence of need in such parishes, did not realize that their 'prosperity' was paid by the expulsion of a notable part of the local labour force.

In the region of Liège such movements had become equally commonplace by the early nineteenth century. According to the prefect of the *département de l'Ourthe*, between 1808 and 1810 an average of 4,075 passports were provided per year, of which roughly 65 per cent were for seasonal workers. Most tried during six or seven months to make a living in the nearby departments of the Roer and Lower-Maas as brickmakers, masons' labourers or paviors, and then returned home. Their motives were the same as those of their French counterparts. Since there were no cottage industries or coal mines in the vicinities of their birthplaces, and since their holdings were too small to support a family, they had to relieve the holding as much as possible of the family's largest consumer of food. The interest of temporary migrants for the later industrialization of the area around Liège can scarcely be overestimated: they formed a reservoir of cheap labour from which entrepreneurs could draw when they lacked local poor, when they had to pay high wages, or when they confronted a recalcitrant work force.

Many cottars from north-western Germany, especially the districts of Hanover and Oldenburg, went to the Northern Netherlands year after year from the early seventeenth century onwards for two month periods in order to do heavy labour in agriculture, the textile industry, or peat cutting. In the mid eighteenth century no less than 27,000 *Hollandgänger* trekked every summer to the Republic. After 1780 their number declined somewhat; nevertheless, around 1810 it still amounted to about 20,000.

There were even villagers who emigrated for years at a time to other countries in the hope of earning enough to buy some livestock or an extra bit of land on their return. Innumerable *manouvriers* from the Auvergne, Limousin, Rouergue, Béarn, and the Pyrenees trekked annually to Andalusia, the towns of the duchy of Sevilla, Aragon, some towns of Old Castile, particularly Valladolid, and some in Galicia. This movement dated from the sixteenth century but, from the 1740s, steadily gained in importance. The migrants earned their bread by carrying water, manning stalls, selling lemonade, as street sweepers, as latrine cleaners. Most were married men between thirty and forty who stayed in Spain until they had saved 300 to 400 *pesos.* The realization of this modest ambition seems to have taken an average of five years. But things did not just end there. Returning migrants had to trek through the barren Sierra of central Spain, which often took a heavy toll of their health, and thence through the mountains, where they ran the danger of robbery by bandits of their hard-earned *pécule.*

How is it possible that foreign poor could find work in a country characterized by structural underemployment? Temporary immigrants were prepared to do anything for a wage which exceeded the subsistence minimum of a single adult. They could be satisfied with a pittance, because they disposed of a tiny piece of land that provided just enough foodstuffs to save their wives and children from starvation. For Spanish day-labourers matters were completely different. They were landless folk, totally dependent on the sale of their labour. For the married among them there was no sense in competition with foreign workers. They would have had to put out the same effort, but not been able to quiet the severe hunger of their families. In such circumstances they often preferred to beg. As the English traveller, Henry Swinburne, remarked in 1776, 'the poor Spaniard won't work unless forced to do so by absolute necessity, for his efforts are not rewarded'.[31]

In short, cottars did nearly everything in their power to secure their means of existence in the countryside and thereby avoid being uprooted or, in any case, delay as long as possible. Only when they had exhausted every possibility were they prepared to abandon their traditional milieu and move to the devourers of men, the towns. Although the present state of investigation into migratory movements in the eighteenth and first half of the nineteenth century does not allow for far-reaching conclusions, it seems incontrovertible that the 'attractive power' of urban centres in most European countries played only a subordinate role, the huge metropoles of London, Paris, and (later) Berlin excepted. The uprooted inhabitant of the countryside, in the words of Witold Kula, was, 'not drawn to the town by the prospect of higher wages. He was driven out of the countryside by hunger.' Various monographs support this proposition. In eighteenth-century Lyon, for example, there was no causal connection between the fluctuations of the urban economy and successive waves of immigration.

It is remarkable that the rural poor often settled into places that had little or nothing to offer. Also, seasonal mobility points out the limited attractive power of the towns: temporary immigration was usually greatest during those months in which urban employment was at its least. At Marseille, more than 50 per cent of the 'floating' proletariat at the end of the *ancien régime* consisted of rural day-labourers, cobblers and tailors, who took themselves to the town in winter in hope of finding shelter and aid there; afterwards they went away again. Many studies, moreover, indicate that urban recruitment was overwhelmingly regional, or even local. More than 50 per cent of the immigrants to eighteenth-century Coblenz came from villages within a radius of 25 km around the town. And the famous Cockerill enterprise at Seraing during 1818 to 1859 recruited around 80 per cent of its labour force from the surrounding countryside. The same holds for Antwerp, where the number of immigrants stemming from the province rose during the first half of the nineteenth century from *c.* 40 per cent to *c.* 60 per cent. The industrial centres of Lancashire also drew their quickly growing population chiefly from nearby rural districts in the century after 1750. Certainly they lodged long-distance migrants, but these came from Ireland and Scotland above all, not from the agrarian regions of southern England. Landlords and their capitalist tenants had every interest in the availability of a large labour force and consequently tried to hinder migration as much as possible. As their workers said: [They] keep us here [on the poor rates] like potatoes in a pit, and only take us out for use when they can no longer do without us.' This lasted until 1834, when restrictions of the Act of Settlement and Removal were abolished; only then did emigration to the great textile centres accelerate.[32]

Unquestionably, integration of the immigrants into the towns was an extremely difficult and often hopeless process. Most had no professional qualifications fit for an urban society, so that they were considered only for the most poorly paid jobs – like the unskilled foreign workers of the twentieth century. Casual labour was the lot of the majority. They were thrown together in the most decayed and unhealthy sections of towns, where lodgings were cheapest. In case of unemployment, illness, or other misfortunes, they could count only on the solidarity of their fellow immigrants, since only after several years' residence could they call on official support. Even then, there were differences in language, bearing, and clothing, 'stigmata' which distinguished them from all native urbanites. The example of Mainz shows how deep the cleavage was between immigrants and the rest of the population: no native artisan was married to a daughter of an immigrant day labourer at the end of the *ancien régime*. Not surprisingly, towns were nothing more than a 'way-station' for many of the uprooted, leaving as quickly and as desperately as they came. At least one-third of the immigrants who were listed in 1817 by the Antwerp registrar's office went elsewhere within ten years; with a few exceptions, they were all unskilled.

Finally, it ought to be remarked that permanent movements from one country to another, and even from one continent to another, assumed increasingly greater proportions from the eighteenth century on. The tragic story of the Irish poor is well-known; equally significant was the massive invasion of East Prussia, the New Mark, Brandenburg, Poland, the Hungarian plains, Romania and the southern steppes of Russia by dispossessed protestants and, in particular, impoverished cottars and handworkers from central Europe. This movement was encouraged by the 'enlightened despots', who tried to lure new immigrants to their relatively thinly populated areas in the conviction that 'a country's wealth is the number of its men'. Frederick the Great not only refunded their travelling expenses but also exempted them from military service. Moreover, he provided farmers on favourable terms with a cottage, equipment and stock, while craftsmen received a workshop, tools and industrial franchises. Around 300,000 established themselves in Prussia during his reign. Emigration to Russia, where Catherine II carried out similar policies, was even more extensive; simultaneously, numerous Russians trekked to Siberia, which by the end of the century harboured no less than 575,000 colonists. Hungary and Poland experienced similarly massive immigration. The district of Coblenz alone saw more than 8 per cent of its total population drain away between 1779 and 1789 to other countries. Though detailed comparisons are impossible, without a doubt the Swiss were more mobile than ever before. Around 300,000 went to foreign lands during the eighteenth century – many as mercenaries in the service of neighbouring lords, others to settle in Russia or America. Increasingly more men who could not lead a human existence in the Old World for political, religious, or simple material reasons sought their salvation in emigration to other continents. It is estimated that one and a half million inhabitants of the British Isles and 200,000 Germans sailed to North America in the eighteenth century. As the number of impoverished rural labourers and cottage workers grew, emigration from Europe gained in importance. In the period 1801 to 1840, one and a half million abandoned the Old World. Most were starvelings driven by extreme need, for whom the destination in fact signified little or nothing. The crisis of the 1840s sparked off the exodus: European emigration leapt to 200,000 and even 300,000 per annum. Never before in history was the breakthrough of a new mode of production coupled with such massive impoverishment and dislocation.

4. The regulation of the labour market

Naturally these tragic developments did not leave public opinion unperturbed. From the mid eighteenth century poverty became one of the main subjects of concern to governments, ecclesiastics, learned societies and middle-class circles throughout Europe. Everywhere inquiries were made into the extent and intensity of the problem, and provincial academies set prizes for essays on its causes and possible solutions. Hundreds of authors applied themselves, producing pamphlets on the numbers and characteristics of the poor, on public assistance versus private charity, on begging, prostitution and related problems. But a stream of words was not the end of it, for in many countries, central and local authorities took practical measures with an eye towards a basic reorganization of poor relief. Some historians have suggested that these changes in social policy reflected the humanitarian motives characteristic of the 'Age of the Enlightenment'. This idealistic vision requires fundamental revision.

Undeniably, the ideas of philosophers such as Condorcet, Godwin, Price and Wolff were prompted by sincere concern for the suffering of the poor. They all acknowledged the dehumanizing living conditions of the lower classes and the tyranny of poor-law administration. Most agreed that destitution was not the result of laziness or individual misfortunes but arose through economic and social abuses. Some even emphasized the *right* of the poor to claim assistance, since the rich had unlawfully appropriated for themselves all material goods. 'By what right', asked Richard Woodward, a rural dean in Ireland (who later became a bishop despite these ideas),

> did they take upon themselves to enact certain laws (for the rich compose the legislative body in every civilised country) which compelled that man to become a member of their society; which precluded him from any share in the land where he was born; any use of its spontaneous fruits, or any dominion over the beasts of the field, on pain of stripes, imprisonment, or

> death? How can they justify their exclusive property in the *common heritage* of mankind unless they consent, in return, for the subsistence of the poor, who were excluded from those common rights by the laws of the rich, to which they were never parties?

Many moral radicals went even further and declared that contemporary society needed total reform. The Anglo-American Jacobin Thomas Paine wrote that, in the so-called civilized lands, when

> we see age going to the workhouse, and youth to the gallows, something must be wrong in the system of government. It would seem by the exterior appearances of such countries, that all was happiness; but there lies hidden from the eye of common observation, a mass of wretchedness that has scarcely any other chance, than to expire in poverty or infamy. Its entrance into life is marked with the presage of its fate; and until this is remedied, it is in vain to punish.

All these ideas, however, had not the least influence on the actual social policy exercised by governments and magistrates, other than as a warning to maintain control over the lower classes.[33]

More and more philanthropists attempted to arouse empathy and compassion for the unfortunate, and their efforts bore fruit. The pictorial arts and literature mirrored a new sensitivity for the needs of the very poor. Greuze and Hogarth did not, like most of their seventeenth-century predecessors, portray grotesque beings, but rather destitution in the flesh and blood reality encountered daily by every burgher. In the century after 1750, presumably more hospitals, foundling homes, poor schools and similar institutions were founded by private donation than in all preceding periods. But all these initiatives indicate that official poor relief was completely inadequate. They show that the charity of the elites centred almost exclusively on the 'respectable' poor: children and the aged, sick and lame. The misery of wage labourers aroused the interests of philanthropists, but mostly interest of a condescending, paternalistic variety. Patronage became the new keyword. Control of the religious and moral behaviour of the poor, control of their personal hygiene, control of the cleanliness and orderliness of their dwellings, control of the attendance at school of their children: in short, all aspects of the daily life of paupers became subject to accurate and continuing surveillance. Popular entertainments became the target of sharp critiques. 'It is . . . found by long experience,' declared Henry Zouch in 1786, 'that when the common people are drawn together upon any public occasion, a variety of mischiefs are certain to ensure : allured by unlawful pastimes, or even by vulgar amusements only, they wantonly waste their time and money, to their own great loss and that of their employers.' There had been such pronouncements in the past. However, henceforth there followed a systematic attack on every traditional diversion which prevented the lower classes – according to employers, authorities, and ecclesiastics – from practising the essential virtues of diligence, sobriety, prudence, and thrift. The Antwerp poor-law administration refused support to anyone who set aside money during the year for fair-days. The same lot fell to paupers too often found in taverns or who in one way or another behaved 'unseemly'. The administration, however, offered something in return : poor families who 'fulfil their domestic and their civic duties the whole year through' received a prize for good-conduct. Protest against these disciplinary methods was ruled out, for, as the directive clearly stipulated, 'by entering the poor-lists, the needy are considered to be minors and are for that reason automatically subject to the custody of the administration'.

According to a detailed report composed by the Antwerp poor-law administration around the mid nineteenth century, the destitution of an old man was to be blamed on his lack of thrift in better years, as well as to the indifference of his children, who refused to support him. This heartlessness was in turn explained by the lack of love with which the aged himself had reared his children : 'Instead of caring for them, he spent his leisure time in the tavern; he taught them to squander their money thoughtlessly on personal and passing wants; he, in other words, set them to give free rein to their whims.' The report went on to ascribe illness and disability to improper hygiene and debauchery, such as the excessive drinking on Sundays and on 'Saint Monday'. Unemployment was seen as the result of illness or disability, if not of incompetence, clumsiness or carelessness. Low wages? Of secondary importance : 'A skilled and orderly working man who does not have too many children and whose wife is thrifty can make ends meet on his wages.' Yet, the poor-law administration recognized that the living standards of the working population had drastically declined and that the opportunity to save was in fact lacking. It was even accepted that 'the overwhelming majority of workers are born, live, and die, if not in poverty, at least in a state which necessitates public support following the least misfortune'. Instead of going further into the matter, the directors chose to take up the moral charter anew. The themes of excess, laziness, and imprudence were played on in detail. The conclusion: 'The foremost cause of poverty is misbehaviour. Let us raise the morality of the lower classes, entailing decent behaviour and appearance, love of family, resignation and courage in the face of adversity, and sobriety in all circumstances; thereby shall we erect the only dike which can resist the high waters of destitution.'[34]

How could it be different? To tackle the social problem by the roots would put in question the whole of society as actually constituted, and that was the very last thing to be considered by authorities and employers. Did not the individual pursuit of profit provide the best guarantee for economic growth? Did not purposeful personal enrichment bring general improvement? But, everyone had to contribute his share. If the poor did not understand this basic principle of economic logic by themselves, then they had to be shown the light – in their own interest, of course.

England

Nowhere else in Europe did social policy change so fundamentally in the century after 1750 as in England, the first country to break through to industrial capitalism. Some historians have ascribed the new measures for poor relief to more sympathetic attitudes among the upper classes with respect to the needy. Although such motives may have motivated social reformers and philanthropists they did not turn the scale. The explanation for the new social policy is far more prosaic.

The Workhouse Test Act of 1723 could function properly only as long as the number of needy stayed within certain limits. Continuing expansion of poverty slowly but surely undermined the system. Since, in general, the whole family had to be accepted into the workhouse, expenses for poor relief rose spectacularly: in 1784 they were around 60 per cent higher than in 1760. The workhouse, moreover, mingled impoverished craftsmen and farmers with the 'scum' of society. Although apparently beneficial, wrote Defoe in 1729, 'they have in some respects an evil tendency, for they mix the good and the bad, and often make reprobates of all alike'. No one, he remarked, was immune from misfortune. If an honourable artisan could not leave anything to his wife and children from which to live, he concluded, 'what a shocking thing it is to think they must be mixed with vagrants, beggars, thieves and night-walkers; to receive their insults, to hear their blasphemous and obscene discourse, to be suffocated with their nastiness, and eat up with their vermin'.[35] Rebellious movements after the middle of the century made the authorities aware of the potential dangers of contacts among the poor of various social backgrounds locked up in the same institution.

Why was it not until 1782 that the principle of out-relief for the able-bodied received statutory implementation? As said above (p. 128), the English textile industry developed a structural shortage of yarn in the first half of the eighteenth century. The problem was only solved by Hargreaves's jenny (*c.* 1765) and Arkwright's water frame (1769). These inventions initiated rapid expansion of yarn production, mirrored in a more than twelvefold increase of cotton consumption between 1770 and 1800. Hence the workhouses lost their economic significance. In some areas they became obstacles to industrial growth. The owners of spinning-mills needed a cheap and 'free' labour force, so they had an interest in the release of the able-bodied poor from the workhouses. A uniform system of public support was premature, nonetheless, because economic conditions varied from place to place. Therefore, Gilbert's Act was not binding: parishes were only encouraged to group together into more viable units to maintain poor-houses for the sick, lame, and aged. Professional 'guardians of the poor', appointed and paid by the parish, had either to help the able-bodied find a job or to ensure that they 'be properly maintained, lodged and provided for until such employment shall be provided', and they had to help out the poor financially if their wages were insufficient.

Little effective support was forthcoming. The responsible authorities generally limited themselves to the distribution of minimal sums, never enough for a pauper to support his family, but when poor harvests led to food riots the authorities realized that more adequate measures were essential. The answer to this growing social problem was Speenhamland.

In 1795 the magistracy of Berkshire concluded that wages were insufficient to maintain an 'industrious man and his family'. At an assembly in Speenhamland parish it was agreed henceforth systematically to adjust relief to match wages, the price of bread and size of family. This 'rate in aid of wages' was not totally new, but the principle was henceforth institutionalized in many parishes. The 'allowance system' had the advantage that wage rises were superfluous (or could at least be kept to a minimum), while recipients became more dependent than ever on the local authorities, who determined payments on a case-by-case basis, employing various methods according to circumstances. The *roundsman system* dictated that the pauper-labourer had to go from house to house seeking work; if taken into service he received a daily portion of food and a small wage, while the parish handed over a supplementary sum to him. In other places, the poor-relief administration concluded contracts with employers, who payed a fixed amount for a set number of pauper labourers; the parish paid the wages of the workers, supplemented by relief funds. Another method was the *labour rate*: a parish rate was levied to cover the support of the able-bodied unemployed, for whose labour services a price was set. Taxpayers had the choice: employ a number of paupers at the appropriate wage or pay the tax. All these expedients amounted to the same thing: 'An unemployed and turbulent populace was being pacified with public allowances, but these allowances were used to restore order by enforcing work, at very low wage levels. Relief in short, served as a support for a disturbed labour market and as a discipline for a disturbed rural society.'[36]

K. Polanyi has argued that Speenhamland hindered the evolution of a 'free' labour market, because it met the growing demand for industrial labour inadequately. As an apology for eighteenth-century authorities he invoked the dictum that 'capitalism arrived unannounced'. In other words, ignorance and lack of insight were responsible for the emergence of a social policy characterized by improperly adjusted labour-regulating functions. Polanyi apparently failed to take into account that the transfer of an uprooted peasantry into industry could only take place without great social tensions if migration could be retarded or stimulated, according to need. Since the factories could not yet absorb all paupers, the upper classes had to carry out a policy of limited and controlled mobility of labour. Hence, the laws of settlement were only gradually changed. Sir William Young's Act forbade parishes in the future to remove a person as long as he did not fall a burden on the local poor relief; the ill and lame could under no conditions be rejected. The Act of 1795 thus offered the able-bodied poor greater security than before, yet in no sense hindered their removal in case of chronic unemployment. More flexible legislation at that moment would undoubtedly have met with serious opposition. Estate-owners and capitalist tenants, encouraged by rising food prices, desired an extensive workforce. Far from blocking economic growth, all these measures appear to have put the upper classes in a position to navigate through the hazardous transition to industrial capitalism without encountering too many obstacles.

When agricultural prices fell drastically after the Napoleonic War and the surplus population in the countryside reached disturbing proportions (due to continuing rationalization of the primary sector), emigration to the towns accelerated. Large-scale mobility of labour was now considered essential, because expenses for poor relief reached previously unknown heights in many parishes, while some industrial centres contended with a shortage of labour. Rebellious movements in rural areas around 1830 tipped the scales. In February 1832 the Whig government proposed a Royal Commission 'to make a diligent and full inquiry into the practical operations of the laws for the relief of the poor in England and Wales'. Early in June 1834 the commissioners delivered their report to Parliament, detailing why and how public support had to be changed. Two months later the New Poor Law was an accomplished fact.

The report of 1834 and the subsequent Act rested on the principle of 'less eligibility'. Provision of relief to the needy was henceforth dependent on the condition 'that his situation on the whole shall not be made really or apparently so eligible as the situation of the independent labourer in the lowest class'. The pauper had to sell his labour at any price, in other words. The Commission left no doubts: 'Every penny bestowed that tends to render the condition of the pauper more eligible than that of the independent labourer, is a bounty on indolence and vice.' Thus the vital minimum was institutionalized. The 'workhouse test', moreover, assured that relief was granted only to those in real need. Some exceptions aside, no support could be given to an able-bodied indigent unless he was prepared to enter a 'well-regulated workhouse'. The Commission members judged that such a step 'would be a self-acting test of the claim of the applicant. . . . If the claimant does not comply with the terms on which relief is given to the destitute, he gets nothing; and if he does comply, the compliance proves the truth of the claim – namely, his destitution.'

In theory, all were free to work or not to work: there was no legal compulsion applied. But an able-bodied poor man received no support unless he worked. The iron discipline of the factory, or that of the workhouse: that was his choice.

Yet the industrialized north did not greet the New Poor Law with undivided enthusiasm. Employment was determined there by a wide variety of factors. Some categories of labourers had become 'superfluous' through advanced mechanization, others through recession. The call to support all needy labourers in workhouses could do nothing else than arouse opposition in such circumstances. The poor rates were considered a sort of insurance policy by entrepreneurs: the reserve army was not only kept alive relatively cheaply during recession but was also readily available in time of economic recovery. Moreover, the connection between employer and employee remained firm in a system of out-relief. Many factory owners agreed with S. T. Coleridge, who argued that 'any extensive commercial and manufacturing system must be accompanied by poor rates; they are the consideration paid by, or on behalf of, capitalists for having labour at demand. It is the price, and nothing else.' Thus the 'workhouse test' was never carried out by poor-law administrations in the industrialized areas of Lancashire and the West Riding.[37]

Apart from its ideological implications, perhaps the foremost result of the New Poor Law was that the mobility of the surplus rural population increased. Most of the restrictions laid down by the Act of Settlement and Removal were abolished. In order to expel 'redundant' wage labourers from the countryside, the workhouses were turned into instruments of terror. 'Our intention', said one official, 'is to make the workhouses as like prisons as possible'; another stated: 'Our object is to establish therein a discipline so severe and repulsive as to make them a terror to the poor and prevent them from entering.' This policy was intended to force the destitute to accept any job in any place for any wage, and anyone who went to the poorhouse instead was branded a misfit and treated as such. The 'moral economy', to use E. P. Thompson's expression, definitively belonged to the past. 'Discipline and integration of the proletariat' was the new motto.[38]

The Southern Netherlands

Until around 1770 there was no question of a coherent and purposeful social policy in the Southern Netherlands. Although the central government had repeatedly proclaimed ordinances in the preceding decades which prohibited the able-bodied poor from begging, empowered officers of justice to punish infractions severely, and made local authorities responsible for relief of the truly needy, most of these regulations were not put into effect. The reorganization of poor relief carried out in the sixteenth century left hardly any trace. The few *tuchthuizen* (see above, p.119) to arise in the seventeenth century lodged only a handful of criminals and prostitutes a century later. The numerous attempts undertaken in the early eighteenth century to create *hôpitaux généraux* on the model of France in the end resulted in the erection of only a single institution with small capacity at Roermond in the lesser developed east of the country.

From 1770 the war on poverty moved on to a new plateau. For a decade and more the government showed intense concern for the problem, under the direction of the minister-plenipotentiary Starhemberg. The causes of this shift were twofold. First, destitution and its accompanying phenomena, such as vagabondage, criminality, and prostitution, reached alarming proportions. Second, the government wanted to stimulate national industry by means of a social policy which met the growing demand of capitalist entrepreneurs for cheap labour.

In 1771 Jean-Jacques Philippe Vilain-Quatorze, first Alderman of Ghent and President of the Estates of Flanders, laid a *Mémoire* before the latter, in which he argued for the institution of a provincial *tuchthuis*. His intentions, influenced by Goswin de Fierlant, a member of the Privy Council, were clear: beggars and vagabonds must not only be punished but also be put to profitable employment. He argued that 'a mass of new workers, abandoning begging and idleness, would tend to diminish the costs of labour'. The ideas of Vilain-Quatorze were favourably received by the central government and brought into practice at Ghent, and the government exhorted the Estates of Brabant to create a similar institution; otherwise, the duchy would be flooded with beggars from Flanders. The Estates of Brabant made some objections but eventually agreed to build a house of correction at Vilvoorde at their own expense. The delegates of the Antwerp bourgeoisie laid down the precondition, however, that the institution manufacture no goods which might damage private entrepreneurs. Brussels manufacturers agreed. Hence, the economic function of both *tuchthuizen* was limited to processing raw materials.

In other provinces, the proposals of Vilain-Quatorze drew even greater opposition. In 1774 François-Joseph Taintenier, Alderman of Ath, drew together all the criticism in his famous *Traité sur la Mendicité*. He declared that entrepreneurs were no match for the competition of prison factories with their supply of cheap labour. He also railed against the confinement of criminals, beggars and the unemployed, of men, women and children, all in one and the same institution; such intermingling could not but augment the 'immorality' of the lower classes. He argued further that it was naturally impossible to bring all paupers into *tuchthuizen*, so that more inclusive measures were required. The profitable employment of the poor, according to Taintenier, had to be realized by way of a coordinated and selective system of out-relief. Only the sick, lame or aged might be 'properly' supported. The able-bodied unemployed had to be satisfied with the bare subsistence minimum, 'just enough not to starve while awaiting the employment by which they could support themselves'. These measures, paired with prohibition of begging, would automatically depress wage levels. An efficient reorganization of poor relief also implied foundation of schools, 'to which the poor must send their children in order to learn to labour regularly'. As for financing, Taintenier proposed bringing all existing funds together in one *aumône générale*; if these resources did not suffice, then a poor tax had to be levied. Last but not least, he declared that *tuchthuizen* could only fulfil a useful function if they were exclusively reserved for incorrigible beggars.

Vilain-Quatorze totally changed his earlier conceptions about poor relief when he read Taintenier's treatise. In 1775 he published a new *Mémoire*, in which he in turn emphasized that only dangerous criminals should be locked up in houses of correction, the workshops of which should in no case compete against existing private enterprises. Moreover, he agreed completely with the thesis of his critic concerning the benefits of out-relief.

The same year, Taintenier published a *Supplément* to his treatise, in which he developed his arguments further. He wrote that the poor could be usefully employed only if the economic potential of the country was fully tapped. Therefore it was necessary to eliminate guild regulations, which were responsible for:

(1) high wages, which damaged the export trade of the Southern Netherlands;
(2) massive unemployment, because many workers did not gain admission to the guilds; and
(3) the lack of technological improvements.

His discourse amounted to a plea for free enterprise. Taintenier clearly perceived that a reorganization of public support would yield fruit only if two basic principles were combined: strict control of the labour force and flexible regulation of the labour market. Hence begging must be forbidden, poor relief centralized, the selection of the needy carried through to the limit, and the levels of assistance held as low as possible. By these means the goals of an 'efficient' social policy, namely expansion of labour supply and depression of wages, could be attained without jeopardizing public order.

Such a programme was only practical in centres where industry offered sufficient employment opportunities. Why forbid begging and centralize poor-relief funds if there was little or nothing to do with the labour force? In such cases local authorities feared that introduction of the new system would merely entail extra costs and upset the precarious social balance, since paupers could not be imprisoned for lack of sufficient industrial provisions. The Brussels magistracy did not mince their words: the creation of an *aumône générale*, they said, was senseless, 'because there are few factories in this town, and those which there are . . . do not have workshops employing a great number of workers'. In these circumstances the proposed reorganization could effect nothing 'positive'. On the contrary, thousands of paupers would request assistance, whereas earlier, restrained by their shame, they did not even beg, and they had been compelled to curtail every expense to make ends meet in the winter or during periods of unemployment. The same arguments were brought forward at Mechelen : there too, the magistrates refused to found an *aumône générale*, because the profitable employment of the poor was ruled out. In short, towns which could not pair control with labour regulation had no interest in bringing Taintenier's programme into practice. Hence, the central government proclaimed no compulsory ordinance on the subject.

Investigating where the ideas of Taintenier found acceptance, it can be seen that economic motives were the significant ones. Subsequent reorganization of poor relief took place at Ath (1772), Kortrijk (1774), Brugge (1776), Ghent (1777), Tournai (1777), Antwerp (1779), Verviers (1782), and Lier (1787). The connection between the growing demands from manufacturers for an extensive, cheap, and docile labour force on one side and the reform of public assistance on the other appears irrefutable: nearly all the centres involved had labour-intensive industries which were in full expansion.

The second quarter of the sixteenth century had witnessed the emergence of a similar social policy, but the system now was elaborated far more thoroughly. More than before, attention focused on the moral discipline of paupers. Certainly, some sixteenth-century poor-relief administrations had made provision of relief dependent on knowledge of certain prayers and religious precepts, while others had set up schools where destitute parents had to send their children on pain of being struck off the poor lists. The significance of all these initiatives was nonetheless limited. In contrast, during the 1770s and 1780s the bourgeoisie did everything in its power to turn the poor into a docile labour force. Sunday schools were established to train paupers' children to submit with blind obedience to civil and spiritual authorities. The new *Catechismusfundaties*, financed by both ecclesiastics and laity, had the same goal. The preaching of Christian ethics, or so many members of the 'establishment' thought, would be the fittest means to neutralize potential class conflicts. Thus the circle was gradually closed: the poor-relief administration cared for the regulation of the labour market; the magistracy maintained public order; and the Church accounted for moral discipline.[39]

The new support regulations were not allotted a long life. At the end of the 1780s, the Southern Netherlands experienced a severe economic and political crisis, worsened by extreme inflation of all essential food stuffs. The new social policy as a result lost its labour-regulating function. Since the number of needy rose to excessive proportions, the expenses for poor relief climbed sky high as well. In these circumstances the bourgeoisie no longer found any advantage in the system of poor relief created in the preceding years. Despite growing poverty, charitable institutions saw their incomes gradually drying up. At the time of the Brabant Revolution of 1789–90, which began as a reaction against the reforms of Joseph II, all the parties involved tried to use the poor in pursuit of their own political interests. While the central government dispensed subsidies left and right to ensure public order, many local authorities withheld the money in order to drive the discontent of the lower classes to the breaking point. There was no longer any coordinated social policy. Not until the annexation of the Southern Netherlands by France were new reforms of public assistance carried out; this reorganization, which in its broad outlines remained in force until 1925, simply copied French poor-relief legislation, to which we now turn.

France

Until the Revolution, decentralization, discontinuity and diversity characterized social policy in eighteenth-century France. Private foundations and voluntary almsgiving formed the cornerstones of the relief system. The state attempted to intervene, proclaiming innumerable ordinances which demanded imprisonment of beggars, employment of the able-bodied poor and punishment of recidivists, yet succeeding governments failed to have all local authorities carry out these measures. In most towns nothing came about because profitable employment of the poor was beyond hope, due to lack of employment opportunities in industry. By the second quarter of the eighteenth century, all centres of more than 5,000 inhabitants had an *hôpital général*, but the great majority of these institutions had a very small capacity – a town of around 50,000 seldom had more than 1,500 hospital beds.

The people admitted to an *hôpital général* consisted chiefly of the aged, infirm and orphaned. This institution, in other words, functioned almost exclusively as an asylum.

Yet the government believed that the *hôpitaux généraux* could be remodelled into efficient workhouses, given sufficient funds. In 1724 a royal edict stipulated that the able-bodied poor who found no employment within fourteen days had to apply immediately to the local *hôpital*, which would provide work in return for bed and board and a little cash. Whoever did not apply voluntarily would be locked away in an *hôpital*-prison, branded with an M (for *mendiant*, beggar), and condemned to two to six months forced labour on a diet of bread and water. Needless to say, the edict remained a dead letter. As Olwen Hufton has indicated:

> No *hôpital* had a prison or personnel capable of superintending vast numbers of able-bodied adults. The government offered to pay for the upkeep of the new internees but it left the vital problems of accommodation, type of work, and personnel to the *intendants*, municipalities, and, in the last analysis, to the *hôpitaux* themselves.

In 1767 the monarchy changed its course. In all provinces, *dépôts de mendicité* were to be created, designed exclusively for beggars and vagabonds. These institutions, the foundation of public assistance until 1789 (a short period excepted), were financed by the government and controlled by the intendants. They were far more repressive than the *hôpitaux généraux*. Living conditions in the *dépôts* were so miserable that many beggars and vagabonds did not survive even short stays: of the 71,760 persons lodged in the *dépôts* between 1767 and 1773, 13,899 (19 per cent) died within a few months of their incarceration. The condition of survivors was so poor, as a result of pitiful hygiene and starvation rations, that profitable employment was out of the question. Those able to work seldom numbered more than 50 per cent. Most internees were unfit for textile manufacture, the main pursuit within the *dépôts*. In general, the latter lodged no more than 30 per cent *ouvriers*, artisans; the remaining 70 per cent consisted of rural daylabourers (30 to 40 per cent), itinerant peddlers (around 10 per cent), and a mixed bag of servants, former soldiers, prostitutes, the unemployed aged and children. The *dépôts* could not by themselves restrain the growing tide of wandering bands. Only one-third of all men, women and children in the *dépôts* in 1789 could be labelled 'dangerous'. In short, these institutions neither played a role of any economic significance nor put an end to aggressive begging and vagabondage.

Nor could the *bureaux des pauvres* and the *ateliers de charité* solve the social problem. After proclamation of the edict of 1762 encouraging the growth of rural industry, the government exhorted bishops, nobles and communal authorities to found new rural *bureaux des pauvres*, where the deserving poor could be given technical training. In most cases, this proved to be only an experiment, while those initiatives which did find concrete shape were shortly abandoned for lack of sufficient funds. The impact of the *ateliers de charité*, which sprouted up ubiquitously in the 1770s, was not much greater. These institutions, financed by the monarchy, were intended to provide the able-bodied poor, primarily those in the countryside, with a supplementary income during those months when there was neither local work nor opportunity for seasonal labour. In the end the whole system amounted to little more than employment of several thousand paupers in public building programmes. The meagre significance of this form of relief can be seen in that all the *ateliers de charité* together provided work for only 31,000 men, women, and children during the hard winter of 1788–89.

The efforts of the monarchy to set the poor to profitable employment produced next to nothing. Artificial efforts of this nature could have no success, since the overwhelming majority of the population was wholly or partially employed in agriculture, industry was in large measure dominated by commercial capital, and the bulk of textiles were produced rurally. Hence most municipal governments were not inclined to found large-scale institutions for public assistance: such initiatives required considerable capital, the chances of profitable employment were negligible, and local authorities could not count on financial help from the central government. Setting aside expenses for foundlings, the monarchy in the 1780s spent little more than six million *livres* on poor relief. In *per capita* terms, the destitute on average received the equivalent of around 6 kg of bread per annum. The creation of a coordinated system of poor relief seemed sensible only in major industrial centres such as Lyon. These towns, however, were flooded with impoverished country-dwellers, so that repression there too secured the upper hand over labour regulation. In a country where hundreds of thousands of the poor depended on seasonal labour, migration could not be controlled. Taking into account all these factors, it comes as no surprise that the war on poverty failed.[40]

The repressive policy of the state fanned the lower classes' hatred for the established orders. Aggressive beggary became a plague. Alms were increasingly extorted by abuse, vomiting, or other ruses which filled their well-to-do 'victims' with abhorrence and fear, especially for physical contact. Many beggars no longer tried to arouse sympathy but faced their benefactors threateningly, unashamedly. Crimes against property rose alarmingly. In Douai, Lille and Valenciennes, the number of thefts and frauds more than doubled during the eighteenth century, and in the countryside banditry turned into a structural feature of the society in the last decades of the *ancien régime*. Bands of violent vagabonds coursed through the rural parishes, often with the passive support of poor *manouvriers*, who were not the least bit sympathetic for their propertied neighbours, payers of starvation wages. Arson and violent assault terrorized the great tenants, who could expect little or no protection from the rural *maréchaussée*: after the reforms of the 1760s, the police force of provincial France all told consisted of only 3,882, of whom 468 were administrators. Most villagers refused to support the *maréchaussée*. How could they rely on a handful of unpaid and often corrupt *cavaliers*? Rather than summoning what was essentially an apparat of repression, country-dwellers chose to buy off the blackmailing vagabonds. A climate of insecurity arose, the *Grande Peur* of 1789 in embryo. It is no exaggeration to say that deficient organization of poor relief accelerated the undermining of the feudal edifice in France.[41]

One of the fundamental articles of the Declaration of the Rights of Man and of the Citizen solemnly declared that 'Public relief is a sacred debt. Society owes subsistence to citizens in misfortune, either by providing work, or by providing the means of existence to those who are unable to work'. The goal of the social legislation was, according to the Convention, 'to provide the means to all Frenchmen to get the prime necessities of life without being dependent on anything other than the laws'. Poor relief was reorganized following rules which were binding for the whole nation, and the expenses were entered into the state budget. Return to the *ancien régime* was to be prevented by nationalization and sale of the property of the old charitable institutions and the monastic orders.

Thermidor restored the old situation. All progressive measures enacted by the Convention were abolished. As Delegate Delecroy argued:

> It is time to rid ourselves of every trace of that extravagant philanthropy, bold no doubt but totally in vain, which had constrained us to busy ourselves with the poor ever since the Constitutional Convention. They have a right to universal sympathy only. Let us establish the principle that the government must not deal with public support other than as example and motivator.

This summarized the social policy carried out in France and Belgium in the next decades. The fundamental right of subsistence for the poor, proclaimed by the Convention, was finished. Once again, they were put in their 'proper' place: propertyless dependence on the voluntary charity of full-fledged citizens, who decided that 'members of society should not concern themselves with supporting the poor but providing the necessities of life for themselves instead'. The law of 7 October 1796 consequently ended the nationalization of poor-relief and established public assistance on a local basis, with the *commune* as the basic unit. 'Commissions for the Civil Hospices' were entrusted with administration of all charitable institutions and hospitals. On 27 November 1796 the last brick was laid: in all *communes*, Charity Bureaus were created to organize out-relief. Nothing remained of revolutionary legislation. Maximal limitation of poor rates was the new motto. As for the able-bodied poor: 'Work and wage, there's the only form of support which suits them.' Henceforth, most French and Belgian towns financed their social policy with *octrois*, indirect taxes levied on a whole series of products – mostly foodstuffs – consumed by the whole community; in other words, the lower classes, hit the heaviest by these taxes, had to pay their own relief.[42]

Central Europe

The 'enlightened despots' of the eighteenth century strove to transform the growing masses of paupers into an industrial labour force. Central Europe offers striking examples of this policy. The princes agreed with the Cameralist J. H. G. von Justi, who maintained in 1755 that 'it is the duty of all to serve the State through zeal and labour'. Nearly everywhere, measures were taken with an eye towards the profitable employment of the lower classes. Determined by military and budgetary factors, these initiatives were based, in large measure, on the mercantilist principles of the preceding century. The *Arbeitshäuser*, workhouses, founded in many towns after 1740 with funds from the authorities, differed in only one respect from earlier experiments: they not only lodged beggars and vagabonds, but also provided work for the poor who 'voluntarily' offered themselves. The Berlin *Arbeitshaus*, for example, founded in 1742 by Frederick the Great, in 1785 put to work 641 detainees and 609 'volunteers': 300 women, 192 men, 71 girls and 46 boys.

Corresponding to the traditional orientation of the mercantilist state, many poorhouses specialized in luxury goods. In Würzburg and Bayreuth, internees worked marble; at Nuremberg, lens grinding was the chosen task – and silicone the inevitable hazard to health; in the military orphanage of Potsdam, the girls made lace; the jewellery industry of Pforzheim almost completely supported itself on a supply of labour from the local poorhouses; so did the glove manufacture of Prague, where the orphanage laboured exclusively for a single entrepreneur, Georg Ludwig Malvieux.

Although some institutions rendered a profit, with everything considered, they were not very fruitful, because intervention by the state could not redress the fundamental weaknesses of a feudal society. Whatever efforts an enlightened despot such as Frederick the Great made, the relations of production remained unaltered. The textile and mining industries of Silesia were dominated by feudal landlords, who drew on the labour of serfs alone. Exports were largely controlled by a small group of capitalist merchants, who obtained monopolies, privileges, and subsidies with the support of the *Junkers*. Within this framework, there was no place for an industrial bourgeoisie, so that the necessary basis for an optimal interaction of economic and social policies was absent.

Lord Malmesbury noted that the King of Prussia could never understand that

> a large treasure lying dormant in his coffers impoverishes his kingdom; that riches increase by circulation; that trade cannot subsist without reciprocal profit; that monopolies and exclusive grants put a stop to emulation, and of course to industry; and, in short, that the real wealth of a sovereign consists in the ease and affluence of his subjects.

Certainly, the mercantilist principle which Frederick the Great effected with a half century's delay favoured the expansion of the Prussian economy and resulted in a favourable balance of trade. Nonetheless, this did not suffice for the foundation of an actual industrial organization. The many manufactures and *Arbeitshäuser* created by the king were artificial islands which could not survive without state support. Luxury goods could be consumed by a small elite only, so that these institutions had no influence on the 'national' economy. Also, most *Arbeitshäuser* simultanously fulfilled the functions of workshop, hospital and prison, which hindered the rational division of labour. The 'social policy' of Frederick the Great accomplished little; terror was the sole result. Living conditions in the *Arbeitshäuser* were so revolting that the deserving poor took recourse there only when totally destitute. Needless to say, these institutions did not counterbalance the alarming increase of begging and vagabondage, above all in the countryside, where the feudal burden grew more and more unbearable. Peasant revolts broke out again and again from the 1770s onwards, clearly indicative that the whole system of poor relief had failed.[43]

Pleas for out-relief may have found a hearing, but such programmes could only succeed in towns where considerable opportunities for employment were available. In areas characterized by feudal and aristocratic structures, there was no hope for success as the example of Austria proves. In 1779 Count Bouquoi founded an *Armeninstitut* on his Bohemian lands, which provided out-relief for all the needy. Since at most one-third of the usual wage was awarded and begging was forbidden, two goals could be attained, according to the Count: 'First, the deserving poor shall be satisfied with the support received and envy no one. Second, no one shall want such alms as long as he works, and consequently no one who is able to work will shirk from it.' Many Austrian towns subsequently followed his example, including Linz and Vienna. In 1784 Joseph II decreed the foundation of similar institutions throughout the monarchy and assigned general direction to Count Bouquoi. The organization everywhere rested on the same principles: prohibition of begging, centralization of relief funds, and minimal provision for sedentary paupers. The system was not allotted a long life. Lacking industry, provision of work for the poor was in most cases excluded, while out-relief brought along a sharp rise in expenses. Some exceptions aside, the *Armeninstitut* languished after the death of Joseph II.

As in other continental countries, an effective social policy appeared attainable only when local authorities and private entrepreneurs joined hands. The economic expansion which some German towns experienced at the end of the eighteenth century gave an opening to such experiments. In 1788, on the proposal of the merchant Kasper Voght, Hamburg created an *Armenanstalt*, based on a combination of out-relief and provision of employment. Hamburg was divided into districts containing roughly equal numbers of paupers. Each district was controlled by overseers, responsible to a central administration comprising five senators and ten other burghers chosen for life. Overseers visited the needy regularly, controlled their incomes, had their health investigated by an official physician, questioned employers and neighbours about their way of life, and registered all these data on printed forms. On the basis of this information a closely reckoned sum was to be dispensed weekly to every needy person. Beggars and vagabonds excepted, no one was directly forced to work. The system, however, gave no other choice: levels of support never exceeded the wages of an unskilled labourer, and families did not receive support for children over six years. The administration left nothing to chance: paupers not employed by manufacturers could spin, sew or knit at home for the *Armenanstalt*. Industrial schools were set up for paupers' children from six to sixteen; on the average, two-thirds of the time there was spent in work, while the rest was devoted to rudimentary training. Although regulation of the labour market was the chief purpose, the administration turned its attention to the social discipline of the needy as well. As the Kiel Professor A. Niemann, a fervent proponent of this system of poor relief, declared in 1793: 'An institution which encourages profitable and useful employment must keep in mind not only the skills of the workers, goods in the warehouse, sales, and pure profits; it must attach an even higher value to the habituation of diligence, the weaning away from laziness . . . and the self-reliance of adolescents.'

Operation of the system, however, was totally dependent on the demand for cheap labour. In Vienna, for example, Voght's programme accomplished nothing in practice, despite the efforts of Emperor Francis II, because it brought more disadvantages than advantages: opportunities for profitable employment of the mass of the destitute were simply not there. The same holds for Munich; on the initiative of Benjamin Thompson (a soldier-of-fortune in command of the Bavarian army, later known as Count Rumford), reform of poor relief on Hamburg's model was carried out in 1790. Given the small number of existing industries, Rumford founded a great *Arbeitshaus* to provide work for the poor. This institution, chiefly designed as a centre for manufacture of military clothing, rendered a profit for several years, but in 1799 it closed. Employment of supported workers systematically depressed other workers' wages, so that poverty grew even further. All these factors explain why few central European towns ultimately instituted out-relief, and why others abandoned the system after a short time. This situation lasted until the nineteenth century, when this form of social policy – known as the Elberfeld System, after the textile centre – found general acceptance in Germany.[44]

CONCLUSION

We have tried to throw some light on three interdependent problems concerning pre-industrial society: the causes of impoverishment, the changes in the composition of the 'marginal' population, and the functions fulfilled by diverse systems of poor relief. All three seemed to be connected with the growth of capitalism. Taking into account the present state of knowledge, it is risky indeed to make generalized statements; nevertheless, it seems clear that some traditional interpretations and methods of analysis can be rejected out of hand.

First, poverty in the *ancien régime* cannot be reduced to a 'natural' phenomenon, inherent in a 'society of scarcity,' determined by technological backwardness and a tendency towards unrestricted demographic growth. To view pre-industrial Europe in terms of cycles of population growth and decline, in terms of 'the immense respiration of a social structure', is to beg the question. How then would the extent of destitution be comparable in areas of both economic advance and backwardness, in periods of both population expansion and stagnation? Social inequality cannot be explained in isolation from class relations. Even a sketchy investigation of the dominant aspects of the feudal mode of production, of commercial capitalism, and of nascent industrial capitalism demonstrates that poverty can be fully understood only as the consequence of an established structure of surplus-extractive relations.

The majority of the medieval peasantry lived permanently at subsistence minima because the feudal mode of production rested on the predominance of small, individual producers subjected to heavy extraction of surplus applied through extra-economic coercion within a political structure marked by its 'parcellization of sovereignty.' This ensemble of components also explains why economic growth had a primarily extensive character (expansion of surface area under cultivation and augmentation of input of labour), which sooner or later had to lead to a general blockage.

The causes of the fourteenth century crisis are to be found neither in external factors nor in 'objective' supply and demand mechanisms, but in the internal contradictions of the feudal mode of production itself.

The structural shortage of labour resulting from demographic collapse and the stiff resistance of village communities against seigneurial reaction put the western European peasantry in a position to erase the stigma of personal dependence. Nonetheless, the social differentiation of the preceding centuries remained and even grew. Two factors were responsible for this development. In the first place, the growing tyranny of the market, with its freedom to buy or to rent land, to cultivate cash crops, etc., meant increasing economic insecurity. In many regions the extension of commercial livestock raising was paired with the dispossession of small peasants, the extinction of rights to the commons, and growing unemployment. Also, the tightening grip of the urban bourgeoisie on the surrounding countryside had an unfavourable impact on the peasantry, since most merchants were interested only in speculative profits.

In the second place and even more significantly, new structures of surplus extraction arose. In France and in Germany west of the Elbe, small peasant proprietors and the absolutist State developed in mutual interdependence, with the result that the peasantry were subjected to a two-fold exploitation: crushing taxation by the Crown on the one hand and the renewal of feudal obligations and the imposition of sharecropping tenures by local landlords in search of a 'second-best strategy' on the other. These burdens undermined not only the economic position of the peasantry but also ruled out technological improvements and, consequently, substantial increases in productivity. Not surprisingly, the daily life of the rural masses in both regions until the end of the *ancien régime* was a daily struggle to avoid destitution, if not starvation. In England, in contrast, a nearly if not absolutely unique agrarian structure came into being, based on consolidated landed estates, divided into large tenant farms, worked by wage labourers. This led to agrarian improvement, which in turn favoured general economic growth. The transformation of agricultural production, however, proletarianized a large segment of the rural population. Innumerable marginal peasants lost their means of existence and were obliged to sell their labour. Hence structural poverty was characteristic of both England and France by 1700, although the former was freed from crises of subsistence.

The manner in which relations of production developed in the industrial sector likewise entailed the proletarianization of broad sectors of the population. Just as in agriculture, urban manufacturing was initially dominated by small or middle-sized commodity-producers. The economic independence of this group was gradually eroded by larger scale craftsmen, and above all, by merchant entrepreneurs who controlled the import of the most important raw materials and the sale of the finished products. In nearly all centres with an important export industry, similar processes ran their course: most craftsmen became dependent on the entrepreneurs and were compelled to surrender their produce to them, reduced *de facto* to wage labourers. The triumph of commercial capitalism brought further reallocation of industrial production and, as a result, the disruption of urban society. Indeed, through the putting-out system, which required little investment in durable means of production, merchant entrepreneurs could withdraw their capital from one town or region, if need be, and transfer it to another. From the economic point of view, such reorientation merely signified compensation, but in social terms it was a disaster: the proletarianized population of the abandoned town encountered the most severe misery.

The transfer of industry to the countryside, begun in the Middle Ages, reached its peak in the seventeenth and eighteenth centuries, when the advancing impoverishment of the peasantry conjoined with a rapidly rising demand for cheap fabrics. Naturally, the growth of rural industry struck urban production heavily and often fatally. In the countryside itself, the extension of the putting-out system dominated by commercial capital not only led to the dissolution of the traditional peasant economy but also undermined the social controls which had previously buttressed a system of late marriage. Every rural area where cottage industry developed on a large scale evolved similarly in the long run: rapid demographic growth, excessive fragmentation of landholdings, sharp rise in rents, continuous pressure on wages, growing self-exploitation by the producers – in short proletarianization and impoverishment. In regions where proto-industrialization was paired to the expansion of 'poverty cultures' such as potatoes, which allowed a family to live off a tiny morsel of ground, these processes were pushed to the extreme. Most serious of all, the proto-industrial system contained the germ of its own decline. Flanders, Saxony, and above all Ireland are striking examples of this inbuilt tendency towards self-destruction.

Yet proto-industrialization paved the way for the definitive breakthrough of industrial capitalism. On the one hand, it accomplished the proletarianization of masses of peasants and artisans and their integration into an extra-local marketing system. On the other hand, employers were sooner or later imprisoned in a 'cost-cage', so that they had to seek out other means to increase production within the bounds of their radius of action. Early passage to the factory system, however, was strongly dependent on organizational factors. If commercial capital dominated cottage industry, then structural renewal generally was absent. Mechanization was initially carried out only where industrial production was at least partially in the hands of independent manufacturers or middlemen unhindered by putting-out merchants.

Nevertheless the rise of the capitalist mode of production in no sense signified the end of cottage industry. The introduction of the machine was not an end in itself for the entrepreneurs, only a means to lower production costs. As long as the low level of wages maintained their competitive edge on the international market, investment in labour-saving devices was absent. Hence industrialization was a step by step process. Mechanization of specific sequences of manufacturing not only degraded socially the artisans involved but also and simultaneously stimulated the growth of handicraft production in other trades. When the workers employed in that sector were in turn replaced by machines they transferred to industries in which handicrafts still predominated, thereby augmenting the impoverishment processes already at work. The notion that in the century after 1750 cottage industries and their concomitant poverty were only residual vestiges of an early period is absolutely unconvincing. The Industrial Revolution was characterized equally by the emergence of a new working class as by the proliferation of 'sweated labour'. Despite the debate on the relative wellbeing of factory workers and handicraft workers, neither of the two systems had favourable or unfavourable social implications. Both were dominated by capitalist relations of production, be it commercial capital or industrial, and for that reason the interrelated development of the domestic system and the factory system in the century after 1750 resulted in massive impoverishment.

It follows that it is pointless to stereotype the pre-industrial poor. Although no period or region was free of poverty, the composition of the relative surplus population varied according to time and place. At first sight, one might hypothesize that the extent of destitution was only liable to small changes between 1300 and 1700 or even 1800. Indeed, the number of those living at subsistence minima can almost always be estimated at 40 or 50 per cent of local, regional, or national population. These figures, however, tell us nothing of the ways in which poverty manifested itself.

The cottars of the thirteenth century who drew an insufficient income from their land to support a family had to get by on casual labour, but still primarily within the network of feudal relations: marginal peasants did not live simply off the sale of their labour, nor could they dispose of their labour in complete 'freedom'. Their morsels of land, no matter how small, released them from the economic laws of the commodity exchange, but from the moment the feudal umbilical cord was cut, production and consumption grew increasingly dependent on the market, with its growing economic insecurity. The gradual transition to the capitalist mode of production meant that the material situation of the peasantry was increasingly determined by external factors. Slowly but surely broad segments of the rural population were pulled out of their relatively self-contained economy and integrated into a growing free labour market. The social consequences of this transition cannot be followed completely in full detail as the sources are incomplete, but all available evidence shows that more and more subsistence peasants made way for a landless proletariat. It was no accident that begging and vagabondage became such a social problem during the 'long sixteenth century', nor that the bulk of all fabrics were produced in rural areas by the end of the seventeenth. Both phenomena indicate the acceleration of the proletarianization and the impoverishment of the peasantry. For the same reasons, the subsequent period witnessed the expansion of the potato and the uprooting of the cottars, finally resulting in large scale migrations from one country to another, even one continent to another.

It should be remarked that in the period studied the size of the landless proletariat nowhere else reached such proportions as on the 'untroubled island'. In Tudor and Stuart England, wage labourers and farm hands represented 25 to 33 per cent of the rural population; at the end of the seventeenth century, 40 per cent of the total population had abandoned agriculture, mostly for industry; and by 1820 the number had climbed to around 60 per cent of the national population, versus scarcely 20 per cent in France. The living conditions of English wage labourers were nonetheless no more enviable than those of subsistence peasants and cottage workers on the continent, still 'enjoying' the fruits of their sliver of land.

The towns not only functioned as refuges for uprooted peasants; they also generated the poor. Indeed, the development of capitalist means of production involved the inexorable proletarianization and eventual impoverishment of nearly all craftsmen. A large body of evidence shows that the proportion of wage labourers in the urban population rose continuously. Figures on the number of fiscally poor or supported poor provide no information on the real extent of urban destitution, let alone poverty; the relevant data mirror only the criteria applied by contemporary authorities. These data, however, may be considered in general to be reliable as minimum figures, because tax collectors and poor relief authorities referred to the most stringent of definitions when categorizing someone as needy or poor. Thus the growing disparity in the division of total wealth and the continuing decline of average *per capita* consumption of food indicates that a growing number of townsmen faced both relative and absolute impoverishment. The eighteenth century authors who equated wage labour with poverty were on the mark.

The structural dependence and vulnerability of the swelling ranks of the proletariat necessitated creation of a well organized system of poor relief. In every region of Europe where capital forced its way into the productive sphere a social policy was brought into being with two dominant functions: control of the relatively superfluous population and regulation of the labour market. The rise of capitalist means of production required the construction of public mechanisms of support, which not only kept the reserve army of the poor under control in order to guarantee political order but also offered the possibility of providing employers sufficiently cheap wage labour at every moment to reach their economic targets. Hence poor relief during the feudal-capitalist transition evolved from a discontinuous and highly undifferentiated source of assistance, chiefly dispensed as private charity on a voluntary basis, to a continuous and selective system, largely maintained by public institutions which often taxed to raise the funds necessary. From the sixteenth century onwards, alternations between flexible and rigorous regulations for support were more and more determined by the changing needs of the market and the variable level of social 'stability'. According to circumstances, the accent was now placed on the duty to work, then on the neutralization of class tensions. The expansion of pauperism was never in and of itself a sufficient condition to call poor relief into existence or to maintain it. The 'miscarriage' of poor laws in certain areas is to be explained by economic and political factors. Medieval and early modern governments and local authorities did not have the intention to wipe out poverty. They merely tried to maintain the social *status quo* and to encourage production. The 'adequacy' of their social policy must be viewed within that restrictive framework.

Many examples demonstrate the validity of this argument. The triumph of commercial capitalism brought with it a reorganization of traditional charity. England, the only country to see the breakthrough of agrarian capitalism, was also the only state which maintained the new social policy in the following centuries and made it work. Nowhere else in early modern Europe was the mobility of the rural population led down the 'correct' paths by legislation. On the continent, most projects for the reform of poor relief during the economic recession of 1630–1750 remained a dead letter, except in France, where a nationwide flurry of revolts led to the 'Great Confinement'. The expansion of centralized production in the century after 1750 gave a new opportunity for fundamental reorganization of social policy in the centres involved. Again it was in England, where nascent industrial capitalism was entering a new phase, that a 'total' system of public support was instituted for the first time in history.

The argument that the growing efficiency of social policy was the result of religious or moral motivations is unsound. It is not that sixteenth-century reformers and eighteenth century philosophers exercised no influence on poor relief; but, in most cases, their ideas were only put into practice when they could be 'translated' into economic or political terms, that is, when the trinity of charity – control – labour regulation coincided with the real or imagined interests of employers and authorities. As for private charity: the empathy of elite groups limited itself to the 'deserving' poor, namely children, the aged, and the ill and infirm. The misery of wage labourers either went unrecognized or was ascribed to laziness or other personal shortcomings.

The crystallization of a new working class went hand in hand with the efforts of the bourgeoisie to impress their system of values on the 'labouring poor'. Hence the emphasis during the Industrial Revolution lay on individual misfortune and the discipline of the *bourgeois manqué*. Preaching the virtues of sobriety, thrift, patience and resignation were the favoured means to assure the docility of the lower classes. A network of paternalistic initiatives consolidated – and simultaneously justified – a fundamental social inequality. The more capitalism strengthened its grip on society, the more that this aspect of social policy came to the fore.

BIBLIOGRAPHY AND NOTES

Abbreviations used

ADH	*Annales de Démographie Historique* (Paris)
AESC	*Annales. Economies. Sociétés. Civilisations* (Paris)
AgHR	*Agricultural History Review* (Reading)
AHEW	Joan Thirsk, ed., *The Agrarian History of England and Wales*, vol. IV (Cambridge, 1967)
AHN	*Acta Historiae Neerlandicae* (Groningen)
AHR	*American Historical Review* (Washington D.C.)
AJS	*American Journal of Sociology* (Chicago)
AR	*Archiv für Reformationsgeschichte* (Gütersloh)
BTFG	*Belgisch Tijdschrift voor Filologie en Geschiedenis* (Brussels)
CEHE	*The Cambridge Economic History of Europe*
EcHE	*The Economic History Review* (Hertfordshire)
ER	*Études Rurales* (Paris)
FEHE	*The Fontana Economic History of Europe*
HESF	F. Braudel and E. Labrousse, eds, *Histoire économique et sociale de la France* (Paris)
HFR	G. Duby and A. Wallon, eds, *Histoire de la France rurale* (Paris)
HG	*Hansische Geschichtsblätter* (Leipzig)
HWJ	*History Workshop Journal* (London)
ICEH	*International Conference of Economic History*
IRSH	*International Review of Social History* (Assen)
JEH	*The Journal of Economic History* (New York)
JIH	*The Journal of Interdisciplinary History* (Pittsburg)
JPS	*The Journal of Peasant Studies* (London)
MA	*Le Moyen Age* (Paris)
PP	*Past and Present* (Oxford)
RH	*Revue Historique* (Paris)
RHEF	*Revue d'Histoire de l'Eglise de France* (Paris)
RHES	*Revue d'Histoire Économique et Sociale* (Paris)
RHMC	*Revue d'Histoire Moderne et Contemporaine* (Paris)
RN	*Revue du Nord* (Lille)

SH	*Social History* (London)
SZG	*Schweizerische Zeitschrift für Geschichte* (Geneva)
TG	*Tijdschrift voor Geschiedenis* (Groningen)
TRHS	*Transactions of the Royal Historical Society* (London)
TSG	*Tijdschrift voor Sociale Geschiedenis* (Amsterdam)
VSWG	*Vierteljahrschrift für Sozial- und Wirtschaftsgeschichte* (Wiesbaden)
ZAA	*Zeitschrift für Agrargeschichte und Agrarsoziologie* (Frankfurt am Main)

General sources

The most comprehensive surveys of economic realities in medieval and early modern Europe are the *Cambridge Economic History of Europe*, vols I–VI (1952–7), and the *Fontana Economic History of Europe, vols* I–IV (1972–5), which have very useful and extensive bibliographies. Of one-author, one-volume works, the best introduction to some basic features of the Europe of the time is presented in C. M. Cipolla, *Before the Industrial Revolution: European society and economy, 1000–1700* (London, 1976). Maurice Dobb, *Studies in the Development of Capitalism* (London, 1946), though somewhat outdated, is still the most brilliant essay on the feudal–capitalist transition. The author's controversial interpretations provoked a valuable debate among Marxist historians: Rodney H. Hilton, ed., *The Transition from Feudalism to Capitalism* (London, 1976). At the time of writing, only the first volume of Fernand Braudel's monumental trilogy on *Capitalism and Material Life, 1400–1800* (London, 1967) has been published. For a succinct synthesis of the author's original ideas on the subject one can turn to F. Braudel, *Afterthoughts on Material Civilization and Capitalism* (Baltimore, 1977).

B. H. Slicher van Bath, *The Agrarian History of Western Europe; A.D. 500–1850* (London, 1963) offers an excellent survey of the agricultural sector. There is an enormous body of scholarly analysis on famine crises. For a summary of recent findings, see Pierre Goubert, 'Historical demography and the reinterpretation of early modern French history: a research review', *JIH*, 1 (1970), 37–48. An eloquent proponent of neo-malthusian models is Wilhelm Abel, *Massenarmut und Hungerkrisen im vorindustriellen Europa. Versuch einer Synopsis* (Hamburg and Berlin, 1974). For a detailed account of the 'centuries-long two-phase movement', see E. Le Roy Ladurie, *Les Paysans de Languedoc* (2 vols, Paris, 1966), now available in an abridged translation, *The Peasants of Languedoc*

(Urbana, Ill, 1974). The weakness of traditional explanations for the pattern of economic development in the Middle Ages and the early modern period has recently been exposed by Robert Brenner, 'Agrarian class structure and economic development in pre-industrial Europe', *PP*, 70 (1976), 30–75 (and debate, *PP*, 78–80).

Of economic histories restricted to particular periods, the following may be consulted with advantage: N. J. G. Pounds, *An Economic History of Medieval Europe* (New York and London, 1974); G. Fourquin, *Histoire économique de l'Occident médiéval* (Paris, 1969); R. Davis, *The Rise of the Atlantic Economies* (London, 1973); H. Kellenbenz, *The Rise of the European Economy. An economic history of continental Europe from the fifteenth to the eighteenth Century* (London, 1976).

Among recent studies of the economy of individual countries, the following should be noted: for England: M. M. Postan, *The Medieval Economy and Society: an economic history of Britain, 1100–1500* (London, 1972); Charles Wilson, *England's Apprenticeship, 1603–1763* (London, 1965); L. A. Clarkson, *The Pre-Industrial Economy in England, 1500–1750* (London, 1971); D. C. Coleman, *The Economy of England 1450–1750* (London, 1977).

For France: F. Braudel and E. Labrousse (eds.), *Histoire économique et sociale de la France*, vols I–II (Paris, 1970–7); G. Duby and A. Wallon, eds., *Histoire de la France rurale*, vols I–II (Paris, 1975–6).

For Germany: H. Aubin and W. Zorn, (eds.), *Handbuch der deutschen Wirtschafts– und Sozialgeschichte,* I, *Von den Frühzeit bis zum Ende des 18. Jahrhunderts* (Stuttgart, 1971): H. Kellenbenz, *Deutsche Wirtschaftsgeschichte,* I, *Von den Anfängen bis zum Ende des 18. Jahrhunderts* (Munich, 1977); W. Abel, *Geschichte der deutschen Landwirtschaft vom frühen Mittelalter bis zum 19. Jahrhundert* (Stuttgart, 1962); G. Franz, *Geschichte des deutschen Bauernstandes vom frühen Mittelalter bis zum 19. Jahrhundert* (Stuttgart, 1970).

For Italy: G. Luzzato, *An Economic History of Italy from the Fall of the Roman Empire to the Beginning of the Sixteenth Century* (London, 1961); C. M. Cipolla, 'The economic decline of Italy', in *The Economic Decline of Empires* (London, 1970), pp. 196–214.

For the Low Countries: J. A. van Houtte, *An Economic History of the Low Countries, 800–1800* (London, 1977); J. H. van Stuyvenberg, ed., *De economisch geschiedenis van Nederland* (Groningen, 1977).

For Scotland: S. G. E. Lythe and J. Butt, *An Economic History of Scotland, 1100–1939* (Glasgow, 1975); T. C. Smout, *A History of the Scottish People, 1560–1830* (London, 1972). For Spain: J. Vicens Vives, *An Economic History of Spain* (Princeton, 1969). For Switzerland: A. Hauser, *Schweizerische Wirtschafts- und Sozialgeschichte* (Zürich, 1961); J.-F. Bergier, *Problèmes de l'histoire économique de la Suisse* (Bern, 1968) and *Naissance et croissance de la Suisse industrielle* (Bern, 1974).

No recent book is devoted to the social history of pre-industrial Europe, but Robert Fossier, *Histoire sociale de l'Occident médiéval* (Paris, 1970), Henry Kamen, *The Iron Century: social change in Europe, 1550–1660* (London, 1971) and Pierre Goubert, *The Ancien Regime*, vol I (New York, 1973), give an almost complete panorama if read consecutively. Ph. Wolff and F. Mauro, *Histoire générale du travail*, II, *L'Âge de l'artisanat, Ve-XVIIIe siècle* (Paris, 1965), offer a comparative survey of working conditions. The quantity and the kind of foods consumed are the best criteria for objective measurement of the standard of living in the period concerned. Important articles on this subject will be found in J.-J. Hémardinquer, ed., *Pour une histoire de l'alimentation* (Paris, 1970) and 'Histoire de l'alimentation', *AESC*, 30 (1975), 402–632 (special issue).

There is no recent book on the general history of poverty and poor relief, but Michel Mollat, *Les pauvres au Moyen Age* (Paris, 1977) and J.-P. Gutton, *La Société et les pauvres en Europe, XVIe–XVIIIe siècles* (Paris, 1974) are useful introductions to the problems. The former is thorough, wideranging, and contains a large bibliography; the latter is an interesting if sketchy essay, with an underdeveloped bibliography. Though providing valuable information on the circumstances of poverty and on public attitudes towards the poor, neither of the two works really explains the basic causes of impoverishment and the successive alterations of social policy.

Numerous monographs deal with poverty and/or poor relief over an extended period of time. For England, the most useful introductions are S. and B. Webb, *English Local Government; English Poor Law History*, vol I, *The Old Poor Law*, (2nd edn., London, 1963); K. De Schweinitz, *England's Road to Social Security* (Philadelphia, 1949); E. M. Leonard, *The Early History of English Poor Relief* (2nd edn, New York, 1965). For France: J.-P. Gutton, *La Société et les pauvres. L'exemple de la généralité de Lyon, 1534–1789* (Paris, 1971). For Germany: G. Ratzinger, *Geschichte der deutschen Armenpflege* (2nd edn, Freiburg i. Br., 1884). For Italy: B. Geremek, 'Renfermement des pauvres en Italie (XIVe–XVIIe siècles). Remarques préliminaires', in *Mélanges en l'honneur de Fernand Braudel* (2 vols., Toulouse, 1973), vol I, 205–17. For the Low Countries: 'Armoede en armenzorg', *TG*, 88 (1975), 449–636 (special issue). For Scotland : A. A. Cormack, *Poor Relief in Scotland* (Aberdeen 1923) and T. Ferguson, *The Dawn of Scottish Social Welfare* (London, 1948). For Spain : V. Rau and F. Saez, eds., *A Pobreza e a Assistência dos Pobres na Peninsula Ibérica durante a Idade Media* (2 vols, Lisbon, 1973) and M. Jimenez Salas, *Historia de la Assistencia Social en España en la Edad Moderna* (Madrid, 1958). For Switzerland : K. Geiser, *Geschichte des Armenwesens im Kanton Bern von der Reformation bis auf die neuere Zeit* (Bern, 1894); A. Briod, *L'Assistance des pauvres dans le Pays de Vaud* (Lausanne, 1926); and A.-M. Dubler, *Armen- und Bettler wesen in der Gemeinen Herrschaft 'Freie Amter', 16. bis 18. Jahrhundert* (Basel, 1970).

Notes

1. Poverty as a social problem was 'discovered' in the United States by Michael Harrington, *The Other America* (New York, 1962). From that time on, sociological and economic contributions have accelerated rapidly. Among recent studies see esp. G. Kolko, *Wealth and Power in America* (New York, 1969); J.-M. Chevalier, *La Pauvreté aux Etats-Unis. Essai d'intégration dans l'analyse économique* (Paris, 1971); and L. Thurow, *Generating Inequality* (New York, 1975). For some European countries, see K. Coates and R. Silburn, *Poverty: the forgotten Englishmen* (London, 1970); J. C. Kincaird, *Poverty and Equality in Britain* (London, 1973); Werkgroep Alternatieve Economie, *Armoede in België* (Antwerp and Utrecht, 1972); J. Roth, *Armut in der Bundesrepublik* (Frankfurt, 1974), L. Fabius, *La France inégale* (Paris, 1975).
2. For a succinct synthesis of Oscar Lewis's views on the 'culture of poverty', one can turn to the article by the same author, 'The culture of poverty', in D. P. Moynihan, ed., *On Understanding Poverty* (New York, 1968), pp. 187–200. See also H. J. Gans, 'Poverty and culture: some basic questions about methods of studying life-styles of the poor', in P. Townsend, ed., *The Concept of Poverty: working papers on methods of investigation and life-styles of the poor in different countries* (London, 1970), pp. 146–64.
3. S. Kuznets, quoted by Clarkson, *The Pre-Industrial Economy in England*, p. 10.
4. G. Uhlhorn, *Die christliche Liebesthätigkeit im Mittelalter* and

Die christliche Liebesthätigkeit seit der Reformation (Stuttgart, 1884–90); L. Lallemand, *Histoire de la charité*, III, *Le Moyen Age, du Xe au XVIe siècle*, IV, *Les Temps Modernes, du XVIe au XIXe siècle* (Paris, 1910–12); W. Liese, *Geschichte der Caritas* (2 vols, Freiburg i. Br., 1922).

5. Cf. J.-L. Goglin, *Les Misérables dans l'Occident médiéval* (Paris, 1976), who starts his exposition with the following enunciation: 'Man has suffered; he suffers, and he will suffer. Material poverty and moral distress, material distress and moral poverty are his companions. The Middle Ages did not escape the rule' (p. 9).
6. A. Dubuc, 'Closing remarks', in F. Krantz and P. M. Hohenberg, eds., *Failed Transitions to Modern Industrial Society: Renaissance Italy and seventeenth-century Holland* (Proceedings of the First International Colloquium of the Interuniversity Centre for European Studies, Montreal, 1975), p. 85.

Chapter 1. Feudalism, poverty and charity

Bibliography

The book which has done most in recent years to illuminate the transition from the ancient mode of production to feudalism is undoubtedly Perry Anderson, *Passages from Antiquity to Feudalism* (London, 1974). Two general surveys cover the expansion of the medieval economy: R. S. Lopez, *The Commercial Revolution of the Middle Ages, 950–1350* (Cambridge, 1976 ed) and L. Génicot, *Le XIIIe siècle européen* (Paris, 1968).

The history of agriculture is exhaustively surveyed by Georges Duby, *Rural Economy and Country Life in the Medieval West* (London, 1968). Among a large number of regional studies, note esp.: for England: M. M. Postan, 'Medieval agrarian society in its prime: England', *CEHE*, vol. I (1966 edn), 549–632; R. Lennard, *Rural England, 1068–1135* (Oxford, 1959); E. A. Kosminsky, *Studies in the Agrarian History of England in the Thirteenth Century* (Oxford, 1956); J. Titow, *English Rural Society, 1200–1350* (London, 1969); R. H. Hilton, *The Decline of Serfdom in Medieval England* (London, 1969). For France: R. Fossier, *La Terre et les hommes en Picardie jusqu'à la fin du XIIIe siècle* (Paris 1968); Guy Bois, *Crise du féodalisme* (Paris, 1976), though covering the later Middle Ages, presents an exceptionally lucid analysis of the basis of the feudal economy. For Germany: Ph. Dollinger, *L'Évolution des classes rurales en Bavière depuis la fin de l'époque carolingienne jusqu'au milieu du XIIIe siècle* (Paris, 1949); H. Dubled, 'Administration et exploitation des terres de la seigneurie rurale en Alsace aux XIe et XII siècles', *VSWG*, 47 (1960), 433–73. For Italy : P. J. Jones, 'Per la storia agraria italiana nel medio evo : lineamenti e problemi', *Rivista Storica Italiana*, 76 (1964), 287–348, and 'From manor to mezzadria : a Tuscan case. Study in the medieval origins of modern agrarian society', in N. Rubinstein, ed., *Florentine Studies* (London, 1968), pp. 193–241. For the Low Countries : B. H. Slicher van Bath, 'The rise of intensive husbandry in the Low Countries', in J. S. Bromley and E. H. Kossmann, eds., *Britain and the Netherlands* (London, 1960), pp. 130–53; A. E. Verhulst, 'Bronnen en problemen betreffende de Vlaamse landbouw in de late middeleeuwen (XIIIe–XVe eeuw)', in *Ceres en Clio* (Wageningen, 1964), pp. 205–33.

There is no recent book on the general history of medieval manufacturing, but Sylvia Thrupp, 'Medieval industry, 1000–1500', *FEHE*, vol. I (1972), 221–73, provides a short survey. On woollen cloth, see the excellent, though somewhat English-centred, article by E. Carus-Wilson, 'The woollen industry', *CEHE*, vol. II (1952), 355–429. See also the collection of articles *Produzione, Commercio e Consumo dei Panni di Lana*, M. Spallanzani, ed., (2 vols, Florence, 1976–7). By far the best introductions to employment relationships are E. Perroy, *Le Travail dans les régions du Nord, du XIe au début du XIV siècle* (2 vols, mimeographed, Paris, 1962) and Bronislaw Geremek, *Le Salariat dans l'artisanat parisien aux XIIIe–XVe siècles. Étude sur le marché de la main-d'oeuvre au Moyen Age* (Paris, 1968). The reinforcement of merchant patricians' control over the towns in the thirteenth century, has been underlined by A. B. Hibbert, 'The Economic Policies of Towns', *CEHE*, vol. III (1963), 157–229. Of the numerous monographs on medieval towns, note esp. David Herlihy, *Pisa in the Early Renaissance: a study of urban growth* (New Haven, 1958) and *Medieval and Renaissance Pistoia: the social history of an Italian town, 1200–1430* (New Haven and London, 1967).

Michel Mollat has edited an important series of specialized articles on various aspects of poverty and poor relief in *Études sur l'histoire de la pauvreté, Moyen Age–XVIe siècle* (2 vols., Paris, 1974). Apart from Mollat's overall survey, cited in the bibliography for the foreword, the following general essays may be consulted with advantage : F. Graus, 'Au bas moyen âge : pauvres des villes et pauvres des campagnes', *AESC*, 6 (1961), 1053–65; K. Bosl, 'Potens und Pauper', in *Frühformen der Gesellschaft im mittelalterlichen Europa* (Munich and Vienna, 1964), pp. 106–34, and 'Armut,

Arbeit, Emanzipation', in *Beiträge zur Wirtschafts– und Sozialgeschichte des Mittelalters. Festschrift für Herbert Helbig* (Cologne and Vienna, 1976), pp. 128–46.

There is a mass of monographs on poverty and/or poor relief. For England, see B. Tierney's classic *Medieval Poor Law: a sketch of canonical theory and its application in England* (Berkeley, 1959) and the interesting article by A. N. May, 'An index of XIIIth-century Peasant Impoverishment?', *EcHR*, 26 (1973), which throws light on the manor court fines as a source of information. For France: J. M. Bienvenu, 'Pauvreté, misères et charité en Anjou aux XIe et XIIe siècles', *MA* 72 (1966), 389–424, 73 (1967), 5–34, 189–216; A. Vauchez, 'La pauvreté volontaire au Moyen Age', *AESC*, 25 (1970), 1566–73; M. Candille, 'Pour un précis d'histoire des institutions charitables', *Bulletin de la Société française d'Histoire des Hôpitaux*, 30 (1974). For Germany: E. Maschke, 'Die Unterschichten der mittelalterlichen Städte Deutschlands', in C. Haase, ed., *Die Stadt des Mittelalters*, III, *Wirtschaft und Gesellschaft* (Darmstadt, 1973); pp. 345–454, is an excellent survey of the present state of knowledge. For Italy: Ch.-M. de La Roncière, 'Pauvres et pauvreté à Florence au XIVe siècle', in Mollat, ed., *Études*, 2, 661–745, is by far the best analysis of urban poverty in its period. For the Low Countries: W. P. Blockmans and W. Prevenier, 'Armoede in de Nederlanden van de 14e tot het midden van de 16e eeuw: bronnen en problemen', *TG*, 88 (1975), 501–38, is an excellent essay, which contains a mass of quantitative information; M.-J. Tits-Dieuaide, 'Les tables des pauvres dans les anciennes principautés belges au Moyen Age', *ibid.*, 562–83, presents a clear picture of poor relief; L. Génicot, 'Sur le nombre des pauvres dans les campagnes médiévales. L'exemple du Namurois', *RH* 258 (1977) 273–88, throws light on the intricate problem of computing the rural poor. For Spain: N. Guglielmi, 'Modos de marginalidad en la Edad Media: Extranjera, pobreza, enfermedad', *Annales de Historia Antigua y Medieval*, 16 (1971), 7–187.

Much work has been done on the history of medieval hospitals. Among the more important general studies are S. Reiche, *Das deutsche Spital und sein Recht im Mittelalter* (2 vols, Stuttgart, 1932); J. Imbert, *Les Hôpitaux en droit canonique* (Paris, 1947); Jesko von Steynitz, *Mittelalterliche Hospitäler der Orden und Städte als Einrichtung der Sozialen Sicherung* (Berlin, 1970). An excellent case study is G. Maréchal, 'Het hospitaalwezen te Brugge in de middeleeuwen. Een institutionele en sociale studie' (2 vols, unpublished Ph.D. thesis, Ghent, 1975).

Notes

1. Kosminksy, *Studies*, p. 301.
2. Bois, *Crise*, pp. 164–70, 216ff, 351–4.
3. Postan, 'Medieval agrarian society', p. 613.
4. Duby, *Rural Economy*, p. 285.
5. Cf. Postan, *The Medieval Economy and Society*, p. 212, characterizes the towns in this period as 'non-feudal islands in the feudal seas'.
6. J. Merrington, 'Town and country in the transition to capitalism', *New Left Review*, 93 (1975), 71–92 (on p. 78). See also Dobb, *Studies*, pp. 27–8, 34, 38–9; A. B. Hibbert, 'The origins of the medieval town patriciate', *PP*, 3 (1953), 15–27; Cl. Cahen, 'A propos de la discussion sur la féodalité', *La Pensée*, 68 (1956), 95–6; Anderson, *Passages*, pp. 150, 193–4; R. H. Hilton, 'Feudalism and the origins of capitalism', *HWJ*, 1 (1976), 16.
7. A. Derville, 'Les draperies flamandes et artésiennes vers 1250–1350', *RN*, 54 (1972), 357–61.
8. See the excellent general account by Hibbert, 'The economic policies of towns', pp. 198–206.
9. Data in this paragraph taken from Herlihy, *Medieval and Renaissance Pistoia*, pp. 181–3; M. Belotte, *La Région de Bar-sur-Seine à la fin du Moyen Age* (Lille, 1973), p. 146; Postan, 'Medieval agrarian society', p. 619; Titow, *English Rural Society*, pp. 78–9; Fossier, *La Terre et les hommes en Picardie*, pp. 646–7; L. Génicot, 'L'étendue des exploitations agricoles dans le comté de Namur à la fin du XIIIe siècle', *ER*, 5–6 (1962), 5–31; J. Mertens, 'De economische en sociale toestand van de opstandelingen uit het Brugse Vrije wier goederen na de slag bij Cassel (1328) verbeurd verklaard werden', *BTFG*, 47 (1969), 1132–53.
10. O. Mus, *Inventaris van het archief van de Commissie van Openbare Onderstand van Ieper. Oud Regime zonder de oorkonden* (Ieper, 1972), pp. 25–30. See also G. Maréchal, 'Motieven achter het ontstaan en de evolutie van de stedelijke hospitalen in de XIIe en XIIIe eeuw', in *Septingentesimum Iubilaeum Hospicii Dicti Belle* (Ieper, 1976), pp. 11–34.

Chapter 2. Crisis, social problems and poor laws

Bibliography

The best general account of the crisis is still L. Génicot, 'Crisis: From the Middle Ages to modern times', *CEHE*, vol. I (1966 edn),

660–741. Two other useful introductions are J. Heers, *L'Occident aux XIVe et XVe siècles. Aspects économiques et sociaux* (Paris, 1966) and H. A. Miskimin, *The Economy of Early Renaissance Europe, 1300–1460* (Englewood Cliffs, N.J., 1969).

A large number of regional and local studies deal with the results of the crisis for the peasantry. For England: J. A. Raftis, 'Social structures in five East Midlands villages', *EcHR*, 2nd ser., 16 (1963), 83–100; F. R. H. du Boulay, 'Who were farming the English Demesnes at the end of the Middle Ages?', *ibid.*, 17 (1964), 443–55; C. Dyer, 'A redistribution of incomes in fifteenth-century England', *PP*, 39 (1968), 11–33; J.-P. Genet, 'Economie et société rurale en Angleterre au XVe siècle d'après les comptes de l'hôpital d'Ewelme', *AESC*, 27 (1972), 1464–70; R. H. Hilton, *The English Peasantry in the Later Middle Ages* (Oxford, 1975). For France, the most thorough general survey is H. Neveux, 'Le temps des malheurs, 1340–1450', *HFR*, vol. II (1975), 41–87; see also A. Rochette, 'Fortunes paysannes du XIVe siècle en Forez', *Études foréziennes* (1972), 143–72, and R. Lavoie 'Endettement et pauvreté en Provence d'après les listes de la justice comtale, XIVe–XVe siècles', *Provence Historique*, 23 (1973), 201–16. For Italy: David Herlihy, 'Population, plague and social change in rural Pistoia, 1205–1430', *EcHR*, 2nd ser., 18 (1965), 227–44, and 'Santa Maria Impruneta: a rural commune in the late Middle Ages', in Rubinstein, ed., *Florentine Studies*, pp. 242–76. For the Low Countries, the best general account is A. Verhulst, 'L'économie rurale de la Flandre et la dépression économique du bas moyen âge', *ER*, 10 (1963), 68–80. See also the recent work of G. Sivéry, *Structures agraires et vie rurale dans le Hainaut à la fin du Moyen Age* (2 vols, Lille, 1973).

On the growing gulf between employers and artisans: R. Sprandel, 'Die Handwerker in den nordwestdeutschen Städten des Spätmittelalters', *HG*, 86 (1968), 37–62; R. de Roover, 'Labour conditions in Florence around 1400: theory, policy and reality', in Rubinstein, ed., *Florentine Studies*, pp. 277–313; E. Maschke, 'Deutsche Städte am Ausgang des Mittelalters', in W. Rausch, ed., *Die Stadt am Ausgang des Mittelalters* (Linz, 1974), pp. 1–44; and J.-P. Sosson, *Les Travaux publics de la ville de Bruges, XIVe–XVe siècles* (Brussels, 1977), which contains a wealth of material. The growth of rural industry is studied by H. Kellenbenz, 'Rural industries from the end of the Middle Ages to the eighteenth century', in P. Earle, ed., *Essays in European Economic History* (Oxford, 1974), pp. 45–88. See also the important article by R. van Uytven, 'Die ländliche Industrie während des Spätmittelalters in den südlichen Niederlanden', in H. Kellenbenz, ed., *Agrarisches Nebenge-*

werbe und Formen der Reagrarisierung im Spätmittelalter und 19/20. Jahrhundert (Stuttgart, 1975), pp. 57–76.

There is a mass of modern work on the redistribution of urban wealth, from which we have listed only a few important items. R. van Uytven and W. Blockmans, 'De noodzaak van een geïntegreerde sociale geschiedenis. Het voorbeeld van de Zuidnederlandse steden in de late middeleeuwen', *TG*, 86 (1971), 276–90, is an exhaustive discussion of the social structures of the Low Countries' towns. Among numerous monographs on the contrast between rich and poor in the German and Swiss towns, note H. Jecht, 'Studien zur gesellschaftlichen Struktur der mittelalterlichen Städte', *VSWG*, 19 (1926), 48–85; H. Reincke, 'Bevölkerungsprobleme der Hansestädte', *HG*, 70 (1951), 1–33; *Untersuchungen zur gesellschaftlichen Struktur der mittelalterlichen Städte in Europa* (Constance and Stuttgart, 1966); E. Maschke and J. Sydow, eds., *Gesellschaftliche Unterschichten in den südwestdeutschen Städten* (Stuttgart, 1967); P. Eitel, *Die oberschwäbischen Reichsstädte im Zeitalter der Zunftherrschaft* (Stuttgart, 1970); and R. Kiessling, *Bürgerliche Gesellschaft und Kirche in Augsburg im Spätmittelalter* (Augsburg, 1971).

Much of the material on poverty and poor relief listed in chapter 1, is relevant to this period. B. Geremek, 'Criminalité, vagabondage, paupérisme : la marginalité à l'aube des temps modernes', *RHMC*, 21 (1974), 337–75, provides a good summary of modern work on social control in the later Middle Ages, and W. J. Courtenay, 'Token coinage and the administration of poor relief during the late Middle Ages', *JIH*, 3 (1972–3), 275–95, draws attention to the lead coins which were given out to the supported poor. By far the best analysis of the circumstances of poverty in its period is B. Geremek, *Les marginaux parisiens aux XIVe et XVe siècles* (Paris, 1976).

Notes

1. P. Vilar, 'Réflexions sur la crise de l'ancien type. Inégalité des récoltes et sous-développement', in *Conjoncture économique, structures sociales. Hommage à Ernest Labrousse* (Paris and The Hague, 1974), pp. 37–58 (on pp. 39–40).
2. Brenner, 'Agrarian class structure', pp. 49–50.
3. A. G. Frank, *Capitalism and Underdevelopment in Latin America* (New York, 1967). The manorial economy of eastern Europe is thoroughly examined by W. Kula, *Théorie économique du système féodal. Pour un modèle de l'économie polonaise, XVIe–XVIIIe siècles* (Paris and The Hague, 1970). See also J. Banaji, 'The peasantry in the feudal mode of pro-

duction: towards an economic model', *JPS*, 3 (1976), 299–320.

4. R. S. Lopez and H. A. Miskimin, 'The economic depression of the Renaissance', *EcHR*, 2nd ser., 14 (1961), 408–26; C. M. Cipolla, 'Economic depression of the Renaissance', *EcHR*, 2nd ser., 16 (1963), 519–24. See also A. R. Bridbury, *Economic Growth: England in the later Middle Ages* (London, 1962).
5. J. Munro, *The Transformation of the Flemish Woollen Industries, ca. 1250–ca. 1400: the response to changing factor costs and market demand* (Mimeographed paper of the Workshop on Quantitative Economic History, University of Leuven, 1971), pp. 7–10, and *idem, Wool, Cloth and Gold. The struggle for bullion in Anglo-Burgundian trade, 1340–1478* (Brussels and Toronto, 1973), pp. 2–3.
6. See esp. H. van der Wee, 'Structural changes and specialization in the industry of the southern Netherlands, 1100–1600', *EcHR*, 2nd ser., 28 (1975), 212–14, and R. van Uytven, 'La Flandre et le Brabant: Terres de promission sous les ducs de Bourgogne?', *RN*, 43 (1961), 313–15. Also Maschke, 'Unterschichten', p. 378, and Sosson, *Les Travaux publics de la ville de Bruges*, pp. 189–201.
7. Data in this paragraph taken from E. Sabbe, 'Grondbezit en landbouw. Economische en social toestanden in de Kastelrij Kortrijk op het einde der XIVe eeuw', *Handelingen van de Koninklijke Geschied- en Oudheidkundige Kring van Kortrijk*, 2nd ser., 15 (1936), 401; Mertens, 'Economische en sociale toestand', pp. 1132–53; Neveux, 'Le temps des malheurs', p. 84; Bois, *Crise*, pp. 138–40.
8. B. H. Putnam, *The Enforcement of the Statutes of Labourers during the First Decade after the Black Death, 1349–1359* (London, 1908).
9. The quotation comes from F. Lütge, 'The fourteenth and fifteenth centuries in social and economic history', in G. Strauss, ed., *Pre-Reformation Germany* (London, 1972), pp. 349–50.
10. See the perceptive remarks of de La Roncière 'Pauvres et pauvreté à Florence', pp. 735–40.
11. On popular revolts in fourteenth-century Europe, see esp. M. Mollat and Ph. Wolff, *Ongles bleus, Jacques et Ciompi. Les révolutions populaires en Europe aux XIVe et XVe siècles* (Paris, 1970); Fossier, *Histoire sociale de l'Occident médiéval*, pp. 354–5; V. Rutenberg, 'Révoltes ou révolutions en Europe aux XIVe–XVe siècles?', *AESC*, 27 (1972), 678–83; R. H. Hilton, *Bond Men Made Free. Medieval peasant movements and the English rising of 1381* (London, 1973).

Chapter 3. Economic growth, impoverishment and social policy

Bibliography

Fernand Braudel, *The Mediterranean and the Mediterranean World in the Age of Philip II* (2 vols, London, 1976 ed) is a great general work which develops many brilliant ideas on the whole compass of European economy and society. For a stimulating if overstated thesis on the importance of the sixteenth-century 'world economy', see Immanuel Wallerstein, *The Modern World-System: capitalist agriculture and the origins of the European world-economy in the sixteenth century* (New York and London, 1974). A good sense of the richness and the weakness of the work is conveyed in the review by Theda Skocpol, 'Wallerstein's world capitalist system : a theoretical and historical critique', *AJS*, 82 (1977), 1075–90.

On agrarian change in England, see R. H. Tawney, *The Agrarian Problem in the Sixteenth Century* (2nd edn, New York and London, 1967), which still stands as the classic statement of the subject. The main modern general work on English agriculture is Joan Thirsk, ed., *The Agrarian History of England and Wales*, vol. IV (Cambridge, 1967). For France : in addition to Le Roy Ladurie's masterpiece *Les Paysans de Languedoc*, cited in the bibliography for the foreword, note L. Merle, *La métairie et l'évolution agraire de la Gâtine poitevine, de la fin du Moyen Age à la Révolution* (Paris, 1958); J. Jacquard, *Société et vie rurale dans le sud de la région parisienne, du milieu du XVIe siècle au milieu du XVIIe siècle* (2 vols, Lille, 1974); H. Neveux, *Les grains du Cambrésis (fin du XIVe– début du XVIIe siècle). Vie et déclin d'une structure économique* (Lille, 1974); and G. Cabourdin, *Terre et hommes en Lorraine, 1550–1635* (2 vols, Nancy 1977). For Germany: D. W. Sabean, *Landbesitz und Gesellschaft am Vorabend des Bauernkriegs* (Stuttgart, 1972). For the Low Countries : Jan de Vries, *The Dutch Rural Economy in the Golden Age, 1500–1700* (New Haven and London, 1974). For Spain : J. Klein, *The Mesta: a study in Spanish economic history, 1273–1836* (Cambridge, Mass., 1920) and N. Salomon, *Le Campagne de Nouvelle Castille à la fin du XVIe siècle d'après les 'Relaciones topograficas'* (Paris, 1964). For Switzerland : O. Sigg, 'Bevölkerungs–, Agrar– und Sozialgeschichtliche Probleme des 16. Jahrhunderts am Beispiel der Zürcher Landschaft', *SZG*, 24 (1974), 1–25.

The increasing grip of the urban bourgeoisie on the countryside is studied by B. Bennassar, *Valladolid au siècle d'or. Une ville de Castille et sa campagne au XVIe siècle* (Paris and The Hague,

1967); Robert Mandrou, *Les Fugger, propriétaires fonciers en Souabe, 1560–1618* (Paris, 1969); and A.-M. Piuz, 'Les relations économiques entre les villes et les campagnes dans les sociétés pré-industrielles', in *Villes et Campagnes, XVe–XXe siècles* (Lyon, 1977), pp. 26–48. See also H. Soly, 'The betrayal of the sixteenth-century bourgeoisie: a myth?', *AHN*, 8 (1975), 31–49.

H. Kellenbenz, 'The organization of industrial production', *CEHE,* vol. V (1977), 462–548, is an excellent survey of sixteenth century urban and rural industries. On the putting-out system, see the old but still valuable work of F. Furger, *Zum Verlagssystem als Organisationsform des Frühkapitalismus im Textilgewerbe* (Stuttgart, 1927) and the recent contribution to the subject by D. C. Coleman, *Industry in Tudor and Stuart England* (London, 1975). Among the more important detailed studies on the social consequences of commercial capitalism are E. Coornaert, *Un centre industriel d'autrefois: la draperie-sayetterie d'Hondschoote, XIVe–XVIIIe* siècles (Paris, 1930); R. Gascon, *Grand commerce et vie urbaine au XVIe siècle. Lyon et ses marchands* (2 vols, Paris and The Hague, 1971); A. Laube, *Studien über den erzgebirgischen Silberbergbau von 1470 bis 1546* (Berlin, 1974). See also H. Soly, *Urbanisme en kapitalisme te Antwerpen in de 16e eeuw. De stedebouwkundige en industriële ondernemingen van Gilbert van Schoonbeke* (Brussels, 1977).

On the impoverishment of the labouring population and the increase in socio-economic inequality: E. Scholliers, *De Levensstandaard in de XVe en XVIe eeuw te Antwerpen* (Antwerp, 1960); B. Geremek, 'La popolazione marginale tra il medioeve e l'era moderna', *Studi Storici* (1968), 623–40; C. R. Friedrichs, 'Capitalism, mobility and class formation in the early modern German city', *PP*, 69 (1975), 24–49; W. G. Hoskins, *The Age of Plunder: King Henry's England, 1500–1547* (London, 1976); R. Gascon, 'Vitalité et inquiétudes urbaines', *HESF*, vol. I (1977), 395–468.

There is an enormous literature on the reorganization of poor relief, from which we have listed only a few items relevant to the causes and effects. The attitudes of humanists and religious reformers towards the poor are examined by M. Bataillon, 'J. L. Vivès, réformateur de la bienfaisance', *Bibliothèque d'Humanisme et Renaissance,* 19 (1952), 140–59; W. R. D. Jones, *The Tudor Commonwealth, 1529–1559* (London, 1970); H. J. Grimm, 'Luther's contributions to sixteenth-century organization of poor relief', *AR*, 61 (1970), 222–34; R. M. Kingdon, 'Social welfare in Calvin's Geneva', *AHR*, 76 (1971), 50–69; H. Scherpner, *Theorie der Fürsorge* (2nd edn, Göttingen, 1974). See also G. Kouskoff, 'Le reflet des préoccupations municipales dans le 'De Republica emendanda' de Fricius Modrevius, maire de Wolborz', in *Théorie et pratique politiques à la Renaissance* (Paris, 1977), pp. 61–74. Of the numerous regional and local monographs, note esp.: for England: J. Pound, *Poverty and Vagrancy in Tudor England* (2nd edn, London, 1973), with a very useful bibliography; P. Clark and P. A. Slack, eds, *Crisis and Order in English Towns, 1500–1700* (London, 1972); A. L. Beier, 'Vagrants and the social order in Elizabethan England', *PP*, 64 (1974), 3–29. For France: M. Fosseyeux, 'Les premiers budgets municipaux d'assistance. La taxe des pauvres au XVIe siècle', *RHEF*, 20 (1934), 407–32; N. Z. Davis, 'Poor relief, humanism and heresy: the case of Lyon', *Studies in Medieval and Renaissance History*, vol. V (1968), 217–75, a most important study. For Germany and Switzerland: A. L. Richter, *Die evangelische Kirchenordnungen des 16. Jahrhunderts* (2 vols, Weimar, 1846) is an important collection of documents, and O. Winckelmann, 'Über die ältesten Armenordnungen der Reformationszeit', *Historische Vierteljahrschrift*, (1914), 187–228, 361–400, has a mass of factual information. For Italy: B. Pullan, *Rich and Poor in Renaissance Venice. The social institutions of a Catholic state to 1620* (Oxford, 1971), is a splendid detailed discussion of social policy. For the Low Countries: H. Soly, 'Economische ontwikkeling en sociale politiek in Europa tijdens de overgang van middeleeuwen naar nieuwe tijden', *TG*, 88 (1975), 584–97, has an almost exhaustive bibliography. See also R. Saint-Cyr Duplessis, 'Charité municipale et autorité publique au XVIe siècle: l'exemple de Lille' *RN*, 59 (1977), 193–220. For Scotland: R. Mitchison, 'The making of the old Scottish poor law', *PP*, 63 (1974), 58–93. For Spain: P. Vilar, 'Les primitifs espagnols de la pensée économique', in *Mélanges Marcel Bataillon* (Paris, 1962), pp. 261–94.

Notes

1. Brenner, 'Agrarian class structure', pp. 61–4, 71–2.
2. Tawney, *The Agrarian Problem*, pp. 287–310 (on p. 307); see also J. Cornwall, *Revolt of the Peasantry, 1549* (London, 1977).
3. A. Everitt, 'Farm labourers', *AHEW*, 406.
4. R. Gascon, 'Immigration et croissance urbaine au XVIe siècle: l'exemple de Lyon (1529–1563)', *AESC*, 25 (1970), 994–7.
5. K. H. Takahashi, 'A contribution to the discussion', in Hilton, ed., *Transition*, pp. 87–97.
6. Braudel, *The Mediterranean*, vol. I, 437.
7. Jan van Houtte, quoted by J. Prinsen, 'Armenzorg te Leiden

in 1577', *Bijdragen en Mededelingen van het Historisch Genootschap te Utrecht*, 26 (1905), 139–40. The other quotations come from C. Hill, 'Pottage for freeborn Englishmen: attitudes to wage-labour', in *Change and Continuity in Seventeenth-Century England* (London, 1974), p. 220. See also J. W. Muller and L. Scharpé, *Spelen van Cornelis Everaert* (Leyden, 1920), and Maschke, 'Deutsche Städte', p. 18.

8. Hoskins, *The Age of Plunder*, p. 29.
9. Information drawn from *ibid.* pp. 31–6, 42–7; Le Roy Ladurie, *Paysans de Languedoc*, pp. 240–3, 263–80; Salomon, *La campagne de Nouvelle Castille*, pp. 261–6; de Vries, *The Dutch Rural economy*, pp. 66–7; Blockmans and Prevenier, 'Armoede in de Nederlanden', pp. 516–17; C. P. Clasen, *Die Wiedertäufer im Herzogtum Württemberg und in benachbarten Herrschaften* (Stuttgart, 1965), pp. 204–10; M. Aymard and H. Bresc, 'Nourritures et consommation en Sicile entre XIVe et XVIIIe siècle', *AESC*, 30 (1975), 594–5. The quotation from Heinrich Müller comes from Braudel, *Capitalism and Material Life*, p. 130.
10. Quoted by Soly, 'Economische ontwikkeling en sociale politiek', p. 587.
11. Data in the previous paragraph taken from N. W. Posthumus, *De geschiedenis van de Leidsche lakenindustrie* (3 vols, The Hague, 1908–39), I, 388–90; Pound, *Poverty*, p. 27 (London); Cipolla, *Before the Industrial Revolution*, p. 18 (Cremona); I. Bog, 'Wachstumsprobleme der oberdeutschen Wirtschaft, 1540–1618', in F. Lütge, ed., *Wirtschaftliche und Soziale Probleme der gewerblichen Entwicklung im 15.–16. und 19. Jahrhundert* (Stuttgart, 1968), p. 61 (Lucerne); Gascon, *Grand commerce,* vol. II, 798; G. Panel, *Documents concernant les pauvres de Rouen* (3 vols, Rouen and Paris, 1917), vol. I, 17–18; Kamen, *The Iron Century*, pp. 388–9. The quotations come from Clark and Slack, eds., *Crisis and Order*, p. 17, and W. R. D. Jones, *The Tudor Commonwealth*, p. 129.
12. Quoted by E. Garin, 'La cité idéale de la Renaissance italienne', in *Les Utopies à la Renaissance. Colloque international* (Brussels and Paris, 1963), p. 13.
13. For further information on the growing cultural chasm between rich and poor, see J. Delumeau, 'Mobilité sociale: riches et pauvres à l'époque de la Renaissance', in D. Roche and E. Labrousse, eds., *Ordres et Classes. Colloque d'histoire sociale* (Paris and The Hague, 1973), pp. 125–34; R. Chartier, 'Les élites et les gueux. Quelques représentations (XVIe–XVIIe

siècles)', *RHMC*, 21 (1974), 376–88; A. Jouanna, *Ordre social. Mythes et hiérarchies dans la France du XVIe siècle* (Paris, 1977), pp. 89–101; R. Muchembled, *Culture populaire et culture des élites dans la France moderne, XVe–XVIIIe siècles* (Paris, 1978), pp. 190–217. The quotations come from J. H. Elliott, *Imperial Spain, 1459–1716* (Harmondsworth, 1975 edn), p. 311 (Cervantes); Everitt, 'Farm labourers', p. 441 (Norfolk poor); C. Hill, 'The many-headed monster', in *Change and Continuity*, pp. 187–8 (Thomas Deloney and Sir Fulke Greville); N. L. Williams, *Sir Walter Ralegh* (London, 1962), p. 139.

14. Cf. H. van der Wee, *The Growth of the Antwerp Market and the European Economy, Fourteenth-Sixteenth Centuries* (3 vols, The Hague, 1963), vol. II, 150–3.
15. The quotations come from W. R. D. Jones, *The Tudor Commonwealth*, pp. 56, 108.
16. See the perceptive remarks of A. N. Galpern, *The Religions of the People in Sixteenth-Century Champagne* (Cambridge, Mass., 1976), p. 103.
17. For a detailed analysis of private charity in the 'long sixteenth century', see W. K. Jordan, *Philanthropy in England, 1480–1660* (London, 1959). The author's failure to deflate his statistics of charitable donations to take into account the substantial change in prices over the period concerned has been criticized by a number of historians. See the recent article by W. G. Bittle and R. Todd Lane, 'Inflation and philanthropy in England: a re-assessment of W. K. Jordan's data', *EcHR*, 2nd ser., 29 (1976), 203–10, which in turn has been subjected to critical attacks by J. F. Hadwin, D. C. Coleman and J. D. Gould, *ibid.*, 31 (1978), 105–28.

Chapter 4. Changing economic patterns and the utility of poverty

Bibliography

Jan de Vries, *The Economy of Europe in an Age of Crisis, 1600–1750* (Cambridge, 1976), provides an excellent survey that makes further bibliography almost superfluous. However, another important general work is P. Léon, *Économies et sociétés préindustrielles*, vol. II, *1650–1780* (Paris, 1970), and the collection of essays edited by T. Aston, *Crisis in Europe, 1560–1660* (London, 1965) is still very useful. For a magisterial reappraisal of the whole compass of European political history, see Perry Anderson, *Lineages of the Absolutiste State* (London, 1974).

On the agrarian structures of England and France: E. L. Jones, ed., *Agriculture and Economic Growth in England, 1650–1815* (London, 1967); J. Thirsk, 'Seventeenth-century agriculture and social change', *AgHR*, 18 (1970), 148–77; Pierre Goubert, 'Le paysan et la terre: seigneurie, tenure, exploitation', *HESF*, vol. II (1970), 119–58; R. Forster, 'Obstacles to agricultural growth in eighteenth-century France', *AHR*, 75 (1970), 1600–15.

Important local and regional studies of industrial production are N. W. Posthumus, *De geschiedenis van de Leidsche lakenindustrie* (3 vols, The Hague, 1908–39); N. B. Stephens, *Seventeenth-Century Exeter: a study of industrial and commercial development, 1625–1688* (Exeter, 1958); Pierre Goubert, *Beauvais et le Beauvaisis, de 1600 à 1730* (Paris, 1960); P. Deyon, *Amiens, capitale provinciale* (Paris and The Hague, 1967); A. K. L. Thijs, *De zijdenijverheid te Antwerpen in de 17e eeuw* (Brussels, 1969); J. Craeybeckx, 'L'industrie de la laine dans les anciens Pays-Bas méridionaux, de la fin du XVIe au début du XVIIIe siècle', in *Produzione . . . dei panni di lana*, pp. 21–43. Franklin Mendels, 'Proto-industrialization: The First Stage of Industrialization', *JEH*, 32 (1972), 241–61, draws attention to the fundamental role played by the rural industries.

Migrations are examined by E. A. Wrigley, 'A simple model of London's importance in changing English society and economy, 1650–1750', *PP*, 37 (1967), 44–70; P. Clark, 'The migrant in Kentish towns, 1580–1640', in Clark and Slack, eds., *Crisis and Order*, pp. 117–63; P. A. Slack, 'Vagrants and vagrancy in England, 1598–1664', *EcHR*, 2nd ser., 27 (1974), 360–79; and J. Patten, 'Patterns of migration and movement of labour to three pre-industrial East Anglian towns', *Journal of Historical Geography*, 2 (1976), 111–29.

Changing attitudes to labour are discussed in E. S. Furniss, *The Position of the Laborer in a System of Nationalism* (Boston, 1920), in G. V. R. Rimlinger, *Welfare Politics and Industrialization in Europe, America and Russia* (New York, 1971), and in the article by A. W. Coats, 'The relief of poverty: attitudes to labour and economic change in England, 1660–1782', *IRSH*, 21 (1976), 98–115.

The book which has done most in recent years to illuminate the 'Great Confinement' is undoubtedly Michel Foucault, *Folie et déraison. Histoire de la folie à l'âge classique* (Paris, 1961). The literature on individual countries is large, and no attempt is made here at an extensive coverage. For England: R. H. Tawney, *Religion and the Rise of Capitalism* (London, 1926), ch 4; C. Hill, 'Puritans and the poor', *PP*, 2 (1952), 32–50; A. L. Beier, 'Poor relief in Warwickshire, 1630–1660', *PP*, 35 (1966), 77–100; P. A. Slack,

'Poverty and politics in Salisbury, 1597–1666', in Clark and Slack, eds, *Crisis and Order*, pp. 164–203; Geoffrey Taylor, *The Problem of Poverty, 1600–1834* (London, 1969). For France: E. Chill, 'Religion and mendicity in seventeenth-century France', *IRSH*, 7 (1962), 400–25; P. Deyon, 'A propos du paupérisme au milieu du XVIIe siècle: peinture et charité chrétienne', *AESC*, 22 (1967), 137–53; J. Depauw, 'Pauvres, pauvres mendiants, mendiants valides ou vagabonds? Les hésitations de la législation royale', *RHMC*, 21 (1974), 401–18; M. Jeorger, 'La structure hospitalière de la France sous l'Ancien Régime', *AESC*, 32 (1977), 1025–51. For Germany: R. von Hippel, 'Beiträge zur Geschichte der Freiheitsstrafe', *Zeitschrift für gesamte Strafrechtswissenschaft*, 18 (1898), 608ff., and H. von Weber, 'Die Entwicklung des Zuchthauswesens in Deutschland im 17. und 18. Jahrhunderts', in *Festschrift Adolf Zycha* (Weimar, 1941), pp. 427ff. For the Low Countries: Th. Sellin, *Pioneering in Penology. The Amsterdam Houses of Correction in the Sixteenth and Seventeenth Centuries* (Philadelphia and London, 1944); A. Hallema, *Geschiedenis van het gevangeniswezen, hoofdzakelijk in Nederland* (The Hague, 1958); *Arm in de Gouden Eeuw* (Amsterdam, Historisch Museum, 1966).

Notes

1. Le Roy Ladurie, *Paysans de Languedoc*, pp. 11, 639–41; 652; Neveux, *Les Grains du Cambrésis*, p. 672.
2. De Vries, *The Economy of Europe*, pp. 64–9. See also Anderson, *Lineages*, pp. 85–112; Merrington, 'Town and country', pp. 82–4; and P. Chaunu, 'L'État', *HESF*, vol. I (1977), 178–89.
3. Brenner, 'Agrarian class structure', pp. 65–6.
4. Quoted by M. James, *Social Problems and Policy during the Puritan Revolution, 1640–1660* (London, 1930), p. 114.
5. C. Hill, *Reformation to Industrial Revolution* (London, 1967), pp. 51, 115–22 (on p. 116).
6. J. S. Cohen and M. L. Weitzman, 'Enclosures and depopulation: a Marxian analysis', in W. N. Parker and E. L. Jones, eds., *European Peasants and their Markets. Essays in agrarian economic history* (Princeton, 1975), pp. 175–6.
7. D. C. Coleman, 'Labour in the English economy of the seventeenth century', *EcHR*, 2nd ser., 8 (1955–6), 280–95 (on p. 283). See also Wilson, *England's Apprenticeship*, pp. 228–9, 231, 239; C. M. L. Bouch and G. P. Jones, *A Short Economic and Social History of the Lake Counties, 1500–1830* (Manchester, 1961), p. 142; A. Everitt, 'Social mobility in early

modern England', *PP*, 33 (1966), 56–7; Clarkson, *The Pre-Industrial Economy in England*, pp. 233–4.

8. Goubert, *Beauvais*, pp. 152–96; Vauban, *Project d'une Dixme Royale 1707*, ed. by E. Coornaert (Paris, 1933), pp. 77–81. The quotation comes from H. M. Solomon, *Public Welfare, Science and Propaganda in Seventeenth-Century France. The innovations of Théophraste Renaudot* (Princeton, 1972), pp. 21–2.
9. The Parliament of Rouen in 1675, quoted by G. Lemarchand, 'Economic crises and social atmosphere in urban society under Louis XIV', in R. F. Kierstead, ed., *State and Society in Seventeenth-Century France* (New York, 1975), p. 242.
10. C. Hill, 'Puritans and the poor', pp. 32–50 (on p. 40).
11. The quotations come from E. Thuau *Raison d'État et pensée politique à l'époque de Richelieu* (Paris, 1966), p. 353; Rimlinger, *Welfare Politics*, p. 17 (Petty); B. Inglis, *Poverty and the Industrial Revolution* (London, 1971), p. 20. See also Furniss, *The Position of the Labourer in a System of Nationalism*, ch. VI.
12. The history of Théophraste Renaudot's *Bureau d'Adresse* forms a striking illustration of these fundamental changes. See Solomon, *Public Welfare*, pp. 39–46, 53, 56–7, 217–18.
13. Anderson, *Lineages*, p. 100. On popular revolts in seventeenth-century France, see esp. P. J. Coveney, ed., *France in Crisis, 1620–1675* (London, 1977), which has a very useful and extensive bibliography.
14. Th. K. Rabb, *The Struggle for Stability in Early Modern Europe* (New York, 1975), p. 93.
15. Quoted by Gutton, *Société . . . Lyon*, pp. 338–9.
16. The quotation from Brewster comes from Wilson, *England's Apprenticeship*, p. 349. The quotations from Cary and Defoe come from De Schweinitz, *England's Road to Social Security*, pp. 53–5.
17. C. Hill, 'Puritans and the poor', p. 43.

Chapter 5. Economic growth, pauperization and the regulation of the labour market

Bibliography

The best overall discussion of the Industrial Revolution is D. S. Landes, *The Unbound Prometheus: technological change and industrial development in Western Europe from 1750 to the present* (Cambridge, 1969). There are innumerable works on the Industrial Revolution in England. Outstanding among them are Paul

Mantoux, *The Industrial Revolution in the Eighteenth Century* (London, 1928), E. J. Hobsbawm, *Industry and Empire* (London, 1968) and Peter Mathias, *The First Industrial Nation* (London, 1969). A. Soboul, *La Civilisation et la Révolution française*, I, *La Crise de l'Ancien Régime* (Paris, 1970) is a superb analysis of the French economy and society on the eve of the Revolution.

On agricultural developments in England, excellent recent works are J. D. Chambers and G. E. Mingay, *The Agricultural Revolution, 1750–1880* (London, 1966), Jones, ed., *Agriculture and Economic Growth*, cited in chapter 4, and G. E. Mingay, ed., *The Agricultural Revolution: changes in agriculture, 1650–1880* (London, 1977). For France, see the comprehensive synthesis of E. Le Roy Ladurie, 'De la crise ultime à la vraie croissance, 1660–1789', *HFR*, vol. II (1975), 359–599. Of the numerous monographs, note esp. P. de Saint Jacob, *Les Paysans de la Bourgogne du Nord au dernier siècle de l'Ancien Régime* (Paris, 1960); A. Poitrineau, *La Vie rurale en basse Auvergne au XVIIIe siècle* (Paris, 1965); and above all Michel Morineau, *Les Faux-semblants d'un démarrage économique: agriculture et démographie en France au XVIIIe siècle* (Paris, 1971). Flemish agriculture is thoroughly surveyed by C. Vandenbroeke, *Agriculture et alimentation dans les Pays-Bas autrichiens* (Ghent and Leuven, 1975).

Peter Kriedte, Hans Medick and Jürgen Schlumbohm, *Industrialisierung vor der Industrialisierung. Gewerbliche Warenproduktion auf dem Land in der Formationsperiode des Kapitalismus* (Göttingen, 1977), is a magisterial theoretical discussion of proto-industrialization, with an exhaustive bibliography. For a summary of Medick's argument, see 'The proto-industrial family economy: the structural function of household and family during the transition from peasant society to industrial capitalism', *SH*, 3 (1976), 291–315. The demographic implications of proto-industrialization are examined in the fine book of David Levine, *Family Formation in an Age of Nascent Capitalism* (New York and London, 1977). Important case studies are: H. Kisch, 'The textile industries in Silesia and the Rhineland: a comparative study in industrialization', *JEH*, 19 (1959), 541–64; R. Braun, *Industrialisierung und Volksleben: Die Veränderungen der Lebensformen in einem ländlichen Industriegebiet vor 1800* (Erlenbach-Zürich and Stuttgart, 1960); J. D. Chambers, 'The rural domestic industries during the period of transition to the factory system, with special reference to the Midland counties of England', in *Second ICEH* (Paris, 1965), pp. 429–55; W. Fischer, 'Stadien und Typen der Industrialisierung in Deutschland', in P. Léon, F. Crouzet and R.

Gascon, eds., *L'Industrialisation en Europe au XIXe siècle* (Paris, 1972), 347–55; A. Klima, 'The role of rural domestic industry in Bohemia in the eighteenth century', *EcHR*, 2nd ser., 27 (1974), 48–56. On the connection between land fragmentation, proto-industrialization and population growth in Flanders: B. Verhaegen, *Contribution à l'histoire économique des Flandres* (2 vols, Leuven, 1961); P. Deprez, 'The demographic development of Flanders during the eighteenth century', in D. V. Glass and D. E. C. Eversley, eds., *Population in History* (London, 1965), pp. 608–31; and Franklin Mendels, 'Agriculture and peasant industry in eighteenth-century Flanders', in Parker and Jones, eds., *European Peasants*, pp. 179–204.

On the socio-economic degradation of the artisans: E. Coornaert, *Les Corporations en France avant 1789* (Paris, 1941); D. Bythell, *The Handloom Weavers* (Cambridge, 1969); M. Garden, 'Ouvriers et artisans au XVIIIe siècle. L'exemple lyonnais et les problèmes de classification', *RHES*, 48 (1970), 28–52; J. Vermaut, 'De textielnijverheid te Brugge en op het platteland in Westelijk Vlaanderen voor 1800. Konjunktuurverloop, organisatie en sociale verhoudingen' (4 vols, unpublished Ph.D. thesis, Ghent, 1974).

The Labour problem is examined in J. Dhondt, 'Note sur les ouvriers industriels gantois à l'époque française', *RN* 36 (1954), 309–24; K. Hinze, *Die Arbeiterfrage zu Beginn des modernen Kapitalismus in Brandenburg-Preussen, 1685–1806* (2nd edn, Berlin, 1963); E. P. Thompson, *The Making of the English Working Class* (Harmondsworth, 1970, edn) and 'Time, work-discipline, and industrial capitalism', *PP*, 38 (1967), 56–97; P. Léon, 'Morcellement et émergence du monde ouvrier', *HESF*, vol. II (1970), 651–89.

The debate on the standard of living during the Industrial Revolution has proved the most sustained single controversy in modern economic history. The articles in which the discussion was conducted for the most part appeared in the pages of the *EcHR*. Supplemented by additional pieces, and excellently introduced by Arthur J. Taylor, they have now been collected under the title *The Standard of Living in Britain in the Industrial Revolution* (London, 1975). See also D. S. Landes, 'The standard of living during the Industrial Revolution', in O. Büsch, W. Fischer and H. Herzfeld, eds., *Industrialisierung und 'Europäische Wirtschaft' im 19. Jahrhundert* (Berlin and New York, 1976), pp. 65–82. For the Continent: C. Vandenbroeke, 'L'alimentation à Gand pendant la première moitié du XIXe siècle', *AESC*, 30 (1975), 584–91, and C. Lis and H. Soly, 'Food consumption in Antwerp between 1807 and 1859:

a contribution to the standard of living debate', *EcHR*, 2nd ser., 30 (1977), 460–86. On the extension of potato cultivation see note 29 below.

There is an enormous literature on poverty and public assistance. For England, the most useful introductions are J. D. Marshall, *The Old Poor Law, 1795–1834* (London, 1968); M. E. Rose, *The English Poor Law, 1780–1930* (London, 1971) and *The Relief of Poverty, 1834–1914* (London, 1972); D. Fraser, ed., *The New Poor Law in the Nineteenth Century* (London, 1976); James Stephen Taylor, 'The impact of pauper settlement, 1691–1834', *PP*, 73 (1976), 42–74. See also K. Polanyi, *The Great Transformation* (Boston, 1957). For France, first to be mentioned is an excellent synthesis: O. Hufton, *The Poor of Eighteenth-Century France, 1750–1789* (Oxford, 1974), which combines a fascinating reconstruction of the lives of the poor with an illuminating survey of public assistance. Two other important studies are J. Kaplow, *The Names of Kings: the Parisian labouring poor in the eighteenth century* (New York, 1972) and L. Chevalier, *Classes laborieuses et classes dangereuses à Paris pendant la première moitié du XIXe siècle* (2nd edn, Paris, 1969); the latter is a superb analysis of the circumstances of poverty, where socio-demographic realities and political ideologies are equally stressed. For Germany: L. Koch, *Wandlungen der Wohlfahrtspflege im Zeitalter der Aufklärung* (Erlangen, 1933) provides detailed information on poor relief, and H. Brunschwig, *La Crise de l'État prussien à la fin du XVIIIe siècle et la genèse de la mentalité romantique* (Paris, 1947) develops brilliant ideas on the social crisis of the waning *ancien régime*. The recent articles by R. Endres, 'Das Armenproblem im Zeitalter des Absolutismus', *Jahrbuch für Frankische Landesforschung*, 34–35 (1975), 1003–20, and E. François, 'Unterschichten und Armut in rheinischen Residenzstädten des 18. Jahrhunderts', *VSWG*, 62 (1975), 433–64, are excellent general surveys, with a large bibliography. For the southern Netherlands, the old but still valuable work of Paul Bonenfant, *Le Problème du paupérisme en Belgique à la fin de l'Ancien Régime* (Brussels, 1934) is a mine of factual information. C. Lis, 'Verarmingsprocessen te Antwerpen, 1750–1850' (4 vols, unpublished Ph.D. thesis, Brussels, 1975) is a detailed analysis of the causes of urban poverty. The same author presents a new interpretation of the reorganization of public assistance: 'Sociale politiek te Antwerpen, 1779. Het controleren van de relatieve overbevolking en het reguleren van de arbeidsmarkt', *TSG*, 5 (1976), 146–66.

Notes

1. W. Fischer, 'Soziale Unterschichten im Zeitalter der Frühindustrialisierung', *IRSH*, 8 (1963), 435; Clarkson, *The Pre-Industrial Economy in England*, p. 234. R. M. Hartwell, 'The consequences of the Industrial Revolution in England for the poor', in *The Long Debate on Poverty. Eight essays on industrialization and the conditions of England* (London, 1972), pp. 3–21; Abel, *Massenarmut*, p. 309.
2. Quoted by F. E. Huggett, *The Land Question and European Society since 1650* (London, 1975), p. 71.
3. J. D. Chambers, 'Enclosure and labour supply in the Industrial Revolution', *EcHR*, 2nd ser., 5 (1953), 336.
4. Hoskins, *The Midland Peasant*, pp. 216–76 (on p. 269).
5. A. J. Youngson, *After the Forty-Five. The economic impact on the Scottish Highlands* (Edinburgh, 1973), pp. 120–90 (on p. 180). See also E. S. Richards, 'Structural change in a regional economy: Sutherland and the Industrial Revolution, 1780–1830', *EcHR*, 2nd ser., 26 (1973), 63–76.
6. A. P. Wadsworth and J. de L. Mann, *The Cotton Trade and Industrial Lancashire, 1600–1780* (Manchester, 1931), pp. 317–22 (on p. 317).
7. Quoted by F. Laude, *Les Classes rurales en Artois à la fin de l'Ancien Régime, 1760–1789* (Lille, 1914), p. 255.
8. Quoted by A. Davies, 'The new agriculture in lower Normandy, 1750–1789', *TRHS*, 5th ser., 8 (1958), 143.
9. Quoted by P. de Saint Jacob, *Les Paysans de la Bourgogne du Nord*, p. 404.
10. Le Roy Ladurie, 'De la crise ultime à la vraie croissance', p. 440.
11. Quoted by J. Mokyr, *Industrialization in the Low Countries, 1795–1850* (New Haven and London, 1976), p. 16.
12. W. A. Lewis, 'Economic development with unlimited supplies of labour', *Manchester School of Economic and Social Studies*, 22 (1954), 139–91.
13. Medick, 'The proto-industrial family economy', pp. 291–315 (on pp. 304–5).
14. Ibid., 306. The successive quotations come from Mokyr, *Industrialization in the Low Countries*, p. 16; P. Bois, *Paysans de l'Ouest* (Le Mans, 1960), p. 521; Braun, *Industrialisierung und Volksleben*, p. 81 : English translation from D. S. Landes, ed., *The Rise of Capitalism* (New York and London, 1966), p. 61.
15. Medick, 'The proto-industrial family economy', pp. 298–9. See

also Jones, ed., *Agriculture and Economic Growth in England*, pp. 24–5, and Landes, *The Unbound Prometheus*, pp. 56–60. The quotation from William Temple comes from Wilson, *England's Apprenticeship*, p. 345.

16. Takahashi, 'A contribution', p. 340.
17. R. G. Wilson, 'The supremacy of the Yorkshire cloth industry in the eighteenth century', in N. B. Harte and K. G. Ponting, eds., *Textile History and Economic History. Essays in honour of Miss J. de L. Mann* (Manchester, 1973), 235–46. See also F. Vigier, *Change and Apathy. Liverpool and Manchester during the Industrial Revolution* (Cambridge, Mass., 1970), pp. 85–7, and D. T. Jenkins, *The West Riding Wool Textile Industry, 1770–1835. A study of fixed capital formation* (Edington, 1975). The quotation from Josiah Tucker comes from Wadsworth and Man, *The Cotton Trade*, p. 384.
18. Clifford Geertz, *Agricultural Involution: the processes of ecological change to Indonesia* (Berkeley and Los Angeles, 1963).
19. Landes, *The Unbound Prometheus*, p. 119. See also J. Bergmann, 'Das Alte Handwerk im Uebergang. Zum Wandel von Struktur und Funktion des Handwerks im Berliner Wirtschaftsraum in vor- und frühindustrieller Zeit', in *Untersuchungen zur Geschichte der frühen Industrialisierung, vornehmlich im Wirtschaftsraum Berlin/Brandenburg* (Berlin, 1971), pp. 262ff., and R. Samuel, 'Workshop of the world: steam power and hand technology in mid-Victorian Britain', *HWJ*, 3 (1977), 6–72.
20. G. W. Hilton, 'The controversy concerning the relief for the handloom weavers', *Explorations in Entrepreneurial History* (1963–4), 166–83.
21. Thompson, *The Making of the English Working Class*, p. 370. The anonymous writer, quoted by Hinze, *Arbeiterfrage*, p. 168; Robert Dale Owen's memoirs, quoted by Inglis, *Poverty*, p. 124.
22. Dhondt, 'Note sur les ouvriers industriels gantois', pp. 309–11.
23. Quoted by Lis, *Verarmingsprocessen*, vol. II, 26. The quotation from Mornet comes from M. Garden, *Lyon et les Lyonnais au XVIIIe siècle* (Paris, 1970), p. 592.
24. Information drawn from Soboul, *La Civilisation et la révolution française*, vol. I, 125–6, and Hufton, *The Poor of Eighteenth-Century France*, pp. 22–4. For further details, see esp. A. Daumard and F. Furet, *Structures et relations sociales à Paris au XVIIIe siècle* (Paris, 1961), pp. 19ff.; J. Kaplow,

Elbeuf during the Revolutionary Period: history and social structure (Baltimore, 1964), pp. 65–9, 89–97; J. Sentou, *Fortunes et groupes sociaux à Toulouse sous la Révolution. Essai d'histoire statistique* (Toulouse, 1969), pp. 71–3, 407–11; Garden, *Lyon et les Lyonnais*, pp. 298ff. The ecclesiastics of Lyon, quoted by Gutton, *Société . . . Lyon*, pp. 76–7. The other quotations come from F. Furet, 'Pour une définition des classes inférieures à l'époque moderne', *AESC*, 18 (1963), 460.

25. Data in this paragraph taken from F.-W. Henning, 'Die Betriebsgrössenstruktur der mitteleuropäischen Landwirtschaft im 18. Jahrhundert und ihr Einfluss auf die ländlichen Einkommensverhältnisse', *ZAA*, 17 (1969), 171–93; Abel, *Massenarmut*, pp. 252–7; François, 'Unterschichten', pp. 434–5, 455–7.
26. See Lis, *Verarmingsprocessen*, vol. II, 48–53, vol. III, 5–91. For the distribution of wealth in Antwerp, see J. De Belder, 'Beroep of bezit als criterium voor de sociale doorsnede. Een aanzet tot uniformisering van reconstructiemethoden', *TSG*, 6 (1976), 266–72. The quotation from Buret comes from Chevalier, *Classes laborieuses*, p. 445.
27. The data in this paragraph is taken from Geoffrey Taylor, *The Problem of Poverty*, pp. 12–13, and Marshall, *The Old Poor Law*, pp. 26–7, 33. The quotations come from Inglis, *Poverty*, pp. 113, 157.
28. T. S. Ashton, 'The standard of life of the workers in England, 1790–1830', *JEH*, 9 (1949), 33. For details on the decline of *per capita* food consumption in Antwerp, see Lis and Soly, 'Food consumption', pp. 460–86.
29. Information drawn from C. Vandenbroeke, 'Cultivation and consumption of the potato in the 17th and 18th century', *AHN*, 5 (1971), 15–39; M. Morineau, 'La pomme de terre au XVIIIe siècle', *AESC*, 25 (1970), 1767–85, and 'Révolution agricole, révolution alimentaire, révolution démographique', *ADH* (1974), 335–69 (on p. 355); F.-W. Henning, 'Stadien und Typen in der Entwicklung der Landwirtschaft in den heutigen Industrieländern' in *Schriften der Gesellschaft für Wirschafts- und Sozialwissenschaften des Landbaues*, 5 (1968), 57; K. H. Connell, 'Land and Population in Ireland', *EcHR*, 2nd ser., 2 (1950), 288–9; J. C. Drummond and A. Wilbraham, *The Englishman's Food: a history of five centuries of English diet* (London, 1958), pp. 180–1. The quotations come from W. Abel, *Massenarmut under Hungerkrisen im vorindustriellen Deutschland* (Göttingen, 1972), p. 65 (List); Smout, *A History of the*

Scottish People, p. 251 (Sinclair); Arthur J. Taylor, *The Standard of Living in Britain*, p. xxxii (Porter).

30. Quoted by Garden, *Lyon et les Lyonnais*, p. 299.

31. Data taken from Hufton, *The Poor of Eighteenth-Century France*, ch. III; E. Hélin, 'Migrations d'ouvriers avant la révolution industrielle', in *Annales du Congrès de Liège. Quarantième Session*, (2 vols, Liège, 1969), vol. I, 174–7; J. Tack, *Die Hollandsgänger in Hannover und Oldenburg. Ein Beitrag zur Geschichte der Arbeiter-Wanderung* (Leipzig, 1902) pp. 11–14, 34–42, 64, 86–97, 137–43, 169–73. Swinburne, quoted by B. Bennassar, *L'Homme espagnol. Attitudes et mentalités du XVIe au XIXe siècle* (Paris, 1975), p. 96.

32. W. Kula, 'Recherches comparatives sur la formation de la classe ouvrière', in *Second ICEH* (Paris and The Hague, 1960), pp. 510–23; M. Garden, 'L'attraction de Lyon à la fin de l'Ancien Régime', *ADH* (1970), 205–22; M. Vovelle, 'Le prolétariat flottant à Marseille sous la Révolution française', *ADH* (1968), 117–23; François, 'Unterschichten', pp. 441–2; N. Caulier-Mathy, 'La composition d'un prolétariat industriel. Le cas de l'entreprise Cockerill', *Revue d'Histoire de la Sidérurgie*, 4 (1963), 218; Lis, *Verarmingsprocessen*, vol. II, 174–9; A. Redford, *Labour Migration in England 1800–1850* (Manchester, 1926), pp. 55–63. The quotation comes from Thompson, *The Making of the English Working Class*, p. 247.

33. Woodward and Paine, quoted by Inglis, *Poverty*, pp. 34, 36.

34. See Lis, *Verarmingsprocessen*, vol. IV, 97–101. The quotation from Henry Zouch comes from R. W. Malcolmson, *Popular Recreations in English Society, 1700–1850* (Cambridge, 1973), p. 95.

35. Quoted by Inglis, *Poverty*, p. 21.

36. F. Fox Piven and Richard A. Cloward, *Regulating the Poor: the functions of public welfare* (London, 1972), pp. 30–1.

37. S. G. and E. O. A. Checkland, eds., *The Poor Law Report of 1834* (Harmondsworth, 1974), *passim* (on pp. 67, 335, 378). See the pertinent remarks of Rimlinger, *Welfare Politics*, pp. 51–4. The quotation from Coleridge comes from Inglis, *Poverty*, p. 338.

38. The quotation comes from Thompson, *The Making of the English Working Class*, p. 295. See also the important article by the same author 'The moral economy of the English crowd in the eighteenth century', *PP*, 50 (1971), 76–136.

39. Lis, 'Sociale politiek', pp. 148–60. See also Y. van den

Berghe, 'De algemene armenkamer te Brugge, 1776–1925. Een poging tot rationaliseren en laïciseren van de armenzorg', *Standen en Landen*, 44 (1968), 269–88, and F. N. Takababaza, 'Le Bureau de Charité à Verviers, 1783–1789', *Bulletin de l'Institut archéologique liégeois*, 84 (1972), 107–24.

40. Hufton, *The Poor of Eighteenth-Century France*, pp. 131–93, 227–4 (on p. 156); Gutton, *Société . . . Lyon*, pp. 435–41, 457–67; Kaplow, *The Names of Kings*, ch. VI.

41. G. Lefèbvre, *La Grande Peur de 1789* (2nd edn, Paris, 1970). See also A. Abbiatecci *et al.*, *Crimes et criminalité en France, XVIIe-XVIIIe siècles* (Paris, 1972); Hufton, *The Poor of Eighteenth-Century France*, part III; P. Deyon, *Le Temps des prisons. Essai sur l'histoire de la délinquance et les origines du système pénitentiaire* (Paris, 1975), pp. 54–60, 73–4, 84–7.

42. F. Dreyfus, *L'Assistance sous la Législation et la Convention, 1791–1795* (Paris, 1905); C. Bloch, 'Notes sur la législation et l'administration de l'assistance de 1789 à l'an VIII', *Bulletin de la Commission de recherches et de publications des documents relatifs à la vie économique de la Révolution* (1908), 232–50; M. Leroy, *Histoire des idées sociales en France*, vol. I, *De Montesquieu à Robespierre* (Paris, 1946), pp. 320ff; A. Soboul, *Histoire de la Révolution française* (2 vols, 2nd edn, Paris, 1972), vol. II, 12, 105, 353–6. The quotation from Delecroy comes from J. van Borm, 'De archieven van de Weldadigheidsbureaus als bron voor de sociale geschiedenis van de XIXe eeuw', *Annalen van het XLIe Congres van de Federatie van de Kringen voor Oudheidkunde en Geschiedenis van België* (Mechelen, 1971), 286–7.

43. Von Justi, quoted by Endres, 'Armenproblem', p. 1012. The quotation from Lord Malmesbury comes from W. O. Henderson, *Studies in the Economic Policy of Frederick the Great* (London, 1963), p. 160.

44. The quotations come from Koch, *Wandlungen der Wohlfahrtspflege*, pp. 150, 234–5.

INDEX OF AUTHORS CITED IN THE BIBLIOGRAPHY AND NOTES

The following list gives the page and note where the work of each author is referred to for the first time and given a full citation. Where more than one work by the same author has been used, the year of each publication is given as well as the page on which it is first cited.

INDEX